American Indian Literature and the Southwest

Frontispiece. Walter Ferguson(?), "Geronimo at the Wheel," 1904.
Courtesy National Archives, Washington, D.C., 75-IC-1.

American Indian Literature and the Southwest

Contexts and Dispositions

Eric Gary Anderson

University of Texas Press
Austin

Requests for permission to reproduce material from this work
should be sent to Permissions, University of Texas Press, Box
7819, Austin, TX 78713-7819.

∞ The paper used in this publication meets the minimum
requirements of American National Standard for Information
Sciences—Permanence of Paper for Printed Library Materials,
ANSI Z39.48-1984.

Library of Congress Cataloging-in-Publication Data

Anderson, Eric Gary, 1960–
    American Indian literature and the Southwest : contexts and
dispositions / Eric Gary Anderson.—1st University of Texas
Press ed.
        p.   cm.
    Includes bibliographical references (p.   ) and index.
    ISBN 0-292-70489-5 (hardcover : alk. paper).—
ISBN 0-292-70488-7 (pbk. : alk. paper)
    1. American literature—Indian authors—History and
criticism.   2. Indians of North America—Southwestern
States—Intellectual life.   3. American literature—
Southwestern States—History and criticism.   4. American
literature—Southwest, New—History and criticism.
5. Southwestern States—In literature.   6. Southwest, New—
In literature.   7. Indians in literature.   I. Title.
PS153.I52A49   1999
810.9'897—dc21   98-24862

Shelley

Contents

Illustrations   ix
Acknowledgments   xi

Introduction. Migration and Displacement in the American
   Southwest   1

1. Mobile Homes: Migration and Resistance in American
   Indian Literature   17

2. Unsettling Frontiers: Billy the Kid and the Outlaw
   Southwest   41

3. Outlawing Apaches: Geronimo and Jason Betzinez   51

4. Photography as Resistance in *Almanac of the Dead*   63

5. Indian Detours, or, Where the Indians Aren't: Management
   and Preservation in the Euro-American Southwest   77

6. Driven to Extraction: McTeague in the Desert   92

7. Mary Austin, Sarah Winnemucca, and the Problems of
   Authority   112

8. Cleaning out the House: Tom Outland, Dead Indians, and
   the First World War   133

9. Krazy Kat I: Contexts and Crossings   147

10. Krazy Kat II: Navajo Aesthetics   169

Conclusion. Cross-Purposes and Purposeful Crossings   187

Notes   197
Works Cited   207
Index   219

Illustrations

1. *The Dingbat Family,* 26 July 1910. Ignatz Mouse beans Krazy Kat for the first time.   156–157

2. Original drawing of Krazy Kat, Offissa Pupp, Ignatz Mouse, and friends, c. 1925.   158

3. *Krazy Kat,* 6 January 1918.   160–161

4. *Krazy Kat,* 22 July 1935.   160–161

5. *Krazy Kat,* 21 September 1921.   162–163

6. *Krazy Kat,* 5 February 1922.   164

7. *Krazy Kat,* 16 April 1922.   166

8. *Krazy Kat,* 11 June 1939.   167

9. *Krazy Kat,* 17 August 1920.   174–175

10. *Krazy Kat,* 3 September 1922.   176

11. *Krazy Kat,* 24 September 1922.   177

12. *Krazy Kat,* 25 January 1942.   179

13. *Krazy Kat,* 11 June 1922.   182

Acknowledgments

This book began as a freshman writing course in central New Jersey. While the sheer physical distance between Rutgers University and the American Southwest sometimes unmoored the dissertation, the classroom roots of the project have always been rock solid. Thanks, first, to the many students who asked after it, helped keep it moving, brought their considerable critical intelligence to bear on it, and reminded me that roots are also routes. I am also grateful to the various colleagues—faculty members, graduate students, and undergraduates—who read drafts of this manuscript and offered useful suggestions: thanks to Rick Batteiger, Susan Brill, William Merrill Decker, Betsy Dudczak, Todd Fuller, Linda Leavell, Leonard Leff, Todd Petersen, Carter Revard, and Ed Walkiewicz. Jeff Walker, our department head, and Carol Moder, our associate head, helped smooth the ground, as did Cecelia Austell, Shirley Bechtel, Kim Marotta, Dale McLaughlin, and Gayle Thomas. George Kearns, Calvin Martin, Kurt Spellmeyer, and especially Ron Christ guided the study through its dissertation stage with just the right balance of rigor and flexibility. In, around, and away from New Jersey, Bob Abboud, Steve Dilks, and Ray Klimek have been fast friends and excellent traveling partners. I have been lucky, too, in my outside readers, who examined the manuscript with extraordinary care and offered challenging and constructive suggestions, many of which I have gratefully and enthusiastically adopted. Thanks, too, to my editor at the University of Texas Press, Theresa J. May, for her unfailing encouragement and good humor.

This project was funded in part by a grant from the Oklahoma Foundation for the Humanities and the National Endowment for the Humanities. It was also supported by two Dean's Incentive Grants, provided by the Oklahoma State University College of Arts and Sciences. Research for this book could not have been completed without the resources and resourcefulness of the Edmon Low Library at Oklahoma State University, especially Special Collections and Interlibrary Services. Special Collections houses the Angie Debo Papers, and I had the distinct honor of working with her personal, annotated copy of *Geronimo's Story of His Life* when researching Chapter 3.

All of these friends, colleagues, and institutions have helped to keep the ground relatively level and the work itself solidly grounded even when it was most actively shifting and growing. So, too, have my parents, Eric and Marion Anderson, who have been generous in their steady encouragement. There would be little or no ground, though, without Shelley Reid, whose patience, good humor, critical insight, knowledge of postmodern technology, and much more helped keep things going in more ways than an acknowledgment and a dedication combined can express.

American Indian Literature
and the Southwest

Introduction

Migration and Displacement in the American Southwest

On or about Independence Day 1947 (so the story goes), an alien spacecraft slammed into a small cliff some thirty miles north of Roswell, New Mexico, ejecting and killing some if not all of its occupants. When local civilians and military investigators reached the scene, they identified the craft as extraterrestrial in origin and the corpses as ungendered "foreign bodies," humanoid but clearly not human. Military officials efficiently and relentlessly cordoned the area, packed up the bodies, collected the wreckage, and threatened all the known witnesses, going so far as to swear them to a permanent, compulsory silence about what they had seen "out there" in the "remote" desert. According to the Roswell mythographers, a campaign of disinformation was set into motion almost immediately, portraying the alien debris as a wrecked weather balloon and categorically denying the existence of alien bodies.[1] In fact, fifty years after the discovery of the wreckage, a new and "conclusive" report was issued by the U.S. Air Force: titled "The Roswell Report, Case Closed," it stands as the first official admission that bodies were recovered from the site, but it identifies them as the remains of life-size crash-test dummies dropped in high-altitude parachute tests.[2] Decrying the absence of material evidence, Roswell conspiracy theorists maintain that "alien" bodies continue to be written over and erased.

In the process of calling attention to absent, invisible bodies that are at once exotic and familiar, these theorists participate in a larger late-twentieth-century American redefinition and recovery of the "alien" intruder as a popular, even domesticated icon. But as they reverse-engineer alien bodies, writing them into existence and redefining them as both national artifacts and national secrets, the Roswell mythographers also wrench their highly particularized aliens out of a variety of long-standing historical and cultural contexts. In privileging microcosmically local New Mexico history and macrocosmically forbidding federal cover-ups, they typically overlook a broad, mobile, southwestern middle ground where "alien"-"native" encounters have been variously played out, encouraged, suppressed, and distorted for a very long time. In starting with Roswell, then, I want to call attention to what this post–World War II myth of the alien both reveals and overlooks, exposing a multiplicity of migratory Euro-American and American Indian "alien" identities.

Perhaps more accurately, this book distributes and redistributes this recent idea of the alien, reading it as a circulating, permeable text rather than confining it—as the Roswell "aliens" are usually confined—inside highly selective, mostly impermeable, remarkably stabilized binary constructions of public spheres and private domains. The questions asked here, like the questions asked by Roswell "researchers," certainly concern who and where the aliens are, but I also stretch these questions around and beyond the researchers' arguments, which typically constrict the issue of southwestern alien identity both culturally and contextually. For example, in the texts I discuss in this work, "alien" identity sometimes refers more to physical places than to human (or humanoid) beings; the "typical New Mexico landscape," writes Navajo-Laguna Pueblo novelist A. A. Carr, "could have doubled as Mars in a cheap sci-fi movie, complete with purple and orange mesas, black volcanic cones, and flat valleys of red sand" (56). As I explain in Chapters 5 and 6, late-nineteenth-century railroad passengers, mostly Euro-Americans, also often regarded formidable southwestern deserts as alien topographies, a response reflected to some extent in the Death Valley passages of Frank Norris's 1899 novel *McTeague*.

More often, the "aliens" I identify are produced by and reflected in migratory interactions between peoples and places: Leslie Marmon Silko's *Almanac of the Dead* (1991), for example, describes a multidimensional, ideologically charged range of encounters between travelers and environments, many of which take on or confer alien status in ways that contravene and unsettle dominant U.S. "border" discourses about "illegal aliens." The primary convergence point in the novel, Tucson, Arizona, is in fact simultaneously an alien site and an American city on the verge of being further alienated, a place where "outsiders" meet, and a home place for the almanac-keepers Lecha and Zeta as well as for Silko herself. "There's something about Tucson, about Arizona, that's so corrupt," Silko tells interviewer Donna Perry. "The land is very beautiful. There's nothing wrong with the earth. . . . but Arizona is totally corrupt" (Perry, 326). But Silko also points out, "I am a part of this. . . . The desert protects me" (Perry, 339). And the complexities of home emerge in part out of the experience of travel: Silko writes, "I did not really learn about my relationship with the land or know where 'home' was until I left Laguna for Tucson" (*Yellow Woman*, 86).

Throughout this book, I read ideas of the "alien" as products of both Euro-American and American Indian cultures in motion, migrating toward, around, and against each other in ways that blur as well as enforce the differences among, for example, S. M. Barrett's Geronimo, Silko's Geronimo, Geronimo's Geronimo, Geronimo's Barrett, and the various Arizonas these figures inhabit, however impermanently. My work on migration has been influenced by James Clifford's reflections on travel: "Virtually everywhere one looks," Clifford argues, "the processes of human movement and encounter are long-established and complex. Cultural centers, discrete regions and territories, do not exist prior to contacts, but are sustained through them, appropriating and disciplining the restless movements of people and things" (3). He contends that no one "is permanently fixed by his or her 'identity'; but neither can one shed specific structures of race and culture, class and caste, gender and sexuality, environment and history" (12). And he regards such "crosscutting determinations" as "sites of worldly travel: difficult encounters and occasions for dialogue" (12).

Along with Clifford, I try to read comparatively, moving across and against various textual and cultural constructions of particular migratory strategies. In multiple, tangled and entangling ways, American Indian and Euro-American Southwests are both solidly grounded and portable, both physical and textual; at the same time and often in the same space, however, the borders flung up by southwestern or southwestering cultures in motion are neither ideologically translucent nor physically or socially stable. Texts— both Indian and non-Indian—that propose and enact uneven, shifting migratory moves therefore receive particularly close attention. These texts sometimes define migration as a resistance or survival strategy rather than as an expansionist inevitability, and they often articulate in some way the problems as well as the possibilities of personal as well as cultural movement. Along the way, characters, authors, texts, and readers variously enter or approach states of alienation, broadly defined, but these displacements typically preserve—and sometimes move toward—the idea, if not always the actuality, of home. Like Silko, to reach—let alone to understand—home, many southwestern peoples from a variety of cultures must travel.

Thus, the canonical Roswell conspiracy narrative is in important ways not simply a "new," post–World War II story. Rather, Roswell's alien bodies should be read specifically in the twined contexts of the American Southwest and a national style of alien management that long predates the summer of 1947. The Southwest represents or approximates a home place—not a "regional" periphery but a center—for a rich variety of Indians and non-Indians, but it also stands restlessly and paradoxically as a place where alien, migratory cultures have been encountering each other and competing against each other for a very long time. Because the cultures that populate these physical and textual Southwests migrate so frequently and creatively, moving metaphorically and metaphysically as well as physically, I urge wariness in the face of southwestering narratives that propose to secure all evidence inside a single, bounded thesis, whether that thesis addresses the alien secrets of the federal government, the frontier processes of an expansionist America, or the revitalization of American Indian tribal peoples.

With caution in mind, then, I have deliberately chosen to work with a collection of highly elastic key words and concepts—"migration," "travel," "resistance," "mobility," "alienation," "colonialism," "postcolonialism"—

all of which cross and recross a variety of actual and imagined borders in a variety of undisciplined as well as disciplinary ways. These terms, as I understand and mobilize them, have historical as well as figurative currency; they work both culturally and textually. They also engage each other in complex ways. The Southwest—to the extent that I can define it from multiple, shifting points of view *and* maintain that it coheres geographically, demographically, ideologically, or argumentatively *as* the Southwest—is a place where "alien" forces (social, cultural, racial, colonial, nuclear, and otherwise) have been set in motion toward, across, through, around, and away from each other for many centuries.

In working toward a multicultural, multidirectional, multidisciplinary Southwest characterized by such difficult migratory interactions and the frequent transformations they produce, I inevitably work against critics and historians inclined toward positioning the region and its cultural products inside one or more bounded spheres, even as they insist that this region defies or at least blurs such boundaries. This book, then, is pointedly and explicitly about a variety of Southwests; I do not insist or hope that the Southwests I describe in Chapter 1 exactly resemble those elucidated in Chapters 9 and 10. These Southwests may very well overlap in particular ways, but it would be presumptuous to equate George Herriman's Arizona, for example, with Wendy Rose's. Moreover, the Southwest's many distinct local characteristics do not preclude comparisons between this region and others. Like many American regions, the Southwest appears to be constantly in motion and constantly moved through; like many American regions, the Southwest functions as a highly active and complicated convergence point that proves difficult to contain inside any one disciplinary or critical sphere.

For example, as various Americanists have convincingly demonstrated, regionalism is a powerfully contingent phenomenon; country and city are entangled with each other and in crucial ways are responsible for each other. Literary and literary-critical representations of regions can and should, therefore, be read both for what they are and for what they are not. For instance, the regions in question are not necessarily marginalized pockets of America in which inhabitants sit still. Sarah Orne Jewett's "A White Heron" (1886, Maine), Hamlin Garland's naturalistic "Up the Coulé" (1891, Wisconsin), and Edward Abbey's *Desert Solitaire* (1968, Utah), for example, construct clearly bounded local environments only to collapse those boundaries: characters "at home" contend with characters from an "outside" realm, and "home" itself is both a stable and a destabilized place, both before and after the entrance of characters from worlds seemingly elsewhere. As June Howard argues, Jewett's work crosses spatial, temporal, and literary-critical boundaries; it "is both more 'modern' (in her concern with circuits and exchange) and more 'nineteenth-century' (in her religious belief and didacticism) than any turn-of-the-century local colorist is conceived to be. And her deep engagement with the byways of a particular region portrays them as already criss-crossed by the tracks of translocal connection" ("Unraveling Regions," 379). Just as urban/industrial figures and elements impinge on the rural (as in "A White Heron" and *Desert Solitaire*), they impinge transculturally on New Mexico (as in the work of Mary Austin, Willa Cather, Herriman, and Silko), often in ways that straddle literary-historical periods.

And of course these transactions do not move in one spatial or temporal direction only: New Mexico, Arizona, and "the Southwest" infiltrate the American nation as well, a process this book will document by looking at a variety of southwestern writers and texts. Over the past century, New Mexico has been overworked and underworked as a "regionalist" site, even to the point of being evacuated of human figures (Georgia O'Keeffe and Cather, Chapters 5 and 8); Arizona has been represented as a convergence point overflowing with human figures from a variety of nations and across a variety of "historical" periods (Silko, Chapters 1 and 4). American writers as different as Geronimo (Chapter 3), Theodore Roosevelt (Chapter 5), and Patricia Limerick (Chapter 5) have perceived and discussed the paradoxes involved in occupying and using the Southwest, attempting to preserve something of its character as a home place without removing it from circulation altogether. Each author discusses both posterity and progress, both national memory and (often conflicting) cultural desires.

Moreover, American Indian texts and cultures have a great deal to say about these and other matters; indeed, the major paradigm of this book—a loosely bounded, migratory Southwest that functions, with varying degrees of fluidity and tension, as a multicultural, multinational convergence point— is first set in motion by Indians. In discussing southwestern American Indian literatures, though, this book adheres to Arnold Krupat's assertion that "contemporary Native American literatures cannot quite be classed among the postcolonial literatures of the world for the simple reason that there is not yet a 'post-' to the colonial status of Native Americans" (*Turn to the Native*, 30). This is not to deny or suppress the tremendous vitality of American Indian political and textual resistances to what Krupat calls "domestic imperialism or internal colonialism" (*Turn to the Native*, 30); neither is it to whitewash the specificities of Indian experiences in Arizona, New Mexico, and adjacent places. It is, however, to urge skepticism and caution rather than an overly optimistic postcolonial positioning of American Indian tribal cultures as they continue to work through the enormous, continuing difficulties of being positioned—stereotyped, reserved, removed, assimilated—both spatially and temporally. In other words, Euro-American and American Indian cultures have, for a long time, been migrating *against* each other.

Of course, in reading places as texts and texts as places, this book does not overlook the specific physical features that distinguish Albuquerque from Tucson, Gallup from Kayenta, or, more broadly, the Southwest from other American regions. Certainly, southwestern topographies and cultures are different from other American regions, and certainly they have been perceived (and not perceived) in light of these differences. But critics and historians have often been more preoccupied with identifying regional coordinates than with critiquing such territorial acts of marking; the topographical and cultural diversity of, for example, "Navajoland" is easy to overlook in favor of generalizations about a (unitary) Navajo "place." When Linda S. Cordell (who does work carefully with such matters), casts the Southwest as the place between Durango, Mexico, and Durango, Colorado, and between Las Vegas, New Mexico, and Las Vegas, Nevada (2), she calls attention to one of the many neat ways in which the region writ large is often plotted. Such demarcations are less crucial, at least to this book, than a critical sense of the instabilities and limitations of such maps and the ideological motivations for demarcating in the first place. Clearly, the Southwest has been the site of colonial manipulations, attempts to impose geopolitical, cultural, religious, juridical, and other boundaries on indigenous peoples already inhabiting a complex, circulating system of bounded and unbounded time and space. Just as clearly, American Indians also often invest ideologically in the places they inhabit. Robert Allen Warrior argues that such investments need to be intensified and perhaps redefined, because "land and community are necessary starting points for the process of coming to a deep perception of the conflicts and challenges that face American Indian people and communities" (85). Again, this book describes some of the ways in which these processes assume and encourage cultural movement; Warrior's argument articulates a similar openness to the intricacies and flexibilities of these interactions between Indian peoples and places.

In describing some of the relationships between physical environments and ideologically driven constructions of borders, I have come to recognize that several of the terms most often mobilized in critical discussions of the Southwest are less than ideal. "Southwest," of course, depends on one's point of view; as Reed Way Dasenbrock remarks, "To ask what Southwestern literature is, one must first ask, What is the Southwest? For whom is it the Southwest? What is the Southwest southwest of?" (123). Somewhat similarly, there are problems with the terms "borders" and "boundaries." Eric J. Sundquist's warning in regard to different cultural geographies/territories applies as well to the Southwest: "the inclusion of the amorphous imaginative and historical terrain of Caribbean and Latin American literary culture within the scope of our thought and criticism requires more than another repetition of the various pieties about crossing boundaries" (793). Moreover, Rafael Pérez-Torres has issued a strong cautionary critical statement about overworking "migration" as a critical concept: "A migratory reading wends between the Scylla of the local and the Charybdis of the total, between the devil that historical and cultural specificity can be and the deep murky seas of essentialization and homogeneity. In short, it steals" (169–170). Pérez-Torres particularly warns against migratory readings that move too easily and construct models "by which difficult cultural and political terrain can be successfully traversed" (170). Critics, especially those who work with ethnic literatures and questions of travel, must actively prohibit fantasized success stories and stolen happy endings.

Sundquist and Pérez-Torres's remarks serve a crucial reminder to critics focusing on American Indian/Euro-American "borders" as well. The Southwest as place and idea has been interpreted, most often by Euro-American historians but also by Euro-American artists, anthropologists, and literary and cultural critics, in no—or few—uncertain terms. However, these interpreters' certainty rests securely on the unintentionally ironic double move of claiming *un*certainty about southwestern geographical borders yet imposing a variety of firm ideological borders, often concerning race, class, and gender. In fact, one of the conventions of nonfiction texts about the Southwest is the disclaimer that the region cannot really be adequately defined or bounded. The authors of a 1980 bibliography of southwestern literature observe, for instance, that "the American Southwest is difficult to define [geographically], because, as J. Frank Dobie once said, the boundaries are themselves 'fluid, expanding and contracting according to the point of view from which the Southwest is viewed and according to whatever common denominator is taken for defining it'" (Anderson, Gaston, and Lee, eds., ix). In 1940, Erna Fergusson wrote that "The Southwest is not, like other sections of the United States, exactly bounded" (3). In 1961, W. Eugene Hollon observed that "Everyone has his own definition of the Southwest. The more one tries to limit and define it, the more elusive the area becomes" (3). In 1971, Lynne I. Perrigo picked up some of the same terms, claiming that "The Southwest has experienced such variety in definition that it is now an elusive entity" (iii). As early as 1903, Mary Austin, reading the California deserts as southwestern topographies, labeled the Death Valley area the Country of Lost Borders (*Land of Little Rain*, 9). And as late as 1987, Patricia Nelson Limerick both reinforces and subverts this discourse when she writes that "we cannot fix exact boundaries for [the West], any more than we can draw precise lines around 'the South,' 'the Midwest,' or that most elusive of regions 'the East'" (*Legacy*, 26). In a sense, the borderlands criticism of Gloria Anzaldúa maintains this long-standing convention; in another, crucial sense, though, Anzaldúa expands prior work in the field significantly by complicating its assumptions about space, time, and identity, calling attention to psychological, sexual, and spiritual "[b]orderlands [that] are physically present wherever two or more cultures edge each other, where people of different races occupy the same territory, where under, lower, middle and upper classes touch, where the space between two individuals shrinks with intimacy" (*Borderlands/La Frontera*, n.p.).

With the exception of Limerick and Anzaldúa, the writers mentioned above simultaneously loosen geographical borders and impose ideological limitations. Hollon's border person is male; Fergusson's ambiguous syntax suggests a border region that is simultaneously not "exactly bounded" and distinct from all other U.S. regions, which are "exactly bounded," thereby instituting what is at best a paradox. Dobie expects one homogenizing "common denominator" at a time rather than a mix of denominators and denominations. In his recent historical study of the transcontinental Spanish frontier of North America, David J. Weber defines frontiers as "zones of interaction between two different cultures—as places where the cultures of the invader and of the invaded contend with one another and with their physical environment to produce a dynamic that is unique to time and place" (11)—but why two cultures and only one oversimplified invader-invaded binary? As many of the chapters that follow suggest, the term "frontier" is, like the terms "borders" and "boundaries," an almost perversely flexible concept; the brilliance of Frederick Jackson Turner's metaphor for American colonial processes has come to seem at least somewhat counterproductive. It tends to encourage dualistic thinking. How, for example, do the complicated tensions among Mexico, the United States, and several distinct, sometimes allied and sometimes warring Apache branches fit inside this paradigm? Despite its malleability, Turner's metaphor severely limits local cultural differences; in the words of Alan Trachtenberg, it "fails to acknowledge cultural multiplicity; in the Southwest alone, Anglo-Americans, Spanish Americans, Roman Catholics, Mormons, and Indians all contributed to a heterogeneous culture" (*Incorporation*, 16–17).

As such revisionist arguments make emphatically clear, the majority of "southwestern" texts express a remarkable critical and historical consensus on the region; its position as a "last frontier" or American periphery has been regarded as secure. Only recently have alternative Southwests been proposed. This book collaborates with these propositions, turning for example to an American Southwest that is as much "American" as it is "Southwest" and as much "Indian" as it is "American." In the comic strip *Krazy Kat* (1913–1944), for example, cartoonist George Herriman imports a variety of urban characters, motifs, dialects, and even architectural structures to the Monument Valley area of Arizona. But, as Chapters 9 and 10 demonstrate, these transactions do not move in only one or two directions. Herriman enjoyed his double status as a traveler through Navajo Country and as a syndicated cartoonist whose work circulated daily and Sunday for many decades, and he enjoyed inventing visual and verbal metaphors for the multicultural engagements his comic strip somewhat subversively celebrated. Like each of the texts I read in this book, *Krazy Kat* reflects, and reflects on, its own migratory movements. More like Silko's fiction than the earlier-twentieth-century writings of Norris, Austin, and Cather, Herriman's art moves toward an implicit and tentative postcolonialism grounded in southwestern places, identified with southwestern Indian peoples, and distributed through national cultural circuits. Of course, Silko's *Almanac of the Dead* (written nearly fifty years after Herriman's death) argues much more explicitly for a radical and unsettling anticolonial retaking of the Americas, but Herriman's multicultural, multidirectional, even multispecies narratives unprogrammatically set in motion similarly fluid crossings and recrossings of a variety of geographical, racial, sexual, and gender boundaries.

American Indian Literature and the Southwest assumes that the Southwest and its peoples, like other American regions and theirs, can and should be read relationally; here is one of the shifting places where metaphors and notions of travel, migration, and movement appear to be more helpful than metaphors of borders and boundaries. In other words, this book does not simply substitute one set of slippery metaphors for another. Of course, in my discussion of some of the ways in which various metaphorical, metaphysical, fantasy Southwests are produced, maintained, and superseded, the term "relationally" does not refer, simply or exclusively, to the relations between Euro-Americans and native peoples. Chapter 1 in particular argues that American Indian peoples are not often enough discussed in relation to each other—that the colonial presence of Europeans and Euro-Americans continues, in a sense, to colonize spoken narratives and written texts about both the Southwest and southwestern Indians.

One of my main goals, with this point in mind, is to situate Euro-American cultural processes and texts in the context of American Indian cultural processes and texts. Most obviously and bluntly, I do so because the Southwest is Indian Country: Indians migrated there, lived there, and moved across and through its various physical environments before Europeans arrived there, and Indians continue to maintain powerful relationships with various southwestern places. Chapters 1 and 4 demonstrate that Silko's *Almanac of the Dead* is, as a migration narrative, both radically inventive and a typical, even traditional American Indian novel. This paradox emerges so richly because Silko encourages readers to situate the novel's transcultural, transnational movements in Indian contexts, keeping in mind that a variety of native cultures have circulated through and across the Southwest for thousands of years. Long before migratory, colonial Europeans arrived in the Americas, Indians were moving through the Southwest, and Indians continue to migrate in purposeful, creative, complex, and adaptable ways. When Euro-American colonials construct seemingly impermeable boundaries around and across a variety of Indian spaces and cultures, Indians often respond (as Silko does) in strategic, even subversive, migratory ways, working to dismantle or at least resist cultural impositions. For instance, Geronimo's dispositions, both as he articulates them and as he is constructed by contemporary Indian writers such as Silko, actively counter the "Geronimo" who has acquired iconic status in dominant American culture. Chapters 3 and 4 argue that Geronimo, as an autobiographer and as an intertribal ally of Silko's, brilliantly resists Euro-American efforts to assimilate, erase, or exhibit him and the Warm Springs Apaches as "preserved" and neutralized museum, textbook, or sideshow Indians.

By recontextualizing southwestern places and cultures, this book illustrates some of the differences between transcultural, migratory, Indian sensibilities and transcultural, migratory Euro-American ones. In Chapters 6, 7, and 8, I turn to three Euro-American literary texts grounded in the Southwest (and more nebulously associated with southwestern Indians) and discuss the texts with Indian migration narratives and strategies in mind. While *McTeague, The Land of Little Rain,* and *The Professor's House* speak in pow-

erful, unsettling ways to Clifford's observation that roots and routes intertwine to construct both personal and cultural identities—an observation true
of Indian cultures as well as of Euro-American—each of these texts imagines
non-Indian identity less as a process than as a decisive, authoritative, or inevitable condition. Walter Benn Michaels has recently discussed "the production
of Tom Outland as the descendant of Anasazi cliff dwellers" (*Our America*,
45), but Cather's characterization of Outland, like Norris's of McTeague and
Austin's of the Paiute basket maker Seyavi and of herself, points toward more
troubling claims about the power relations of "alien"-"native" encounters in
the late-nineteenth- and early-twentieth-century Southwest. Still, though, all
three writers go deeper into southwestern places than most of their contemporaries, and both Austin and Cather at least attempt to approach Indian cultures with the conviction that these cultures, though dead (as in Cather) or
partially appropriated (as in Austin), are worth incorporating into literary reflections on the present shape and direction of America.

This book also constructs a trans*disciplinary* context for both American
and American Indian literatures, not only because such disciplinary crossings enact what the book says about the region writ large, but also because
they help expose the transnational complexities of both literatures. As Amy
Kaplan contends,

> American nationality can still be taken for granted as a monolithic and
> self-contained whole, no matter how diverse and conflicted, if it remains
> implicitly defined by its internal social relations, and not in political
> struggles for power with other cultures and nations, struggles which
> make America's conceptual and geographic borders fluid, contested, and
> historically changing. ("'Left Alone'," 15)

I so strongly emphasize migration throughout this book because it so directly
reveals the motives, practices, and ideologies of different disciplines, cultures,
and indeed nations—although, unlike Kaplan, I read migration as a flexible
paradigm for a flexible American Southwest that is itself both regional and
transnational. The phrase "internal social relations" includes rather than excludes an enormous and seemingly endless range of international political
struggles between the United States and most, if not all, American Indian
nations. Geronimo, in *Geronimo's Story of His Life*, suggests as much when
he remarks, "The boundary lines established at different times between Mexico and the United States did not conform to the boundary lines of these
Apache tribes, of course, and the Indians soon saw and took advantage of the
international questions arising from the conflicting interests of the two governments" (14). In addition to the "official" U.S.-Mexico border, there are the
different national and international borders acknowledged and exploited by
the Apaches.

As I have begun to suggest, then, in the grounded yet portable Southwest
I read throughout this book, contested borders are not stable (physically
and socially) and not translucent (ideologically). What they *are* is difficult to

describe but perhaps possible to locate, occasionally and inconsistently, in the elusive, migratory textual and cultural moments I splice together. What they are, then—and where the aliens are—is perhaps best exemplified by the shifting, eclectic, fluid yet disruptive quality of this book itself, as it moves through, across, and around a mix of cultures, nations, disciplines, ideologies, and texts.

To exemplify these shifting constructions and practices of migration, I want to return to the opening paragraphs of this introduction and pursue a little further the recontextualization of the canonical Roswell conspiracy narrative. Some twenty-five years after the alleged UFO wreck at Roswell, self-styled "researchers" began the double-edged project of uncovering "suppressed" details and working out the technology of the purported cover-up. In many of the post-Watergate Roswell narratives, the aliens are naturalized; according to one story, two doctors are said to have speculated that the alien bodies they examined "might have been mutilated by predators and . . . looked as if they had been exposed to the elements on the high desert" (Randle and Schmitt, 67). Integrated into New Mexico ecosystems, the aliens are also, in other accounts, humanized and domesticated, construed not as frightening monsters but as accident victims and, at times, mourning survivors. These "humanlike" qualities are mobilized as a way of likening "them" to "us" without eradicating various physiological ways in which the alien continues to be alien: its different skin colors, different types of hair (or oddly hairless bodies), different body sizes and shapes, different hands and fingers, different types of clothing. But Kevin Randle and Donald Schmitt accomplish this balancing act by essentializing and "purifying" both humans and aliens, overlooking social constructions such as race, class, and gender. The characteristics listed above—skin color and hair, in particular—appear to racialize the aliens, but in Randle and Schmitt's hands, both "human" and "alien" are reduced to generic, raceless categories. "Human," for example, comes to stand for everything and nothing: "They were smaller than human and they were thinner than human" (142).

Like other canonical late-twentieth-century American conspiracy narratives—the John F. Kennedy assassination furnishes perhaps the best examples—the Roswell story mobilizes its reductiveness strategically, demonizing the conspirators and sympathizing with the conspired-against. The Roswell locals and, by extension, all American civilians who are lied to are defined, along with the extraterrestrials, as victims of this incident. Typically, the narrative rages against Higher Powers that, in the Roswell conspiracy theory, serve as antagonists not of aliens but of home cultures, American selves; U.S. officials, not extraterrestrials, menace individual citizens and small communities such as Roswell. "We" become alien-ated; in an odd twist, the foreign bodies themselves, the "original" aliens, are domesticated and even allied with the citizenry at large, to the point where the July 1997 fiftieth-anniversary celebration in Roswell was explicitly marketed as a tourist festival to stimulate the struggling local economy. The aliens join the Roswell locals as business partners, political allies, profiteers. They are friends; they are cute, stuffed-toy versions of aliens. Because their presence, in all its intimate foreignness, has been covered up, they paradoxically move closer to those of "us" who look under the covers.

Correspondingly, the technicians of the domestic military propaganda machine are frightening, shadowy figures who maintain its dark, tantalizing secrets, its storehouses of collected (and covered-up, denied) evidence of all sorts of things, its dark hangars and subterranean complexes, its acts of psychological terrorism and denial. In every conspiracy narrative there is, somewhere, a locked door, a dusty closet, a drawerful of mythic artifacts, a collection of closed spaces, and, conversely, a sweeping if not pathological desire to open these interior spaces, to in a sense reverse prior national narratives of colonial closure in the name of an estranged postcolonialism, to redefine conquest as encounter, and perhaps, finally, to expose actual, rather than imagined, alien bodies—but as what? Generic aliens? Marketable aliens? Ideological familiars? Millennial anxieties? Meanwhile, the actual site of the alleged wreck undergoes its own particular trauma. Frequently, in conspiracy narratives, the physical site of the "original" crime or event is both revisited and displaced. As cultural geographer Kenneth E. Foote points out, sites of violent and tragic events "play an active role in their own interpretation" (5), but communities must decide how, or whether, to memorialize these highly charged places. Foote finds that, depending on the degree of shame or guilt experienced by residents of the places in question, the sites are variously sanctified, designated, rectified, and obliterated (7); obviously, two of these four general options involve erasure of some or all of the memories attached to the place. For all the attention given to the Roswell incident, the site of the crash has been contested, and, fifty years later, remains unmarked and in a sense deflected or erased.

Despite the absence of visible public ratification of the crash site, most Roswell commentators see the incident—the wreck itself, combined with "upper-level" silencings of it—as a watershed and even as a first. Roswell marks the first time alien bodies were discovered, examined, perhaps autopsied, perhaps maintained alive; the first time an alien ship was recovered and studied; the first time the military engaged in evasive action regarding UFOs. Conspiracy theorists make spectacular claims for the event and its consequences: Randle and Schmitt, for example, claim that the Roswell incident "might be considered the major event of the last one thousand years" (3) and value the cover-up as "one of the most successful military disinformation operations of all time" (36), safeguarding "the greatest secret of the twentieth century" (109). In a Roswell text that predates Randle and Schmitt's by fourteen years, Charles Berlitz and William L. Moore write that perhaps at this very moment [1980] we sit at the verge of the greatest news story of the twentieth century, the first contact with live (or dead) extraterrestrials. This occurrence, if true, would be at least comparable to Columbus's encounter with the startled natives on his visit to the New World. Except for one thing. In this case we would be the startled natives. (139–140)

These Roswell stories themselves operate as a reenactment of alien invasion (or, in Berlitz and Moore's more complacent term, "visit"), not least because they invariably erase or severely diminish American Indians—here, a vague collection of "startled natives"—even as the emergence of Roswell conspiracy theory coincides with the emergences of the American Indian movement and the Chicano/a movement.

The very exceptionalism of claims such as Randle and Schmitt's and Berlitz and Moore's is predictable and unexceptional. In fact, whether the Roswell story is true, false, both, or neither, it describes one in a long series of alien entries into the American Southwest and one in a long series of cultural mythologies: of the West, of the desert, of the frontier, of aliens and alienation, of the status—the preservation and contamination—of national memory, of America itself. The aliens *are* like the Euro-Americans who ultimately domesticate them. And the Roswell narratives *do* get involved in a cover-up, but it is not the cover-up the researchers think it is. Like many other southwestern texts, the Roswell conspiracy narratives do a remarkably efficient job of suppressing certain contexts in favor of others. The larger point, made in a variety of ways throughout this book, is that the story of "alien" invasion of the Southwest is not exclusively a twentieth-century story and is not strictly a contest between a single, specific New Mexico locality and a generalized, symbolic, "secret" federal realm of military and political officialdom—a contest mediated, in a sense, by extraterrestrial bodies. Moreover, the tactical displacements and reinventions of Euro-American "aliens" as explorers, missionaries, sanctified colonialists, and extraterrestrials (to name no more) all suppress or diminish actual, documented transcultural encounters between migratory Euro-American cultures and migratory American Indian cultures.

In other words, the identity of the "alien" shifts radically as historical and cultural contexts shift, but the purpose or function of the "alien" does not. To southwestern American Indians, the aliens are first other, migrating Indian tribes, then Spanish colonials, and then Europeans and Euro-Americans in general. To Euro-American colonials, the aliens are natives, "savages," Mexicans. In conventional Anglo-Saxon, Turneresque myths of the Wild West, the aliens are women; nonwhite, non-Protestant, or non-Anglo men; and, as Chapters 2 and 3 demonstrate, mythic outlaws who resist and disrupt their own marginalization. The alien can be incoming or he/she/it can be already there. The alien can be a Navajo woman in a town full of white male cowboys in transit or a Mexican crossing from Ciudad Juárez to El Paso, the latter a man or woman ostensibly defined less ethnically than legally. The alien can be Billy the Kid or Geronimo; Norris's hulking dentist, McTeague, or Cather's Indian mummy, Mother Eve; Austin's Country of Lost Borders or, for that matter, Austin's courageous yet self-promoting Austin.

Silko, unlike most of the other writers and artists discussed in this book, directly takes up the problem of Euro-Americans as alien invaders of the American Southwest—as de facto and at times intently programmatic conspirators whose alien wreckage continues to obstruct and mystify both the "region" and the migratory yet grounded indigenous peoples who live there. Compared to *Almanac of the Dead,* in other words, the generic, revisionist narratives of the Roswell UFO crash and subsequent cover-up *only* go so far as to suggest an alliance between aliens, Roswell locals, and American citizens. Randle and Schmitt never compare alien invasions from outer space with alien invasions such as those Silko both critiques and sets in motion, invasions from the East, West, North, and South. Neither do the Roswell "researchers" understand or explore this post–World War II alien invasion story as a paradigmatic southwestern event; while "desolate" terrain, weathered locals, and a vague sense of cultural isolation characterize the Southwest of the Roswell narrative, the region is in other ways surprisingly dislodged from the story. "Roswell" comes to seem oddly unimplicated and dis-positioned in its own historical and cultural contexts. Particularly in *Almanac of the Dead,* though, Silko's subversive work with and against Euro-American technology speaks indirectly to the constricted version of Roswell—and, more importantly, Silko articulates the complex relationships between a variety of cultural processes and dispositions, including unsettlement and resettlement, displacement and replacement, "alien" and "native" identities. She argues that migratory cultures are politically viable, and she directly links the act of Indian migration with the retaking of the Americas.

William Cronon, George Miles, and Jay Gitlin have proposed a particular way of understanding the history of the American West, a method that acknowledges multiple Wests and multiple ways of traveling to and from these Wests. In their discussion, they introduce a process called *"species shifting,* the movement of alien organisms into ecosystems from which they were once absent. Such organisms were the most visible proof that a frontier area had become linked to the rest of the world in a new way" (11). As another paradigm for the complexities of southwestern as well as western history, species shifting clearly applies to phenomena as diverse as the Roswell conspiracy theories and a wide array of Indian and non-Indian narratives about the Southwest, including several I discuss in this book and several I do not.

A. A. Carr's Navajo-vampire novel, *Eye Killers,* briefly discussed in the conclusion, explores transcultural ideas of the alien by transplanting a group of migratory vampires (and by extension, European myths) to New Mexico, where they encounter contemporary Navajos and Euro-Americans (and, again

by extension, their particular cultural myths). Vampires and skinwalkers together enable Carr to discuss issues of blood in new ways; he suggests that
the mixing of blood may itself take part in the migratory processes of identity
formation and displacement that are paradigmatic of the Southwest. Carr not
only delivers three species-shifting vampires to New Mexico, he also confers
a powerful though still surrogate "Indian" identity on a Euro-American high
school English teacher, who is given permission to perform a Navajo ceremony and act as a Navajo warrior. And Michael Roanhorse, a Navajo elder,
transforms into Coyote after being bitten by one of the vampires, encounters
Changing Woman, and travels throughout—and out of—the novel, carrying
the most powerful vampire's remains to a sacred Navajo place as the book
comes to a close. The mythic European vampire, then, is subsumed into
places, cultures, and stories explicitly and unpredictably defined as Indian.

American Indian Literature and the Southwest focuses primarily on the
Southwest as Indian country, but as even a brief discussion of *Eye Killers*
and a slightly more extended reading of Roswell make clear, it is difficult to
consider Indian country without also bringing to bear the various complex
transcultural migrations and alliances that, in crucial ways, characterize the
places I circulate through in this text. These places, like the peoples and cultures that cross and recross them both physically and textually, tend to be
very much in motion in a variety of ways; they are not only the destinations
of migrants or the way stations of colonials passing through from elsewhere
but also textual inventions that, read singly or comparatively, shift and travel
and elude generalizations. The diversity and complexity of intertribal cultural movements alone render the most commonly ventilated, historically
certified East-to-West trajectory and critical perspective very limited. This
book reveals numerous *dis*positions—temperaments, ideologies, unsettlings,
and resettlings of roots and routes—that characterize or otherwise affect
southwestern places and peoples. Without losing sight of the actualities of
southwestern migrations, the crossings and recrossings of particular places by
particular peoples, I trust "migration" as a metaphor that is elastic enough to
do justice to these complex, kinetic interactions among peoples, places, and
cultures justice. More often than not, these migratory texts actively unsettle
a variety of positionings of the Southwest and compel, perhaps, reconsidera-
tions of those positionings and the assumptions that drive them.

The Southwest, after all, is the site of Betonie's hogan (in Silko's *Ceremony,* a place of healing and reorientation) and the site of the Bates Motel
(in Alfred Hitchcock's version of *Psycho,*[3] a place of terror and killing). Both
structures are situated on or near roads, the better to interact with travelers.
Indeed, one of Norman Bates's many big problems is a peculiar, twisted variation on Clifford's paradigm of roots and routes: the new interstate highway
bypasses his motel, which is located on an older route, and this apparent
obsolescence infects and intensifies his already fraught sense of genealogy.
Betonie, on the other hand, fills his hogan with multicultural detritus: the
telephone books, calendars, and medicines that, along with the physical

position of his home place on top of a hill overlooking Gallup, New Mexico, help him to keep track of things, to watch and watch over the people as they travel to and through Gallup's mean streets, culverts, and bars. As this last pair of texts suggests, the narratives and examples discussed in this book may at first seem eclectic at best. But such migratory critical acts make possible a variety of transcultural, transdisciplinary moves that in turn allow the construction of a crucial, alternative literary and cultural history of an ever-shifting, Indian-American Southwest.

1 Mobile Homes

Migration and Resistance in American Indian Literature

In broad terms, migrations—sometimes forced, sometimes voluntary, always complicated, often between and across and through a variety of places and cultures—continuously define many cultures in the Americas and in the world. That is, migrations are, paradoxically, constants, a perception James Clifford arrives at in his recent work *Routes* when he contends that global culture is typified by travel, the complex entanglements of migratory routes and genealogical roots. Centers and borders alike are constantly shifting transcultural constructions created out of mobility and maintained as provisionally "open" cities and boundaries, however vexed these encounters and however policed these ephemeral borders. But it is also clear that few of these migratory cultures have met with as much hostility from other, competing migratory cultures as have American Indians since 1492. These tangled, entangling migrations against each other, as recorded and critiqued in late-nineteenth- and twentieth-century Euro-American and Indian texts of a variety of forms and media, constitute the subject of this book.

I read the American Southwest as a sort of paradigmatic site, in part because of the frequency and intensity of the various, competing migrations through it, in part because, as the archaeologists say, the region's many cultures tend to preserve themselves well, for better and for worse. Some Euro-American modernists, for example, migrated against both indigenous cultures and literary expatriates who went in "the other direction," transatlantically rather than transcontinentally. It is perhaps a cliché (as well as an odd move politically) to present Spanish colonials as a sort of corrective to the earlier, prevailing literary-historical view that Europeans migrated only to Massachusetts. But, as is pointed out in the Introduction, it is not yet a cliché to read the Southwest as a place both solidly grounded and portable, a place where migratory cultures have, physically and textually, contested borders that are neither translucent (as ideological constructions) nor stable (as physical or social constructions). This book enters into this shifting, elusive, often unarticulated third possibility, an unevenly postcolonial space.

Wendy Rose's "poems about traveling" (*Bone Dance*, xv) provide a useful starting place because they sketch out a migratory worldview that is characteristic not only of American Indian literature but also of multicultural southwestern literature. In her 1977 poem "To Some Few Hopi Ancestors," she links the changing songs of Hopi ancestors to the changing circumstances of Hopi descendants who have moved "to Winslow, to Sherman,/to Oakland, to all the spokes/that have left earth's middle" (*Bone Dance*, 16). Rose, a mixed-blood Hopi/Miwok Indian born in Oakland and raised in the city rather than on the reservation, writes many such stories of personal and cultural travel; in these migration stories, she represents contemporary American Indian experience as a series of emergences and recedings, movings out and homings in, removals and survivals. Like a remarkable number of native writers, Rose measures her tribal identity against the distances, both physical and psychic, she has traveled (or been propelled) "away" from it, while at the same time reaffirming this identity in the very act of acknowledging its capacity for change, redefining "tribal" spatially and temporally.

A quick glance at the contents of her volume *Bone Dance: New and Selected Poems, 1965–1993* (1994) reveals poems set in or otherwise associated with Iowa City ("Incident at a Hamburger Stand: Iowa City"), the urban West ("What Distinguishes Sunset in Seattle from Sunset in Chicago"), South Dakota ("Mount Rushmore"), Santa Barbara ("Excavation at Santa Barbara Mission"), Tasmania ("Truganinny"), El Salvador ("The Day They Cleaned Up the Border: El Salvador"), and Wounded Knee ("December"). She has also published two entire volumes of travel poems: *What the Mohawk Made the Hopi Say* (1993), about the American journeys made by Rose and Mohawk poet Maurice Kenny; and *What Happened When the Hopi Hit New York* (1982), with poems about Denver, Alaska, Iowa City, Chicago, New Orleans, Vermont, New Hampshire, Connecticut, and of course New York City. The titles of both volumes explicitly link travel to transcultural encounters and transcultural encounters to stories, the textual places that record and often complicate the questions and problems involved in writing an emerging, mobile Indian identity in all of its complexity and multiplicity. In addition to documenting the difficulties of a migratory pan-Indianism, Rose's traveling is particularly powerful and particularly fraught with conflicts between her self-image and her "image as an Indian" because, as she has written in her autobiographical piece "Neon Scars," she continues to search for her Hopi roots, for "a comfortable identity" (253):

> It would certainly be better for my image as an Indian poet to manufacture something and let you believe in my traditional, loving, spiritual childhood where every winter evening was spent immersed in storytelling and ceremony, where the actions of every day continually told me I was valued. (261)

In what ways does the rootlessness of a difficult childhood translate into a series of travels and travel poems? Is it appropriate even to ask this question, let alone possible to develop a response that avoids overburdening or overdetermining "travel," a metaphor whose elasticity makes it easy to stretch so extensively that it risks snapping?[1] And in what ways can such a mobile American poetry simultaneously embody a rooted southwestern sensibility?

Regarding travel as the process or processes of traveling into or through cultures and locating connections between cultures and stories, Rose has found, that "As my travels increased and I began to see a little more of the world and its people on their home turf, I felt more and more a sense of being linked not only to Native American issues, but to related concerns on a global level" (*Bone Dance*, xv). She seems to travel away from, instead of toward, particular American regions. Her Indian identity emerges relationally, not exclusively from a sense of a single, rooted home place and a single tribe but rather from the multiple routes she has traveled and the great variety of people and cultures she has encountered. Along the way, her reflections on travel also include sharp critiques of the routes and motives of counter-traveling colonial powers, whether European or Euro-American, or men suppressing women, parents abusing children, or even some part of Rose herself, as in "Subway Graffiti: An Anthropologist's Impressions," where the speaker of the poem acknowledges her "probing/colonial tongue" (*Bone Dance*, 45). In the introduction to *Bone Dance*, she writes that "halfbreedness is a condition of history, a result of experience, of dislocations and reunions, and of choices made for better or worse" (xvi). She has spoken of her half-breed identity as a traveling "from one half-home to the other" (Coltelli, 122) and describes herself as "an urban, Pan-Indian kind of person" who "grew up with Indian people from all over the country, all different tribes. Some of them had lived on reservations and some of them had spent their whole lives in the city" (Coltelli, 123). Even so, in moving toward and away from these half-homes, in traveling toward and away from other Indians themselves in transit, in articulating these "dislocations and reunions" throughout her life and work, Rose defines a politically charged and at times paradoxical poetics of Hopi and intertribal traveling space: "My hands are still Hopi/and will keep me home/moving back and forth" (*Bone Dance*, 41). What is home? Where is home? And who lives there? "Moved to another planet, home," she writes in "Neon Scars" (255). "I have balanced my bones/between the petroglyph/and the mobile home," between Southwest and Northeast and various other places and peoples across an ever-moving tribal cartography (*Bone Dance*, 42).

Rose speaks as a Hopi, a poet, and an anthropologist when she writes of balancing her bones, positioning herself physically, psychically, and multiculturally as she finds ways to productively entangle the languages of both the petroglyph and the mobile home. These seemingly disparate languages come together for Rose, and for various other southwestern American Indian writers, as rich metaphors for a rootedness that doubles as a routedness.[2] Home places are grounded *and* portable. Both house trailers and Indian rock carvings mark and inhabit particular spaces more often passed through than permanently settled in. And both are signs of mobility; much remains unknown about the purposes of petroglyphs, but as Colin Calloway points out, "rock carvings on the Colorado River Reservation in Arizona . . . belong to an ancient system of markers that pointed Indian runners to trails spanning vast distances" (135). Indeed, the paradoxes of migratory stability and stable mobility are not exclusively Hopi. Laguna Pueblo Indian writer Paula Gunn

Allen, in "The Autobiography of a Confluence," sees mixed-blood identity as characteristic of the state of New Mexico as well as of her own relations; she regards these personal and cultural hybridities as paradoxes encapsulated by stories that are both roads and fences. Albert Yava (Hopi-Tewa) reads petroglyphs as signatures, "evidence of the clans on their migrations" (71). Writing of Zuni rock art, M. Jane Young emphasizes the cultural significance of figures made by individual inscribers; the markers participate in a "dialectic relationship" across "the permeable boundaries between past and present" and record "a movement back and forth between the beings of the myth time and those of today. Thus, for the Zunis, markers in the landscape evoke not so much one's personal past—idiosyncratic events known to only a few, but those events that make up the past of the entire tribe—the time of the beginning when various events happened that now influence the shape of the present" (233–234). Similarly, Young claims that "the very ambiguity of form and meaning of a number of rock art figures . . . allows for a fluidity of meaning and the creative use of the imagination in constructing cultural interpretations" (233). Clearly, she regards literacy in petroglyphs as a migratory process.

Leslie Marmon Silko adds, "Pictographs and petroglyphs of constellations or elk or antelope draw their magic in part from the process wherein the focus of all prayer and concentration is upon the thing itself, which, in its turn, guides the hunter's hand" (*Yellow Woman*, 28–29). Like Young, Silko sees petroglyphs not only as fixed signs but also as important parts of a topography already in motion: "Survival depended upon harmony and cooperation not only among human beings, but also among all things—the animate and the less animate, since rocks and mountains were known on occasion to move" (*Yellow Woman*, 29). In a sense, both the hunters and the land are grounded; in a sense, both the hunters and the land are in motion, passing through. Indians do get lost sometimes, but "[l]ost travelers and lost piñon-nut gatherers have been saved by sighting a rock formation they recognize only because they once heard a hunting story describing this rock formation" (*Yellow Woman*, 32). Stories, themselves in motion, describe grounded landmarks; hunters remember the stories, understanding them as maps that move in a variety of directions, transecting time and space. Silko writes, "Indeed, stories are most frequently recalled as people are passing by a specific geographical feature or the exact location where a story took place" (*Yellow Woman*, 33). To be literate in petroglyphs—literate in the land as in the stories—is to be comfortable with travel or migration and able to survive its vicissitudes. Mobile homes, in tribal historical contexts, are nothing new.

In summary, as Rose constructs a mobile identity of her own as a Hopi, an anthropologist, a teacher, a writer, and a woman, she develops a sense, always in process, of the relations between a variety of personal and cultural identities. She writes,

> My father told me . . . that Hopi earth does contain my roots and I am, indeed, from that land. Because the roots are there, I will find them. But

when I find them, he said, I must rebuild myself as a Hopi. I am not merely a conduit, but a participant. I am not a victim, but a woman. ("Neon Scars," 261)

Travel is not simply or exclusively a quest for a single, unimplicated self that somehow detaches from the gender of the traveler, the places she visits, or the peoples she encounters. As a process of reconstruction, travel is unpredictable and potentially dangerous; Creek poet Joy Harjo writes, in her autobiographical piece "Ordinary Spirit":

> Each time I write I am in a different and wild place, and travel toward something I do not know the name of. Each poem is a jumping-off edge and I am not safe, but I take more risks and understand better now how to take them. They do not always work, but when they do it is worth it. (265)

Far from idealizing mobility, Harjo, like Rose and Silko, sees it as a mixed blessing that provides both options and restrictions. It introduces paradoxes of stasis and movement (the mobile home), legibility and indecipherability (the petroglyph). In traveling, these American Indian women poets risk re-building themselves as they struggle to translate their travels into memory, language, and an understanding of tribal identity as a process of moving to, from, and through southwestern home places.

Rose's understanding of herself as a participant also reinforces the idea that she is not alone in writing about her travels; she does not see herself as, for example, the heroic or exceptional writer of romance or legend, questing for holy grails or roaming toward sanctioned happy endings. In contrast, she appreciates and has written sympathetically about Coyote's lone wanderings and seemingly random encounters along road after road after never-ending road (see "Coyote," in *Bone Dance*, 108). When Rose travels, and when she reflects on her experiences in transit and in transition, she joins or is joined by not only her pan-Indian friends but also many other American Indian storytellers and writers, whether autobiographers recording forced removals (to boarding schools, U.S. agencies, or other new territories), novelists imagining characters and cultures in constant and conflicted motion, or storytellers describing emergences from world to world. Travel is an essential condition of American Indian literature in general; as many of this book's examples indicate, Indian writers often combine rather than separate their "local" (or "regional") and their "migratory" identities. Black Elk traveled to England by his own choice, as part of Buffalo Bill's Wild West show; N. Scott Momaday and Silko describe the repercussions of protagonists' traumatic experiences overseas in World War II; Abel and Tayo (as well as Momaday's Set) also travel to and from tribal home places, often carrying with them a sense of discon-nectedness from much of what "home" signifies; Zitkala-Ša retells the experience of journeying away from home to Indian boarding school; Jason Betzinez writes of the Warm Springs Apaches' "wandering kind of life" (29) and travels often even after his assimilation into Euro-American culture; Ella

Deloria's *Waterlily* begins with a journey from one camp to the next; characters in the fiction of Sherman Alexie, A. A. Carr, Anna Lee Walters, Silko, Louis Owens, and Louise Erdrich take road trips; Alexie and James Welch describe horse-taking parties; Walters's *Ghost Singer* at times seems to be the first American Indian novel about airports as well as a remarkable narrative about the "travels" of depatriated Indian remains and of contemporary Indians who set in motion multiregional intertribal convergences; Sarah Winnemucca records her amazing travel adventures in *Life among the Piutes*; like Joy Harjo, cosmopolitan Indian poets Simon Ortiz, Jim Barnes, and Carter Revard all travel widely and write traveling poems; in his "Report to the Nation," Revard, an Osage Rhodes scholar, claimed the Eiffel Tower for the Osage.

Coyote, to name but a single trickster figure, is of course an archtraveler who just keeps going along, no matter what happens. So too do *images* of Indians travel, for better and for worse, in both predictable and surprising directions; while these images are often created and regulated by non-Indians, they are nonetheless difficult to separate entirely from various issues and strategies mobilized by American Indian writers. Indian critiques of European and Euro-American immigrations to the Americas also belong in this discussion, even though some of these critiques take the broad disciplinary forms of history, theology, or prophecy rather than the broad literary forms of fiction, autobiography, or poetry.[3] This immense indigenous literature of travel and migration has been underappreciated as a body of work; it has also been underestimated as a political strategy, particularly in the Southwest, where Euro-American migratory styles and motives intervene so problematically with Indians in motion. As Silko suggests in *Almanac of the Dead* and in fleeting places elsewhere (see *Yellow Woman*), these shifting strategies of resistance-in-motion have in a sense been successful beyond words.

Clifford writes that for him, one particular European-Indian "travel conjuncture . . . has, to my thinking at least, come to occupy a paradigmatic place":

> Call it the "Squanto effect." Squanto was the Indian who greeted the pilgrims in 1620 in Plymouth, Massachusetts, who helped them through a hard winter, and who spoke good English. To imagine the full effect of this meeting, you have to remember what the "New World" was like in 1620: you could smell the pines fifty miles out to sea. Think of coming into a new place like that and having the uncanny experience of running into a Patuxet just back from Europe. (18–19)

In this evocative passage, Clifford does not "imagine the full effect of this meeting" because he only imagines how the incoming Europeans might have felt about it; as a result, he presents Squanto as an unrepresentative Indian, an extraordinary means of redefining a sturdily canonical cultural encounter.

Clifford critiques "nomadology"—"the breakdown of everything into every-thing" (44)—as yet another way to romanticize peoples in motion, to glorify (in this instance) American Indians (typically Plains Indians) as noble savages with fine horses and spectacular headdresses who went anywhere at any time. But he also romanticizes Squanto and the incoming Europeans who encounter him, and this romantic inflection needs to be regarded as an integral part of the paradigm Clifford presents.

Far from being so exotic, however, Squanto exemplifies a long-standing if intracontinental indigenous habit of travel and migration, with a well-established system of trade and language exchange. That is, Native American tribal cultures were migratory before the arrival of European explorers and colonists; their status as peoples-in-motion does not originate with and thus depend on the incoming and often intrusive movements of these colonial cultures. Indeed, Clifford's Squanto stands on the shore as a traveling precursor to the pilgrims as well as an "alien" or "savage" being. In this sense, he also exemplifies an important point: the historical and cultural contexts of American Indian migration are very broad. For this reason in this chapter my discussion ranges beyond the American Southwest while suggesting that the very prevalence of migration, as both physical and narrative act, loosens "regional" borders in any case. At the same time, it is important to keep in mind both that tribal peoples maintain strong attachments to particular places and that the pilgrims who met Squanto were traveling westward, if not south-westward. While it is not possible to precisely describe the ideological shape of any of "their" Wests and Southwests, it is surely possible to imagine the pilgrims regarding Squanto as an arresting physical and ideological manifestation—perhaps even an incarnation—of that landed and politically charged American space. And it is possible to imagine Squanto's knowledge of multiple, wide-ranging, migratory exchanges of material goods, languages, routes, and roots.

Certainly it is important to proceed cautiously in negotiating the various pitfalls of writing about tribal peoples who traveled—with varying degrees of skill, luck, and intertribal exchange—while continuously fashioning and maintaining culturally particular ways of life, including of course oral traditions. For example, some tribal stories have not, for a variety of reasons, been shared with Europeans and Euro-Americans, while others have been lost. Faced with willed as well as unwilled absences in their historical narratives, Euro-American scholars sometimes fill in the "blanks" of "prehistory" in rather imaginative ways, despite the cautions and admonitions of native scholars like Vine Deloria Jr.[4] One example to which Deloria turns is Paul Martin's Pleistocene overkill theory, here summarized usefully by Calvin Luther Martin:

> [W]herever sapient man and woman migrated over the face of the earth, penetrating continents and subcontinents and major islands that had never before witnessed this new version of *Homo*, there soon followed a

paroxysm of mega-mammalian destruction and extinction of unprecedented proportions. . . . What was new was extinction without replacement by similarly adapted species. (*In the Spirit,* 33)[5]

Deloria observes, "Not all scholars endorse this idea, at least partially because it is ludicrous, but the popular mind . . . now cites the theory during discussions of Indian hunting and fishing rights as a means of proving that the blame for declining game resources should be placed on the Indians and not on themselves" ("Afterword," 433). In addition to this ideologically loaded tactic, Martin's overkill thesis also in a sense discredits Indian mobility itself, regarding it not as a means to productive interaction between human persons and animal persons but rather as a sort of bungling migratory excess, the Pleistocene equivalent of gangland massacres.

As many native and non-native historians have made clear, cultural exchanges and migrations had been happening for countless years before European colonials arrived and influenced, spatially as well as temporally, the patterns and purposes of indigenous cultures in motion. But many native thinkers reject the Euro-American theory of native immigration across a long-vanished Bering land bridge from Siberia to Alaska and from there into North, Central, and South America.[6] Given the absence of concrete evidence, Deloria observes of this theory, "We can be certain of only one thing: the Bering Strait theory is preferred by the whites and consequently becomes accepted as scientific fact" (433). Deloria argues that, for white scientists, Christian theology—here, the Christian Creation story and its trappings, including its insistence on a particular post-Creation migratory demographics—transmutes into scientific theory (433). Additionally, the Bering Strait theory in effect identifies Indians as immigrants, removing their status as indigenous peoples and thereby altering the status of colonialist whites as agents of dispossession. (If Native Americans weren't the original possessors, then they can hardly see themselves, or be seen, as dispossessed.) As such, the Bering Strait theory serves, ironically, as precisely what it denies: evidence of European and Euro-American attempts to control the status of indigenous peoples as defined by their (alleged, actual, voluntary, compulsory) movements. The Bering Strait theory (with Indians as immigrants, moving from west to east and north to south) dispossesses American Indians as surehandedly as the imperialist myths of westward expansion (with Europeans and Euro-Americans as destroyers moving from east to west and north to south).

My approach to tribal travels differs from both the Bering Strait theory and Clifford's Squanto effect in that I link physical and textual migrations while also attempting, to the extent possible, to resituate these migrations in intertribal contexts that remain important to a variety of contemporary Indian writers. Many Indians disregard Beringia in favor of tribal knowledge that locates the people in a particular geographical (and metaphysical) place from the beginning; as Calloway writes, "Many tribal legends fix the origins of particular Indian peoples firmly in their historic homeland" (134). Silko complicates this observation to some extent when she points out,

> The Emergence was an emergence into a precise cultural identity. Thus, the Pueblo stories about the Emergence and Migration are not to be taken as literally as the anthropologists might wish. Prominent geographical features and landmarks that are mentioned in the narratives exist for ritual purposes, not because the Laguna people actually journeyed south for hundreds of years. (*Yellow Woman*, 36)

But giving tribal priority to specifically located origin stories does not rule out the narrative experience of migration: many origin stories themselves are migration stories in which the people move up through a succession of clearly mapped worlds, descend from the sky, or otherwise travel to the specific originary place. From these stories and their tellers, many Indians know places they have never seen face-to-face. Moreover, Albert Yava, from Tewa Village in northern Arizona, says, "One thing we can be sure of is that people weren't just moving down from the north. They were travelling in all directions" (37). It is also clear from a variety of Indian and non-Indian sources that this continent was crisscrossed with pathways that brought tribes richly, productively, and frequently into contact with each other. And they still do. Rose is one example, and, as Patricia Clark Smith points out, Harjo is another: Harjo's "work traces the modern Pan-Indian trails criss-crossing the country, no longer trade routes in the old way, but circuits—the pow-wow circuit, the academic-feminist lecture circuit, the poetry-reading circuit. The primacy of travel in her works probably makes her . . . the most typical of contemporary American Indian writers" (143).

Calloway, a Euro-American historian focusing on interactions between Indians and European colonists in early America, explains the importance of intertribal activity on the "old" circuits. In a chapter titled "New Nomads and True Nomads," he explains that the American "continent was laced with well-traveled trails" (135), some of which have been transformed into U.S. roads and highways, including, for example, U.S. Highway 11 through the Appalachian Mountains (136). Silko corroborates: "The Laguna Pueblo migration stories refer to specific places—mesas, springs, or cottonwood trees—not only locations that can be visited still, but also locations that lie directly on the state highway route linking Paguate village with Laguna village" (*Yellow Woman*, 35). Streams and rivers were also used as travel routes. These paths served a variety of purposes:

> Diplomats and messengers covered enormous distances along such paths. People visited friends and relatives for social, economic, and ceremonial purposes. . . . Travelers frequently met others on the trail, smoked with them, and shared hospitality before continuing on their journeys. (Calloway, 136)

In *Writing without Words*, a volume on indigenous Mesoamerican cultures, various contributors (particularly Elizabeth Hill Boone and Dana Leibsohn) make clear that Indians have been excellent, imaginative cartographers for a long time. In fact, European explorers and travelers often relied on native maps and guides, although, as Calloway observes, when "Europeans produced maps of their own . . . they also helped dispossess Indians and render them invisible" (137). Ironically, Europeans often used Indian trails as immigration routes; conduits between known Indian locations became the avenues of "re-location" and dislocation.

In addition, Indian stories often describe a world in which human beings are not the only migrating peoples; Silko recalls deer hunt stories that "contained information of critical importance about the behavior and migration patterns of mule deer. Hunting stories carefully described key landmarks and locations of fresh water. Thus, a deer-hunt story might also serve as a map" (*Yellow Woman*, 32). A Dene and Inuit myth about caribou also keeps close track of animal migration. As Sean Kane explains,

> This myth seemed like superstitious knowledge to wildlife biologists sent to study what appeared to be a dramatic decline in the numbers of the Kaminuriak herd in the early seventies. The biologists attributed the decline to overhunting. But the Dene people knew better. Their myth tells of a great hole in the ground into which the caribou periodically disappear. The hole is covered by a caribou skin and two rabbits guard it. When the time is right, the two rabbits will pull the skin away and the caribou will return from their spirit world. (42)

The upshot of Kane's story is that "Native experience, accumulated over ages and organized mythically into informal and flexible systems with natural variation accepted, is better able to account for northern unpredictability" (43). In 1982, "the rabbits pulled the caribou skin aside and the Kaminuriak herd exploded from a supposed precipitous decline to an estimated 200,000 animals. It turned out that the basic [Western scientific] assumptions about caribou biology were wrong" (43). Without demonizing Science or resorting to stereotypes of noble savages mystically attuned to Nature, I want to emphasize that native oral storytellers and contemporary writers often acknowledge powerful and intricate interactions between animals and humans, crossings of permeable boundaries toward mutually courteous and helpful compacts (treaties, perhaps). Animal and human peoples have the extraordinary capacity to move closer to one another and to honor these reciprocally beneficial exchanges in a rich variety of songs and stories. For a variety of reasons, these exchanges happen less frequently as tribal involvement with Euro-American cultures increases; in James Welch's novel *Fools Crow* (1986), for example, human characters not yet fully exposed to white soldiers and settlers still interact with Frog Chief and Raven as well as with mythic figures such as Feather Woman, and even then, only a select few humans are so honored. Even as American soldiers and settlers encroach on the Pikunis' home places, imposing various forms of boundaries in the process, the Pikunis maintain and continue to negotiate various, particular physical and metaphysical borders.

Some of the most vital permeable boundaries can still be located in origin stories. In the creation stories of many North American Indian tribes, human and animal peoples migrate, sometimes exchanging physical forms along the way; these migrations often bring the people to the place they identify historically as their homeland. To borrow Clifford's formulation, roots interconnect with routes, and to be rooted means also to be routed. These interconnections are often discussed in autobiographies by American Indians, in part because the autobiographer sees his or her life as inseparably intertwined with the life of the larger whole, the clan or tribe. Yava in his autobiography, *Big Falling Snow*, says,

> It is hard to put down something with myself as a center of interest—that is, to say I did this or that. It makes me out as important, which isn't the way I see it. We Tewas and Hopis don't think of ourselves that way. In our histories and traditions we don't have individual heroes with names to remember. (4)

The roots, like the routes and like the stories about both, are communal, and Yava works hard in this autobiography to preserve as much of that communal quality and function as is possible. Speaking of the traveling history of his people, he says that "adding it all up you can say that [the various Hopi clans] came from just about every direction" (36). As he points out, "[I]t's clear that the modern Hopis are descendants of numerous different groups, including Plains Indians, that merged after gravitating to this place" (36). Yava links this tribal historical knowledge to the Hopi creation stories, another form of historical intelligence: "[T]he beginning of our earthly experience was when the people emerged from the underworld. . . . The clans separated and went in different directions, but eventually they converged here" (37). Problems within or between clans also caused migrations; when the people fell into contention, "evil ways," they would sometimes "pack up and leave" (37). Earlier, the Hopi migrated up through the First, Second, and Third Worlds, finally traveling "up inside the bamboo stalk" (40) to the Fourth World, where they presently live. During these originary times, the people also shifted species identities: "Way back in the distant past, the ancestors of humans were living down below in a world under the earth. They weren't humans yet. . . . They lived in darkness, behaving like bugs" (38). Later, they evolved, "but they were still animals in form . . . some with tails, some without" (38). In tribal creation stories, the physical, geographical migration often coincides with a sort of bodily migration, whether shape-shifting or the type of evolution described by Yava and the Hopi. Becoming a true human, a real person, is a process that occurs across both time and space. Identity, both personal and tribal, emerges as a result of migration.

Yava makes clear that different clans have different versions of creation, and also emphasizes that not all Hopi accept the "standard" creation story he tells here and that tribes have knowledge of, and sometimes are involved in, other tribes' creation stories. In other words, the stories are not monolithic but rather are discussed and contested as well as communally remembered and preserved, and the contacts between tribes, brought about by traveling, actively inform the people's sense of who and where they are. As Yava remarks, "We Hopis . . . can't be explained so easily" (36).

Particularly intriguing is the status of migration in Navajo creation stories. The Navajo, as Andrew Wiget writes,

> came to the Southwest, most anthropologists believe, around A.D. 1500 from the Canadian Yukon, Athabascan peoples who knew nothing of agriculture or the Emergence myth. Under the pressure of forced association with Pueblo refugees from the Spanish reconquest following the Pueblo Revolt of 1680, they became agriculturalists and adapted the Pueblo Emergence story to their own purposes, later refining it through contact with the Hopi and the Zuni. For these borrowings they unabashedly give credit in their origin myth, acknowledging that when they emerged they met the Kisani, "house dwellers" or Puebloans, who were already living there, a people with hair cut straight across their brows who taught them about agriculture. (11)

As the Navajo migrate from northwest to southwest, their Emergence story follows suit, accompanying them and, like the storytellers, adapting to the new and very different sacred and secular geography of present-day New Mexico and Arizona. Paul Zolbrod, like Wiget, links the Navajo acquisition of agriculture to their adaptations of "the accompanying emergence mythology" (31); the migratory culture's idea of itself is capable of being changed, influenced by Pueblo technology but also by a dialogic commitment to both groundedness (the new home place) and mobility. The Navajo do not adapt at the expense of themselves; they should not be regarded simply or strictly as adaptive peoples.

Calloway distinguishes between native migration stories, which "explained how they came to be where they were" (135), and the gradual formation of cultural identities that link and root Indians to particular places. In part, Calloway (like various other Euro-American historians and anthropologists) attempts to reconstruct a poetics of tribal life in "the world of the Indian peoples before the arrival of Columbus," to quote the subtitle to Alvin M. Josephy's *America in 1492*. This reconstruction is difficult to accomplish, for obvious reasons. Deloria keeps close tabs on Euro-American reconstruction efforts, often exposing them as ideologically motivated fantasies; he also explains why Euro-American "scholars have had a difficult time piecing together the maps of pre-Discovery America" (*God Is Red*, 102–103):

> [E]ven the closest approach to the Western idea of history by an Indian tribe was yet a goodly distance from Western historical conceptions. What appears to have survived as a tribal conception of history almost

everywhere was the description of conditions under which the people lived and the location in which they lived. Migrations from one place to another were phrased in terms descriptive of why they moved. Exactly when they moved was, again, "a long time ago." (*God Is Red*, 102)

Compare the remarks of a Euro-American historian, Francis Jennings:

> Though much remains conjectural, it is certain that migration in North America [before 1492] was not a one-way street, nor was acculturation. Migrations from the North and Northwest were a constant over many generations, unavoidably encountering the northward-moving descendants of migrants from the South. (358)

Jennings's qualification, "much remains conjectural," and his pitting of "conjecture" against "certainty" both reveal much about an approach reluctant to accord full validity to imaginative, tribal historical reconstructions of the interactions between the place and the people who lived there. Western historical methodology overrules tribal stories; intertribal encounters are imagined as "unavoidable" rather than tactical.

Given the uninvolving quality of much textbook historical prose written by Euro-Americans as well as the pitfalls of "nomadology"—the temptation to slide into fantasy, romance, overgeneralization, and other such excesses— I would simply point out that cultural encounters and exchanges did not begin with the arrival of European invaders on American shores. And American Indian literature has, for a long time, had a great deal to do with travel and migration. The ideologies (and, with Silko particularly, the political resistances) of Indian migration stories should be compared to the ideologies actively at work in Euro-American migrations as well as in Euro-American historiographical and critical responses to Indian migration, including my own.

There is a dynamic relationship between grounded, rooted home places and an American Indian traveling intelligence, an intelligence of travel; further, there is a great deal of creative interplay between tribal and textual migrations, and this interplay is often reflected in crossings between oral and written native literatures. Rose and Harjo embody and exemplify these migratory relationships and so does N. Scott Momaday, who has long held the conviction that this dynamic is central to his identity as a Kiowa. Although Momaday imaginatively supports the Bering land bridge theory, he has written that "It is tempting to associate the hollow log [of Kiowa origin stories, through which Kiowa people migrated into this continent] with the passage to America, the peopling of the Americas, to find in it a metaphorical reflection of the land bridge" ("Becoming of the Native," 17). Momaday creatively (and, to some readers, controversially) links the Kiowa origin story to a larger idea of Indian dispersal or diffusion throughout this continent and thereby links Native American literature to native migration in a way that needs to be thought through more fully than it has been.

Momaday himself has traveled extensively, and his travels have become a solid part of his identity as a canonical writer. He was born in Lawton, Oklahoma, and grew up in a variety of places: Navajo country, Jemez Pueblo, Santa Fe and Albuquerque, and Fort Defiance, Virginia. Awarded the Ph.D. from Stanford University, he has held teaching positions in Santa Barbara, Berkeley, Palo Alto, and Tucson; he has exhibited his paintings in the United States, Switzerland, Germany, and elsewhere; he spent the spring semester of 1974 as visiting professor of American literature at the University of Moscow. All of this information is worth considering in the context of trans-world migrations in the creation stories Momaday returns to as well as in the interconnections, in his life and art, between routes and roots. As Charles L. Woodard argues, Momaday's clearly articulated "idea of the importance of place is . . . not contradicted by [his] nomadism" (48). *The Way to Rainy Mountain* perhaps enacts a sort of imaginative, formal and stylistic migration by moving among and across three parallel "levels" of narrative, including Momaday's physical and imaginative retracings of historical Kiowa migrations. And throughout his written work, Momaday reflects on and represents himself, with depth and complexity, as a Kiowa Indian writer in motion.

Momaday's journeys, writes Woodard, are "not linear and permanent, as is so often true of modern displacements, but circular and, in interesting ways, continuous. . . . One returns to one's native landscape whenever possible, to renew oneself. But the return is as importantly spiritual, and can be accomplished through the oral tradition" (48). In this sense, the repetition of stories from one text to another—one of the characteristics of Momaday's work as well as Silko's—can be understood as a form of migratory return and renewal. There is also, as is reflected in statements Momaday makes in interviews, the sheer joy of traveling:

> Well, the greatest light upon landscape that I know of is in the Southwest. I have never seen light such as one sees in northern New Mexico. . . . And I've seen wondrous light in Russia. I've been in Soviet central Asia, where in the foothills of the Himalayas there is wonderful light. I've also been in the Virgin Islands, where there is another kind of light, and in the Arctic, where there is yet another kind of light. So all of these are interesting to me. (Woodard, 182)

Class issues come into play here as well: Momaday, unlike many American Indian writers, let alone nonwriters, has the prestige, finances, and leisure time necessary to undertake so many world travels. For other Indian writers, a decision to live or travel off the reservation raises very complicated issues; a decision to relocate a hundred miles away from the reservation is difficult enough. While keeping in mind the power relations involved in determining and maintaining the cultural "status" of Indian writers, I want to emphasize these various forms of cultural movement for the purposes of this study, as one way of redefining, and pluralizing, ideas and practices of "literary movement." A literary movement can be labeled "modernism," but it can also be described as a physical and/or textual journey from one place to another. Sherman Alexie's movements from Spokane to Seattle and from relative obscurity to national recognition are both relevant to his writing itself. Locating him in relation to a literary "school" or period may be less important than coming to terms with other movements he has experienced and written about. Similarly, the "Southwest" should be regarded as a grounded yet fluid home place that can and should be in motion; as physically concrete and sensually vital as Momaday's Southwest is, for example, there is also something amorphous and shifting about it. In his first novel, he figures this conjunction deftly as a house made of dawn and a man, Abel, running.

In particular, this book will move around and through the work—primarily the fiction but also the photography theory—of Leslie Marmon Silko, whose most recent novel, *Almanac of the Dead*, is simultaneously the most extraordinary and most paradigmatic contemporary Native American migration narrative. Before turning to Silko, though, I want to read Paula Gunn Allen's autobiographical narrative, "The Autobiography of a Confluence," which interconnects suggestively with much of Silko's work, even though Allen has distanced herself from Silko to some extent, criticizing her for revealing too much, in *Ceremony*, of Laguna Pueblo Indian ceremonies (see Allen, "Special Problems").[7] A. Lavonne Ruoff explains that Laguna Pueblo origin stories describe a series of tribal migrations, including various interminglings of migrating tribes. The Laguna tribe itself "came southward from the Mesa Verde region," periodically moved about this southerly region, invited other clans to join them at Old Laguna, and then, in the late 1600s, was joined by "immigrants [who] came chiefly from Zia, Cochiti, and Domingo, but a few came from Jemez, Zuni, and Hopi" ("Ritual and Renewal," 70). Over time, Navajos married into the tribe, and Spanish colonizers came through; one result of all of these cultural encounters and exchanges is a hybridity brought about by intercultural exchanges and interracial marriages.

Allen has spoken and written a great deal about her particular mixed-blood genealogy. As she tells interviewer Donna Perry,

> My background was very diverse. My father is Lebanese and my mother is Laguna and Scottish. She was raised a Presbyterian and a heathen and my father was raised as a Maronite Roman Catholic. He grew up speaking Arabic and Spanish, and when she was tiny she spoke Laguna. But since her mother married a German immigrant and they moved to Cubero [New Mexico], a Spanish-speaking town, when Mother was quite small, she forgot Laguna and learned Spanish and English. (interview, 2)

In the interview with Perry, Allen also speaks about her identities as an Indian academic, as a novelist, and as a "ceremonial lesbian," adeptly negotiating between and across "a lot of voices" and "many different personae" (3) toward a strong sense of who she is and what she does (see, e.g., Allen's essay

"*Hwame, Koshkalaka,* and the Rest: Lesbians in American Indian Cultures," in *Sacred Hoop,* particularly 257–258). As she makes abundantly clear in "The Autobiography of a Confluence," her sense of herself is inseparable from her senses of place, of tribe, and of the road. She is at, and she is, a confluence.

Allen emphasizes this transitional quality in the shifts between the various sections that constitute her autobiographical essay. These sections are titled "Tucson: First Night"; "Stories Are Roads, Stories Are Fences"; "The Highway Is Forever"; "The Road Is Stories, Is Dreams"; and "On the Road." Because the Southwest is "the confluence of cultures, the headwaters of Mexico" ("Autobiography," 145), a place distinguished by the movements of peoples across and through it, a southwestern Indian like Allen can call herself a "multicultural event" (Coltelli, 16) who powerfully remembers the New Mexico highways and roads that carry enormous metaphorical freight and autobiographical significance. The story of Allen's life is many stories of traveling, watching, and remembering these roads and the fluid connections or dangerous colonizations that are so inextricably a part of their paradoxical merging of stasis (the road stands still) and mobility (the road enables movement): "My life is the pause. The space between. The not this, not that, not the other. The place that the others go around. Or around about. It's more a Möbius strip than a line" ("Autobiography," 151). Some of us, she writes,

> live on the road that the dead walk down. We ride it out of town and back. By its meanders we discover what is there, what is not. By its power we are drawn into a confluence of minds, of beings, of perceptions, of styles. It is a singularly powerful place, the road that runs across the middle of the lands, the roads that run, everywhere, bordering the Big Arroyo that leads to the other place, that connects us to it and them to us. (153–154)

Allen concludes "The Autobiography of a Confluence" by saying,

> Essentially, my life, like my work, is a journey-in-between, a road. . . . In my mind, as in my dreams, every road I have traveled, every street I have lived on, has been connected in some primal way to The Road, as we called it, like Plato in our innocence. That Road has many dimensions; it exists on many planes; and on every plane it leads to the wilderness, the mountain, as on every plane it leads to the city, to the village, and to the place beneath where Iyatiku waits, where the four rivers meet, where I am going, where I am from. (154)

To be and to remember being Indian, being Laguna, Allen turns to the roads and The Road that effect and figure the processes of coming and going, the multicultural place as multidirectional space. In traveling and in locating the connections between roads, she paradoxically and typically finds the confluences that double as self-identity. In traveling these routes, whatever routes, she returns to her roots. Similarly, Silko makes a variety of complex connections between selves and places; like Allen, Silko values the confluences and enters into them actively. Typically, she articulates the intricacy of her sense of self by locating it spatially and textually: to think about who she is, Silko tells stories about where she has been, where she is, and how she gets there. For both Allen and Silko, travelers bring stories, travelers are stories, and stories travel. Identity travels, stories are identity, and traveling is identity.

Silko has traveled, for example, to Ketchikan, Alaska, where she lived between 1976 and 1978 and where she wrote *Ceremony*, and she took a three-week trip to China by invitation of the Chinese Writers Association (Coltelli, 146, and Barnes, 61). "Yellow Woman" in all of its various incarnations in *Storyteller* alone is certainly a kind of travel story as well as a kind of captivity narrative; it tells of a woman wandering outside the bounds of the community and eventually, importantly, returning. After she tries out several stories on her husband in the poem "Storytelling," he leaves her, and she doesn't blame him: "I could have told/the story/better than I did" (*Storyteller*, 98). Still, she brings stories back with her, and he listens to them before deciding that they are not very persuasive. The traveler returns with stories that can confer and change identity, particularly self-identity; as Melody Graulich writes, "Walking away from her everyday identity as daughter, wife, and mother, she takes possession of transgressive feelings and desires by recognizing them in the stories she has heard, by blurring the boundaries between herself and Yellow Woman" (14). But these stories, and the identities that perhaps hinge on and in them, must be told and retold; in negotiating these boundaries, she must also negotiate home audiences. As Silko has written elsewhere, "through the stories we *hear* who we are" (*Yellow Woman*, 30, emphasis added).

Driving Silko's firmly canonized first novel, *Ceremony* (1977), are the perception, narration, and celebration of emerging, shifting, highly complicated patterns. These patterns, inherent in specific places and intricately wound up in stories, teach characters, storytellers, and readers alike how to read and respond to catastrophic local and global concerns. Travel is intimately bound up in this process. What confuses Tayo is the apparent blurring and overlapping of different places: he sees relationships between the South Pacific jungle and the New Mexico Pueblo; he feels that his curse against the wet jungle rebounds and causes the drought that afflicts postwar Laguna Pueblo. He sees his uncle Josiah's face superimposed on the body of a Japanese soldier in the Philippines. Along with this sense of storywebs comes a sense of entanglement; at times the delicacy and strength of webs double as the confusion and disorientation of tangles. The proximity and extremity of the danger help dramatize the great power of the patterns as well as the vitality of native traditions, provided that these traditions are understood as highly flexible and at the same time, finally, legible, coherent, cohesive.

Jana Sequoya-Magdaleno complicates *Ceremony* further still, arguing that

> At the narrative level, the contradictions personified by the protagonist are resolved in terms of his accommodation within the sacred traditions of the Laguna (Tayo's entrance into the society of the Kiva); at the performative level of reader reception, the repositioning of the sacred clan story

within the secular terms of the literary market generates new framing conditions that accommodate the canonization of *Ceremony* as a representative text of pedagogical multiculturalism. (107)

Sequoya-Magdaleno critiques and troubles the position of the recreational reader of *Ceremony*, refusing to allow that reader the complacency of, in effect, staying at home while at the same time vicariously participating in a sacred ceremony that—according to Betonie's definitions and exemplified by Tayo's practices—travels. The controversies over Silko's publication of sacred knowledge also militate against such recreational readings of the novel, but they unsettle flexible, migratory readers as well, especially if those readers have not been formally accommodated within Laguna sacred traditions. In this sense, *Ceremony* raises extraordinarily complex questions of travel and identity.

In *Place and Vision,* Robert M. Nelson discusses some of these questions as he methodically details where Tayo goes and how the novel moves through a secular and sacred geography; Nelson explains why people, places, and stories interconnect as they do. Clearly, *Ceremony* has a great deal to do with movement, and this movement to some extent brings people, places, and texts closer to each other. In other ways, the book critiques this vague ideal of cultural harmony, particularly by moving farther and farther away from strictly Euro-American characters and designs as it gets deeper into a ceremony that urges "no boundaries, only transitions" (Silko, *Ceremony,* 246). The movements between worlds; the transatlantic movements from Laguna Pueblo to the South Pacific; the Bataan Death March; the movement through metaphysical "windows" into what appears to be a mythic time and place peopled by Ts'eh and Tayo and Mountain Lion, the Hunter; Tayo's movement, on foot and with striking stamina and sensory alertness, toward the novel and ceremony's climax at Trinity Site; the significantly limited movements of Indian men in beat-up pickup trucks, trapped in similarly dilapidated nostalgic secular ceremonies; the negotiations among characters, ceremonies, and readers, particularly non-Laguna readers; all of these and more speak to the complex ways in which Silko investigates the political, cultural, and literary ramifications of migratory experience.

Silko's most daring and complex treatise-narrative about migration is clearly *Almanac of the Dead* (1991). In this enormous 763-page novel, she almost immediately questions what "Southwest" means and to whom. One of the ways she does so is to set characters and cultures in migratory movement and to circulate the stories they tell and the rumors they generate, so that textual and ideological migrations intertwine in complex ways, across Maya codices, characters' stories, and Silko's narrative. Through this process, she also reconfigures "Native American literature" and "American literature" radically. In a 1992 review of *Almanac of the Dead*, Joy Harjo makes this very point, seeing the novel as an extension and at the same time an "exploded version" of *Ceremony* and a book that "change[s] the shape and concept of the American novel. It will never be the same" ("World Is Round," 209, 207). Silko does so in part simply by describing trajectories that do not strictly or even primarily point east-west; like Albert Yava, she sees that the people "were traveling in all directions" (Yava, 37), though on a larger scale, in "massive human migrations from continent to continent" (*Almanac,* 511). Like Yava, Silko understands why people travel. More so than Yava, she reveals and critiques the extraordinary multicultural, multinational, ideological characteristics of many qualitatively different migrations.

Inside the covers of the novel is printed a map that makes clear that the region does not signify on an east-west axis only, as though the place only comes visible when approached or perceived from outside it and to the north or northeast. This map also pledges no particular national allegiances to the United States or to Mexico: the national border is drawn thick, looks more impermeable and daunting than permeable or romantic, and "MEXICO" appears in boldface capital letters while "UNITED STATES" does not appear at all. Silko allies herself intertribally with Native America and Native Americans; in the process, she remains critical of the United States and Mexico without regarding them as permanent presences or permanent dangers in the Americas. Indeed, that overdrawn Mexico-U.S. border almost seems a caricature, as thick and bold and absolutely linear as it is. Silko knows full well that borders and border patrols are nothing to laugh about in the 1990s, and "borders haven't worked" (*Yellow Woman,* 122), but she sees such regulatory acts of racist, nationalistic surveillance as symptomatic of a badly eroded system on the way out, frightening to encounter in the form of border police but possible to elude, especially in the 1990s with an indigenous "mass migration . . . already under way" (*Yellow Woman,* 122), and impossible to stop. She works toward disempowering the border, which "is fast becoming a militarized zone" (*Yellow Woman,* 107), and those who attempt to control this border; she participates in an intertribal political and cultural resistance that creatively links forms of prophecy, migration, and narrative.

On Silko's map Tucson, Arizona, is clearly a major convergence point, its name duly capitalized and printed in boldface. Tucson is a place people go from and (more frequently, in this novel) go to, but for some of those people, it lies north by northeast or east rather than southwest. As Reed Way Dasenbrock asks, "What is the Southwest? For whom is it the Southwest? What is the Southwest southwest of?" (123) Granted, there are distinct and distinctive topographies there that make it possible to demarcate the Southwest as a region and southwestern literature as regionalist literature, but for Silko, the "Southwest" looks to be most significantly a place in motion and a place people move to and through. The Southwest is, perhaps preeminently, a migration place and convergence point, a confluence—which, as Paula Gunn Allen makes clear, involves both people and place in its creation and maintenance, in all the dynamic, unpredictable flux of embodied and narrated traditions. Further, the map is not restricted to space and geography but also serves as a temporal map, a "five-hundred-year map" that insistently honors and returns to much older indigenous texts that stand unintimidated by such Western linear-historical markers (Silko's map acknowledges them but refuses to be governed or redrawn by them). And in the novel, Silko frequently diminishes that five hundred years, pointing out that it is neither a particularly long time nor a particularly sturdy time frame when regarded in the context of Indian habitations of the land. "Five hundred years, or five lifetimes, were nothing to people who had already lived in the Americas for twenty or thirty thousand years" (631). Sherman Alexie in *The Lone Ranger and Tonto Fistfight in Heaven* critiques that five-hundred-year time span by referring frequently to it; Silko undercuts Columbus and his consequences by moving beyond him.

As I have begun to argue, learning how to read this map has something to do with learning how to read *Almanac of the Dead* itself. Far from being drawn to scale, the map defies cartographical convention, compressing and distorting whatever version of Truth (topographical, demographic, ideological) maps convey in the first place; the map models the book in this regard, since *Almanac of the Dead* defiantly and happily makes and breaks its own rules rather than observing fidelity to Western "scales" and other standards of measurement. Writing of Nahua identity, Dana Leibsohn argues that "cartographic histories [render] visible a series of ideological propositions" by way of images that "privilege certain memories, setting out a visual framework for indigenous constructions of identity" (161). On these maps of Cuauhtinchan, "Visually, identity takes form in a geographic setting molded by the demands of historical event and memory. It is not necessarily constituted around a stable tableau of sites. Nor does it depend solely upon one set of boundaries or landmarks" (179). Leibsohn's work on these Central Mexican cartographic histories overlaps to some extent with Silko's work in *Almanac of the Dead*, which ranges widely across and through Mexican history and territory. Both Leibsohn and Silko are well aware that maps are ideological statements; in refusing the pretense of cartographic neutrality, Silko uses this map to reinforce the indigenous political resistance that fuels the novel.

For example, except for the thick line between Mexico and the (unnamed) United States, and the Atlantic and Pacific coastlines, the map gives no borderlines: the states of Arizona, New Mexico, and California are not "represented," and neither are any Mexican states. The act of not naming the United States is significant as well; there is enough space to do so on the map, but Silko chooses not to, perhaps suggesting that names of nations themselves function as boundary markers, or, in this instance, binaries, and that "Mexico" is enough. In any event, she decenters U.S. nationalism as much as she can on this map, not only by leaving the States unnamed but also by pluralizing "the Americas" in three of the four boxed insets, in which Silko further politicizes the cartography by adding ideologically explicit historical statements. Empty spaces on maps are important parts of cartographic histories, legible emptinesses that also carry ideological weight as they partially refigure colonial geography as anticolonial space. Similarly, Silko's act of replacing explanations of cartographic symbols ("how to read this map") with political statements ("how to read this map") dares to represent not only the past and present but also the future as it folds into and reconnects with prophecies made long ago.

Typically, maps reveal the names of territories but do not unpack the act of naming by explaining how it happened and who was responsible. While the map in *Almanac of the Dead* avoids naming the United States and demarcating a variety of subdivisions (state and local borders), it does name more than fifty figures and characters (including Geronimo, John Dillinger, the First Black Indians, gangsters from New Jersey, and a Yupik woman named Rose). She carefully links these names to a variety of mostly "southwestern" places, charting the movements of characters between San Diego, Tucson, Tuxtla Gutierrez, and various other sites. Peopled as few maps truly are, Silko's map suggests that even the most malevolent and disconnected characters in the novel are to be understood in relation to places, even if the characters themselves badly misuse the land and misunderstand the importance of place. Silko does not list the name of every character who appears in the book, but the names given cut across past and present, social classes and nationalities, genders and sexualities and races. Although Silko offers a handful of brief sentences (in addition to the inset statements) that may be read as kernels of narratives—"Seese seeks help," "Sterling accidentally goes to Tucson"—the map mainly establishes connections between names and places, implying that stories will emerge from these relationships, whether the people are traveling or at home. This place-centeredness, even in the midst of processes of migration, is axiomatic to Silko and to some of the characters in *Almanac of the Dead*. And, as has been true throughout Silko's thinking and writing over the past twenty-plus years, the characters who interact creatively, respectfully, and receptively with the land are the most able and culturally responsible characters.

Even so, many of these people—most—do not remain in a single place throughout their lives or throughout the novel. Almost anybody in the novel can migrate, and almost everybody does; migration in and of itself is not a valued or devalued act. In other words, migration does not calcify into a moral or ideological absolute, in the sense that all migratory characters are "heroic," "criminal," "political," "authentic," or whatever; their motives vary, as do their abilities, and Silko does not simplify or otherwise soothe readers seeking narratives easily recognizable as "Indian" or "non-Indian." What matters is why people migrate, and what their migrations bring about. Real-estate developer Leah Blue, who has moved to Arizona from Cherry Hill, New Jersey, with her gangster husband, Max, fantasizes about building a heavily irrigated desert town to be called Venice, Arizona. Dealing with a corrupt, deeply conservative federal judge, she unscrupulously arranges to fix the outcome of a water-rights suit brought by local Indians. In contrast, Calabazas, a Yaqui Indian and a smuggler who lives in Tucson, has crossed the U.S.-Mexico border countless times. In an "Indian style" oration to his friend and coworker Root, Calabazas remarks,

> We don't believe in boundaries. Borders. Nothing like that. We are here thousands of years before the first whites. We are here before maps or quit claims. We know where we belong on this earth. We have always moved freely. North-south. East-west. We pay no attention to what isn't real. Imaginary lines. Imaginary minutes and hours. Written law. We recognize none of that. And we carry a great many things back and forth. We don't see any border. We have been here and this has continued thousands of years. We don't stop. No one stops us. (216)

Speaking of "the past" without resorting to a past tense and insisting on a pluralized tribal identity, Calabazas articulates an ideologically charged worldview that merges space, time, and text both as arbitrary Euro-American imports and as powerful indigenous concepts. Unlike Leah Blue, who seeks to disrupt the land and people by imposing profit-making constructions designed by and for outsiders, Calabazas speaks of a fluidity that involves both the people and the land in a continuing process that depends in part on "thousands of years" of cooperation and alliance. Mobility for Calabazas involves both unbounded crossings and a grounded, continuous tribal sense of self that in turn enables a clear sense of Euro-Americans' imaginary constructions of space, land, time, and history. His words insist on both polarity and fluidity.

For Silko, migration links integrally to Euro-American exploitation and to native "defiance and resistance" that further develops into multicultural alliances. In some ways *Almanac of the Dead* charts (or predicts) cultural movements similar to the Euro-American movements (migrations, invasions, appropriations, and so forth) that will be discussed later in this book. In various other ways, Silko radically revises and critiques these movements as she centers not on Euro-American ideas and needs but rather, much more so, on the thoughts and actions of an energetic coalition of indigenous peoples including men and women; Maya, Lakota, Hopi, and Yaqui; homeless Vietnam veterans led by a white Euro-American called Rambo and an African American named Clinton; a Korean computer genius somewhat curiously named Awa Gee; eco-terrorists such as Eco-Grizzly and Eco-Coyote; and many others.

Both the Almanac of the Dead and *Almanac of the Dead* are prophetic texts, and their prophecies are portable. Silko's major prophecy crosses temporal, spatial, and textual boundaries (as well as the borders of race, class, gender, and age), surviving in a punctuated and fragmentary yet still powerful collection of documents. In the novel, Silko writes, simply, "One day a story will arrive in your town" (578). On the map, in the box titled "Prophecy," she gives a necessarily abbreviated explanation of this story's contexts: "When Europeans arrived, the Maya, Azteca, Inca cultures had already built great cities and vast networks of roads. Ancient prophecies foretold the arrival of Europeans in the Americas. The ancient prophecies also foretell the disappearance of all things European." And in another of the boxes, she also emphasizes the connections between ancient and future, time and space, encoding and deciphering: "Through the decipherment of ancient tribal texts of the Americas the Almanac of the Dead foretells the future of all the Americas. The future is encoded in arcane symbols and old narratives." Prophecy carries historical validity; additionally, Silko's *Almanac of the Dead* bears a complex relationship to *the* Almanac of the Dead, so that readers of Silko's novel may be tempted to link her to the prophets, just as readers of *Ceremony* frequently associate Silko with Thought Woman.

According to the prophecies encoded in the Almanac and discussed in the *Almanac*, indigenous peoples will retake the land and/or the land will be returned. Because the people have never really left, this is not an act of recovery as much as a process of reclaiming that involves major shifts in political and cultural empowerment: "Now it was up to the poorest tribal people and survivors of European genocide to show the remaining humans how all could share and live together on earth, ravished as she was" (749). As the novel ends, huge masses of indigenous peoples ("illegal aliens" in a very different discourse) are moving northward across the current Mexico-U.S. line while, at roughly the same time, others from a variety of native and nonnative cultures also converge on Tucson. As these emerging political alliances take shape, Silko insists that the migratory native peoples of the Americas are long-standing and even permanent; in contrast, Euro-America is transient, and its alien visitation will not last forever. As Mayan revolutionary Angelita/La Escapía reflects,

> The old people had stories that said . . . that it was only a matter of time and things European would gradually fade from the American continents. History would catch up with the white man whether the Indians did anything or not. History was the sacred text. The most complete history was the most powerful force. (316)

She argues that Euro-Americans will inevitably disappear from the Americas and Indians will inevitably regain their sovereignty; she sees that these demographic and political shifts will necessarily involve migrations.

The Almanac, then, is very much alive and in motion, though "of the dead" and unknown to the great majority of people, both Indian and non-Indian, who are involved in some way in its prophecies of migrations. What the Almanac prophesies doubles as what has been happening for a long time: the living Almanac of the Dead folds linear time and otherwise challenges the destroyers who seek to impose a terminal "Reign of Death-Eye Dog." By the end of the novel, Trigg, Max Blue, Jamey, Tiny, Greenlee, Menardo, Iliana, David, and Bartolomeo are all dead. Serlo's work on a racially "pure" biosphere has been infiltrated and disrupted by eco-terrorists, who, along with eco-kamikazes, have also been blowing up U.S. property. And in an important meeting in Room 1212 during the International Holistic Healers Convention, a multicultural group of people converges and begins to forge an alliance. Lecha (a Yaqui woman and former television psychic who helps keep the Almanac), Clinton (an African American Vietnam veteran who seeks to link the tribal peoples of Africa and the Americas toward a takeover of America), Calabazas (the aging but still sharp Yaqui Indian and drug smuggler discussed earlier in this chapter), an unnamed African man, Rose (a Yupik woman), Mosca (an Indian man with a spirit in his shoulder), Angelita (the Mayan revolutionary leader), Wilson Weasel Tail (a Lakota poet and ex-lawyer), the Barefoot Hopi (an ex-con working to develop a network of prisoners and others who will also work to take back America)—all of these characters finally meet in the same place, and their convergence is very important, not because everyone automatically agrees on everything (they don't), but because they all understand the crucial relationship between mobility and a new, multitribal sovereignty.

As they meet, the twin brothers Tacho and El Feo are leading masses of people from the south to the north, into the present-day United States. Silko foregrounds neither this migration nor the workings of the Almanac itself; in fact, many readers feel derailed by the book's emphasis on grisly, ugly, violent, altogether horrifying images of dead babies, hungry capitalists, sexual trysts between the conservative Judge Arne and his basset hounds, snuff videos, and many other atrocities that bespeak profound dislocation (see for example St. Clair, "Uneasy Ethnocentrism" and "Death of Love/Love of Death"). However, *Almanac of the Dead* provides counterarguments to these atrocities even before the first chapter begins; Silko's five-hundred-year map places Euro-American excesses in the context of an Indian history and resistance that has been in motion since long before the first arrival of Death-Eye Dog. And these migratory indigenous cultures will not only survive but flourish long after the last Euro-American disappears from this hemisphere. Sterling's return to Laguna Pueblo connects, in its own modest but vitally important way, to these larger, scarier, and at the same time hopeful movements; he sits near the giant stone snake and listens to it, and its reappearance connects to his as he reconnects with his home-in-motion and, with the snake, looks south "in the direction from which the twin brothers and the people would come" (763).

2 Unsettling Frontiers

Billy the Kid and the Outlaw Southwest

Toward the end of *Almanac of the Dead*, politically inflected prophecies help to set in motion large-scale migrations from south to north. These mostly indigenous migratory peoples purposefully cross a variety of physical and imaginary borders constructed by a variety of Euro-Mexican and Euro-American officials, and in the process work toward a coherent, reemerging sense of both tribal and intertribal identity. Moreover, as this intertribal alliance moves across large geopolitical spaces, the people also expect to move across hundreds of years: the Indian history of the Americas already comprehends vast physical spaces and tens of thousands of years, and the prophecies urge a continuation of that history as they affirm the temporal as well as the spatial coordinates of a future specifically defined as Indian. The Almanac of the Dead prophecies, themselves migratory, cross national and technological borders, ending up (for now) at the Tucson ranch of Lecha and Zeta, who transfer them from parchment to computer disk.

In a sense, then, the people who walk from the south to the north and from fragmentation to cohesion follow in the almanac's steps; like the almanac, the Indian migration is also understood, depending on who you ask, as revolutionary, marketable, and illegal. The migrants regard themselves as moving outside one system of laws to move back toward another. Fearful Euro-Americans see the migrants as outlaws in a different sense, but the emerging migratory Indian community is so huge that it overturns prevailing Western expectations about outlaws: that they act as isolated lone gunmen, for example, or as members of small, short-term, mostly apolitical gangs rather than huge, long-term political alliances. The complexities of outlawing preoccupy Silko and *Almanac of the Dead* in more ways than this; they also characterize a great deal of southwestern history, including its affectionate treatments of Billy the Kid and the physical and textual southwestering moves made by nonnative emigrants who effect discoveries of the nation or nations in the region.

Toward the close of "The Significance of the Frontier in American History," Frederick Jackson Turner banishes the western outlaw to footnote 49:

> I have refrained from dwelling on the lawless characteristics of the frontier, because they are sufficiently well known. The gambler and desper-

ado, the regulators of the Carolinas and the vigilantes of California, are types of that line of scum that the waves of advancing civilization bore before them, and of the growth of spontaneous organs of authority where legal authority was absent. (32–33)

About a dozen years before Turner first publicized his frontier thesis in 1893, Pat Garrett shot and killed perhaps the most famous southwestern outlaw, Billy the Kid, in a Fort Sumner, New Mexico Territory, bedroom. This transaction, one of a vast number of violent acts in the territorial American Southwest, underscores that it was still, in 1881, very much a frontier zone. As Robert Utley describes it, for example, the territory of New Mexico (still more than thirty years away from statehood)

> was a land of vast distances; of rugged mountains, parched deserts, and grassy plains; and of a cultural medley of Hispanic, Anglo, and Indian that did not always mix well. . . . New Mexico was also a land of rudimentary transportation, of isolation and parochialism, of poverty and privation relieved by only nominal prosperity, of centuries-old cultural institutions and infant political and economic institutions, of ineffective government, and of endemic violence. (*Billy the Kid*, 3)

Like New Mexico Territory, Mexico and the territory of Arizona were border zones punctuated by multicultural encounters and violence. In their autobiographies, Geronimo and his relative, Jason Betzinez, recount frequent border crossings and recrossings by both Apaches and Mexicans on raids and war parties against each other.[1] Another Apache autobiographer, James Kaywaykla, remarks that "Until I was about ten years old [approximately 1883] I did not know that people died except by violence. This is because I am an Apache" (xiii). Into this already dangerous environment came mobile "adventurers" such as Billy the Kid, who were able to blend in, finding or making room to practice a sort of uneven recklessness, an often unpremeditated violence that nonetheless helped keep the western outback unsettled. Witness, for example, their "casual view of suffering and death," their often unreflective responses to confusing social arrangements, and their use of the territory's formidable terrain for hiding out and for numerous "accidental" killings (Utley, *Billy the Kid*, 4).

This alliance of the physical frontier and the frontier criminal kicked up a problem for Turner, whose faith in the steady progress of American civilization westward rested on the assumption that outlaws would not survive that migration for long, that each successive region's savageries and barbarisms would yield to the inevitable, inexorable waves of civilization. But, to Turner's distaste and disappointment, these waves hurled up a freakish realm of "scum" and stopgap "spontaneous organs of [dubious] authority," some of which had acquired national celebrity status even before he presented his paper. The forces of civilization and the natural laws envisioned by Turner and others would have to be strong indeed to tame biology and sanitize this barely mentionable environment; that he writes little about the Southwest suggests, for one thing, that its natural frontiers and mix of inhabitants might not co-operate so readily with his metaphorical frontier's closing.

In Utley's words, the outlaws "rocked New Mexico with violence and lawlessness" (*Billy the Kid*, 4). Turner sees these unspeakable figures as un-civilized, ungendered, borderline traitorous forces who actively obstruct and disrupt the steady westward advance of American civilization; in a sense, he groups outlaws with Indians while inviting speculation about how the west-ering migrations of "scum" compete against the Indian-hating migrations of "law-abiding" Americans. As Richard Drinnon argues, in Turner's writings, American Indians "subsisted as natural objects, extensions of the nature that had to be subdued, impediments that had to be removed from the irresistible march to the West" (462). Euro-American residents in the territorial South-west frequently regarded Indians as outlaws or worse and bestialized them: "There is a royalty for wolf scalps and why not Indian scalps," the *Las Vegas (New Mexico) Daily Optic* asked its readers; "let them be hunted to death. . . . We kill mad dogs and mountain lions on sight. Of the beast and the Indian which is the worst?" (Weigle and White, 288). Similarly, Turner's quasi-biological metaphors for outlawry seem to suggest that the frontier process, in which even the lawless participate, has been naturalized rather than fully understood as an ideologically charged cultural process. All in all, local and national debate about Indians, outlaws, and emigrants was of course much more complex than these quotations from Turner and the *Daily Optic* let on. In the context of this book's larger argument, this chapter and the next will focus on the physical and textual mobility of territorial outlaws like Billy the Kid and Indians like Geronimo, in part by discussing some of the ways in which this mobility is transformed into legends that are themselves highly elastic and capable of demonizing, romanticizing, and otherwise recirculating the figures of the outlaw, the Apache, and the places they inhabit—the very frontier that Turner declared closed.

The outlaws of the Southwest were no more completely bad than the law-men were completely virtuous: just as the outlaws often vacillated between deviltry and more "civilized" occupations, the agents of law and order raised hell and broke their own laws, and members of both groups worked, hid, and rioted in a variety of "uncivilized" environments. In the Lincoln County, New Mexico Territory, wars of the 1870s, in which Billy the Kid participated, both "sides claimed to be instruments of the law," both sides deputized allies illegally, and both sides committed cold-blooded murders. "Under color of law, both sides . . . engage[d] in a great deal of unlawful activity" (Utley, *Billy the Kid*, 56). Both sides fell in and out of favor with local and federal authori-ties, including territorial governor Lew Wallace, who, when he wasn't work-ing on *Ben Hur*, was first bargaining with Billy the Kid and then signing his death warrant.

Geronimo, of course, was only captured—as distinct from surrendering—once, and that, as Angie Debo points out, by a ruse (107). Soldiers and Indian agents varied in ability and ethics; some, like General O. O. Howard, treated the Apaches fairly and earned their respect, while others, like General George

Crook, received Geronimo's scorn: "I think that General Crook's death was sent by the Almighty as a punishment for the many evil deeds he committed" (Geronimo, 139–140). But Betzinez, who later came to terms with much of Euro-American culture, writes of the same man, "We actually loved General Crook, and even today think of him, and talk about him, with genuine affection" (121). Kaywaykla takes more of a middle ground, saying that Crook "was an enemy, yes, but he was an honorable enemy. His promise was good; his understanding of Apaches was fair" (150). As Betzinez understates to his predominantly Euro-American readership, "All was not harmony at all times in the Apache tribe" (67–68). In fact, S. M. Barrett interpolates a chapter into *Geronimo's Story of His Life* (1906) in which he explains that Apaches banished from the tribe for crimes often came to be regarded as outlaws: "Frequently these outlaw Indians banded together and committed depredations which were charged against the regular tribe. . . . [T]hese bands frequently provoked the wrath of the tribe and secured their own destruction" (Geronimo, 30). And Theodore Roosevelt contends in "Across the Navajo Desert,"

> The lawless Indians are the worst menace to the others among the Navajos and Utes; and very serious harm has been done by well-meaning Eastern philanthropists who have encouraged and protected these criminals. I have known some startling cases of this kind. (209)

Outlawry in the Southwest was not necessarily contingent on Euro-Americans or on simple polarizations of "Indian" and "white" as racialized cultural stances. The point is obvious but important to rearticulate precisely because it warns against constructing historiographical master narratives of the places and the peoples in question.

To turn away from Billy the Kid and the Apaches for a moment,

> [t]he celebrated Wyatt Earp, stern-eyed guardian of law and order in so many Westerns, had once been an outlaw himself, indicted by a grand jury on a horse-stealing charge. [In 1881] Wyatt and his brothers were hired to keep the peace in Tombstone, Arizona, a task they conducted with a certain light-fingered permissiveness toward the roaring trades of gambling and prostitution. Their opponents referred to them as the Fighting Pimps. (Brownlow, 280)

As Kevin Brownlow remarks, "The dividing line between lawmen and outlaws in the West was, to put it mildly, blurred" (280)—as was the line between, for example, "renegade" Apaches and the Apache scouts who pursued and sometimes guarded them. These shifting, hazy borderlands of law and disorder are well captured in western films such as *My Darling Clementine*, John Ford's 1946 treatment of the Wyatt Earp story. In this film, Doc Holliday embodies a complex, confusing mixture of virtues and vices; Doc, though clearly a thief and a killer who intimidates the Tombstone citizenry, seems equally at home as a medical and civic hero, struggling to save the life of his mortally wounded Mexican lover and accompanying the lawman Earp to the OK Corral. Earp's fictional character has more than one dimension, too: he is

played by Henry Fonda, familiar to movie audiences as a versatile yet characteristically homespun actor who also portrayed Gil Carter (*The Ox-Bow Incident,* 1943), Charles Pike (*The Lady Eve,* 1941), Tom Joad (*The Grapes of
Wrath,* 1940), Abraham Lincoln (*Young Mr. Lincoln,* 1939), and the outlaw
Frank James (twice). When the bare beams of the first Tombstone church go
up in *My Darling Clementine,* silhouetted against the Arizona desert sky, the
church-raising is celebrated not with a sermon but with a dance attended by
the entire community—including Earp, the avenging lawman who, for a little
while, exchanges gun battles for awkward, comic dance steps.

At the very least, the range and complexity of many western outlaws,
lawmen, soldiers, Indians, actors, and territories—in both actual and fictionalized manifestations—represent and embody an argument against the
Turner thesis. Even in the late nineteenth century, when Turner was prepar-
ing and delivering his ideas, these often disruptive, unpredictable forces were
complicating the inexorable advance of civilization as Turner understood and
theorized it and were helping to maintain an unruly frontier rather than participating in its closing. The western presence of such "scum" before the
official "closing of the frontier" (1890) could of course be used to back up
Turner's contentions; outlaws, vigilantes, and "savages" were to be expected
in "precivilized" places, and the vanquishing of these "bad" people was typically seen as indisputable proof of civilization's advance. But the continued
activities of actual western outlaws after 1890, as well as the lingering presence of outlaws as icons, of ghostly, fictionalized Billy the Kids and Wyatt
Earps, of Geronimo riding in President Theodore Roosevelt's inaugural parade
and agreeing to present himself to white spectators as a commercial property,
badger Turner's thesis; for in another sense, the persistence of crime and
criminal legends gives powerful evidence of post-1890 frontier conditions.

Put another way, Turner offers a strong explanation of westward expansion and settlement, seeing it as a clear, steady, sequential process; western
outlaws such as Billy the Kid, many of whose actions are still hotly debated
and thoroughly unclear, unwittingly point up the disorderly, random, still-
unsettled side of much frontier experience. And Indians such as Geronimo,
although captured and exhibited (in part) as evidence of U.S. imperialism, also
continue to disrupt the easy binaries of "civilization" and "savagery" long
after their capture. They do so in part by producing autobiographical texts
that register their continuing resistance to U.S. policies and in part by helping
to encourage resistance in the hearts and minds of those who come after, including American Indian writers such as Jimmie Durham and, most notably,
Leslie Marmon Silko.

The Billy the Kid legend often seems more open-ended than the frontier thesis. Rather than turning predictable and closing things down, Billy the Kid
usually surprises as he is reinvented over and over again; a decade or two older
than Turner's essay, the Kid as icon has been much more flexible and adapt-

able than the frontier thesis as paradigm. His legend, based in part on his early death (he was twenty-two) combined with his unusually bad temper, was coming into being at about the same time Turner was declaring the frontier closed. In the same year that the census marked the official, statistical closing of the frontier, Francis W. Doughty published, in the New York Detective Library, one of many dime novels about the outlaw, *Old King Brady and Billy the Kid; or, the Great Detective's Chase* (1890). Books such as Doughty's, published in the wake of Billy the Kid's death, dramatized and debated what Turner theorized: the contest between civilization and frontier. Generally promoting the forces of law and domesticity while interpreting American history in the Turner/ Roosevelt manner, these books nonetheless also reproduced and perpetuated the frontier that historians were declaring closed, civilized, eradicated. These books provided their readers, many of them easterners, with neither a peaceful agrarian West nor a successful, urbanizing, "civilized" West; instead, they focused on precisely the qualities that Turner pronounced dead. Sometimes Billy the Kid was painted as the archfiend and Garrett glamorized as the hero; sometimes their roles were reversed. Sometimes the iconographers complicated such polarizations. But typically, the frontier was glamorized as an exciting, unruly spectacle, sometimes mythic, often romanticized, and generally, in its capacity for imaginative reconstruction and its transformation of local history into legend and national concerns into marketable appetites, a fit prototype for the Southwest as aesthetic spectacle.[2]

Billy the Kid's long and varied afterlife, then, bears witness to a powerful popular image of an active, open frontier. His malleable frontier rides alongside the more monumental metaphorical frontier of Turner's, harrying and disrupting the historian's claims about American character and American history. Further, these conflicting readings of the West and Southwest, more so than either narrative considered separately and thus out of context, are signally important to the gradual development of a southwestern frontier aesthetic that typically combines and blurs elements of outlawry and settlement, among other things. As richly as Silko works with Indian history and Indian prophecy in *Almanac of the Dead*, she also bases her representation of southwestern outlawry in part on these shifting, blurred Euro-American cultural processes of constructing and deconstructing frontiers.

Clearly, a great many other writers more than compensate for Turner's refusal to elaborate on Wild West outlaws and territorial violence. His thesis is predicated on his decision that "scum" taint a history assumed to be already magisterially in progress; he does not theorize a frontier in which a variety of people move cross-culturally toward the construction of multiple, arrhythmic histories. As Richard White explains,

> The nationally imagined West depended on the mass media, and the popularity of western stories with the mass media was in part serendipitous. Anglo American settlement of the West happened to take place

simultaneously with the rise of penny newspapers, dime novels, and sen-
sationalist journals such as the *National Police Gazette*. . . . [M]ass media, a mass audience, and mass western migration all bumped into each
other, as it were, at a given historical moment. (620)

What results is a frontier condition characterized by its unpredictable cultural collisions and exchanges. Just as Roosevelt, Frederic Remington, and
others were popularizing a bracing and upright West in prose works and paintings, a whole industry of dime novels depicted and sometimes romanticized
the corruption, chaos, and outlawry of the same region; between 1881 and
1906, for example, some 270 dime novels appeared in the James gang series
alone (Tatum, 44; see also G. Edward White). Other western figures, among
them Billy the Kid, were well represented in all their satanic attractiveness in
the dime novels: there were approximately fifteen Billy the Kid dime novels
between 1881 and 1906. By 1965, conservative estimates place the Billy the
Kid bibliography at more than eight hundred items, including more than forty
movies (Tatum, 5). Moreover, contemporary commentators on the death of
Billy the Kid were much more forthcoming than Turner about addressing
western outlawry. As Kent Steckmesser observes, "The Kid's death was national news" (71); amplifying this statement, Richard White points out that
"The actual Billy the Kid was a relatively inconsequential gunman and stock
thief. . . . He was, however, by the time of his death a national figure of sorts
because the *National Police Gazette* and mass-circulation eastern papers reported the story of his crimes. In New York City eight newspapers published
notices of the Kid's death" (625). Alleged by some to have migrated from New
York City to New Mexico as a youth, Billy the Kid continues to migrate after
his death; as one result of this process, ideas of the Southwest, along with
southwestern texts, become more visible, more prominent, and more under-
standable as part of the American nation.

The multitude of newspaper reports, with their already hazy combinations of fact and legend, paved the way for the variety of "pseudo-biographical
dime novels" (Steckmesser, 75) as well as an aggressively fictionalized work
titled *The Authentic Life of Billy, the Kid* (1882). Credited on the title page to
none other than Pat Garrett himself, this account was in fact mostly written
by the local postmaster, Ash Upson, whom Utley describes as "a restless jour-
nalist who loved words, people, and the bottle, in reverse order" (*Billy the Kid*,
20). From very early on, "authentic" advertises not historiographical "fact"
but a merging and mixing of fact and fiction, with each pressurizing and vali-
dating the other. Precisely because he was and is so mobile, so able and ready
to cross and blur the boundaries of fact and fiction, history and legend, Billy
as cultural icon takes on complex significance and aesthetic potentiality.
Even the circumstances of his death remain uncertain, and indeed the fact of
his death was, within more or less reasonable limits, disputed; as late as 1950,
the Texas codger "Brushy Bill" Roberts claimed to be Billy the Kid (Tatum,
123–124). Did the Kid conspire in inventing the stories of his own death? In

March 1882, some eight months after Pat Garrett's bedroom ambush, a posted notice in Las Vegas, New Mexico, warned away "thieves, thugs, fakirs, and bunco steerers" (Steckmesser, 70) and named, among other badmen, Billy the Kid. As Steckmesser remarks, "The good citizens sought to banish him even in death" (70). Or was their error a tacit acknowledgment of his imaginable presence?

Though *Authentic Life* attempts to soften the Kid's image as a satanically villainous wretch, most of Turner's contemporaries agreed with him that such outlaws were, not to mince words, scum. Writing at approximately the same time as Turner, Frank Hall describes Billy as "the most desperate and bloody-minded civilized white man that ever cursed the border with his crimes" and concluded, "The earth was well rid of him" (Steckmesser, 81). Heinous as Billy the Kid clearly is, he nonetheless qualifies as "civilized," his whiteness duly noted and mobilized in his defense even as he is otherwise vilified as indefensible: "civilized white man" implies, in the logic of racialized polarities, "uncivilized" or "savage" Indian. In two books, written in 1897 and 1901, the popular western historian Emerson Hough—a friend of Garrett's—calls upon other polarizations when he characterizes the Kid as an animal and, as Steckmesser puts it, an "archfiend" (81). The very quotable Hough embellished the "animal" tag by explaining that "the soul of some fierce and far-off carnivore got into the body of this little man" (Tatum, 56). Even so, the energy expended on these lurid statements suggests that "this little man" is interestingly fiendish, as compelling as he is repulsive.

Despite Turner's footnoted refusal to speak of outlaws, then, the outlaw as satanic antihero was a well-known and very popular figure, and as the "archfiend" of them all, Billy the Kid was fast attaining the status of national legend. Readers were fascinated, for example, by the psychopathic energy of an outlaw who was both so very bad and so very young. Soon after his death at age twenty-two, the legends began to take shape; Billy was said to have boasted that he killed one man for each of those twenty-two years. (In fact, the best estimates credit him with four killings of his own, as well as complicity in five other murders [Tatum, 34; Utley, *Billy the Kid*, 203–204]. From early on, the legend and its makers have interesting conversations with the facts and fact mongers.) The early popular interest in Billy the Kid, from his death in 1881 until around 1910, lingered over his exaggerated deviltry and defiance of social proprieties, the Mansonesque, fictive "dipping his finger into the blood of his victims" and a wavering between male and female clothing (Tatum, 45, 46, 48). Stephen Tatum writes that "the Kid was generally perceived [in these years] as the romance story's villainous foil to the hero's progress through a depraved landscape" (55), and as such, he appears to stand in the way of manifest destiny and the workings of westward expansion as theorized by Turner. But at the same time, the stories about Billy the Kid draw attention to and illuminate (however distortedly) a region, the Southwest, that Turner pays little attention to, with or without outlaws. In other words, the writers who attempt to come to terms with unruly southwestern outlaw elements also help integrate the Southwest itself into America. Even

the early popular historians of the Kid, who agree with Turner that such outlaws were bad sorts indeed, propose at the same time the beginnings of a more
open-ended and disorderly (though exaggerated) Southwest. The quick translations of Billy the Kid into a type, a metaphor, even an icon mark the origins
of a legend very successful at persuading American readers to imagine, remake, and in some way participate in the previously disregarded American
Southwest.

Given this emerging national public interest in outlaws and their regional
environs, it is not entirely surprising to find the satanic Billy transforming
into a saintlier and more sentimentalized hero beginning early in the twentieth century. Arizona and New Mexico were granted statehood in 1912, and at
about the same time dime novel Westerns began to make their way to Hollywood, where often-romanticized backward glances at the more violent years
of settlement were quickly gaining in popularity. The Southwest becomes in
these years still more visible to still more audiences. John Cawelti notes the
Western's "unique adaptability to film" (42); more specifically, Tatum argues
that "the movies did the most to establish the Kid as a figure in popular culture" (107). Indeed, the book most influential and important in reshaping the
Billy the Kid legend was compared to and made into a movie. Chicago news-
paperman Walter Noble Burns's *Saga of Billy the Kid*, published in 1926, became a best-seller; selecting it for the Book of the Month Club, a judge remarked that it conveyed "the vivid reality of the moving pictures without the
infusion of false sentiment" (Tatum, 102). Four years later, in 1930, it was
reworked into the MGM movie *Billy the Kid*, directed by King Vidor. In his
reshaping of the legend, Burns paints Billy as an American Robin Hood, actively blurs history and fiction, and plays up the local Mexican and New
Mexican folklore, in part so that he can align Robin Hood with the locals who
believed in Billy (Steckmesser, 86–87). In the process, Burns makes intriguing
cross-cultural connections between the Kid and some of the frontier cultures
he inhabits; Billy's alliance with the local Mexican population has in fact become a strong part of the legend. At the same time, Burns powerfully defamil-
iarizes the notorious outlaw by reconstituting him as attractively heroic
and even virtuous, although he does so by reversing rather than dismantling
readily available binaries.

Richard White, working closely with Tatum, argues that this

> new Kid, too, eventually became a means to revitalize rather than under-
> mine [1920s–1930s American] society. In the thirties, with the country in
> the midst of the Depression, it was easy to make the Kid a Robin Hood de-
> fending ordinary Americans against corrupt capitalists who were driving
> the country to ruin. He is, however, if not a conservative, at least a New
> Deal liberal; he destroys evil bankers but not banks. The Kid becomes Pat
> Garrett; he becomes the Virginian. He defends American ideals. (626)

Burns's *Saga* performs a crucial role in reworking not only the outlaw but also
the American Southwest, not only in reaffirming that the Southwest can be
reworked and re-created but also in dramatizing and popularizing yet another

revision and reopening of the frontier Turner deemed closed nearly two generations earlier. For one thing, Burns demonstrates and confirms Billy the Kid's ability to change over time, to be a "flexible container" (Tatum, 11) and a complex aesthetic property. All in all, the frontier, allied with its favorite outlaw son, functions from the early 1880s on as a metaphor, a fiction, a myth, a place where history and legend, fact and fiction, law and order, settlement and open space blur in the imagination—a place, in short, reproduced yet reinvented, aesthetically valued, and characterized by the literal and figurative mobility of its occupants. Problematic as it certainly is, this frontier is nonetheless, in some ways, energetically created and sustained in a variety of American popular-culture discourses, enabling region and nation to make limited yet volatile contact.

Writes Tatum, "Discovering the Kid throughout the years since his death in 1881 has usually meant discovering the appeals of the West and the Western, the historical landscape and the aesthetic context within which the Kid both resides and rides. Such appeals continue to preoccupy us and beckon to us, even though we no longer confront the conditions of frontier existence" (13). Tatum replicates and supports, perhaps more than he realizes, the Turner thesis; though the various reinventions of Billy the Kid certainly point up contrasts between frontier and contemporary conditions, they also encourage comparisons.[3] Images of the Kid reopen and perpetuate frontier conditions because frontier conditions are as subject to redefinition as is the Kid; Turner, insisting that the process of westward expansion closes the frontier, leaves no room for such redefinitions, even though his metaphor of the frontier is itself an act of great imaginative power and redefinition. Perhaps there is something teasingly criminal about not only frontier conditions but also frontier redefinitions. Whether these white outlaws come to seem safer and somehow more appealing than Indian "outlaws" such as Geronimo is a tricky question. Clearly, though, the aesthetic careers of the white outlaw and the American Southwest get under way in large part because of the imaginableness and, ironically, the cooperation of its most visible outlaw as his mythic incarnations tangle with the mythic movements of the frontier thesis.

3 Outlawing Apaches

Geronimo and Jason Betzinez

The iconic white Euro-American outlaw's controlled yet relatively flexible textual dispositions differentiate him from the iconic Indian "outlaw," who must much more forcefully and creatively resist the impositions of both political and textual authorities. Geronimo narrated his autobiography to Apache interpreter Asa Daklugie and Euro-American educator S. M. Barrett in 1905–1906; *Geronimo's Story of His Life* appeared in print in 1906, after a series of bureaucratic maneuvers that seem almost comical in retrospect, except that they clearly demonstrate the entanglement and containment that epitomized Geronimo's life under U.S. government supervision. Concern over this Apache autobiography reached to the highest levels of the U.S. government, and this clear textual evidence of early-twentieth-century power relations may tempt late-twentieth-century readers to focus on U.S. interference with Apache life rather than Apache resistance to U.S. forces. The autobiography dramatizes both, though, as it develops the radical argument that Apache-U.S. relations should be diminished, not maintained in their 1906 form and certainly not expanded.

After securing the cautious approval of President Theodore Roosevelt, contingent on the inclusion of nervous, defensive footnotes "disclaiming responsibility for adverse criticism of any [Euro-American] persons mentioned by Geronimo" (xxii), Barrett finally managed to see the book through to publication. Both Barrett and Geronimo express their gratitude to Roosevelt, but their reasons for doing so differ, as do their expectations of what constitutes a "proper" text. Geronimo's statement of thanks appears in the final chapter of the text; it calls explicit attention to a serious imbalance of power and at the same time undercuts presidential power: "I am thankful that the President of the United States has given me permission to tell my story. I hope that he and those in authority under him will read my story and judge whether my people have been rightly treated" (213). In other words, all the prior judgments made by U.S. authorities—including those in all the documents printed and otherwise described in Geronimo's text—do not stand as the final word on the status of the Apaches. In fact, Roosevelt has not yet judged the Apaches in that he has not judged them rightly. Geronimo makes quite clear that even his storytelling falls under the subjugation of the president; his words as well as his deeds are under surveillance. Still, he positions himself as a counter-authority who tells his story because it will enable U.S. leaders to make the right judgments. Barrett, in contrast, thanks Roosevelt in the foreword to the text: "I especially desire . . . to say that without the kindly advice and assistance of President Theodore Roosevelt this book could not have been written" (vi). And Barrett means written, not published: he had to ask federal permission simply to sit with Geronimo and Daklugie and take down words. Barrett's and Geronimo's statements of thanks in a sense frame the text, but Geronimo's carries considerably more rhetorical weight and subversive potential.

In his discussion of how the text was produced, Barrett describes Geronimo's injunction, "Write what I have spoken" (xxi), his unwillingness to answer questions immediately, his refusal to talk when a stenographer was present—in short, his insistence on upholding some of the conventions of oral storytelling even in the process of making a book. As Barrett laments, Geronimo "left us to remember and write the story without one bit of assistance" (xxi). Another way of seeing Geronimo's method is as a sort of initiation—of Barrett and of his readers, as well as, perhaps, his Carlisle-educated interpreter—into an (admittedly modified) Apache narrative style and tradition. (Geronimo was approximately seventy-six years old when he told the story of his life; Barrett was forty and Daklugie thirty-five or thirty-six.) Barrett, anticipating readerly disorientation, apologizes for this situation: "The fact that Geronimo has told the story in his own way is doubtless the only excuse necessary to offer for the many unconventional features of this work" (xxvii). But these features are also highly conventional, Apachean; for instance, as David Brumble, III, and others have noted, Geronimo decides to begin with the "Origin of the Apache Indians" and the "Subdivisions of the Apache Tribe" before arriving at the conventional Western autobiographical beginning, "I was born," in his third chapter (see Brumble, 54, 168). Carter Revard further points out that Geronimo truly begins in, and at, the beginning, offering a "*Genesis*-like history of his world's creation, his people's creation and deliverance, of their land's creation, of why they are called Apaches, [and] of what it means to be taken from the land created for the people" ("History," 85). As Revard observes, "Geronimo ranged . . . from the cosmic through the geologic to tribal, subtribal, family, and then only, last and in full context, to the 'individual' self that was Geronimo" ("History," 85). From its first publication, this text has played out the tension between what Geronimo intends and what Barrett expects—or, perhaps more precisely, between two conflicting understandings of what constitutes a proper "text" and proper "contexts."

Thus far, *Geronimo's Story of His Life* has most often been read in the context of other Native American autobiographies, under the rubric of what might be called autobiography theory. Many of the critics who have studied Barrett's Geronimo and, to a significantly lesser extent, Geronimo's Barrett have noted a variety of cross-cultural complexities in the text as well as in its production. Brumble, for example, repeatedly remarks that the text begins with tribal history before turning to Geronimo's personal autobiography. Even the title of the work, with its third-person pronoun, contravenes Western autobiographical convention to some extent.[1] Still, though, as Greg Sarris argues, scholars and critics of Native American autobiography can lose sight of Geronimo's Geronimo if they remain too wedded to Euro-American perspectives and expectations: "If [Arnold] Krupat, for example, in his encounter with *Geronimo's Story of His Life*, had in fact considered Apache history, culture, and language, particularly as presented by Apache Indians orally or otherwise, he might have seen himself as present and gained a broader understanding of the text" (90). Sarris argues that various scholars of Native American literature unwittingly

> replicate in practice that which characterizes not only certain non-Indian editors' manner of dealing with Indians but also that of an entire European and Euro-American populace of which these editors and scholars are a part. The Indians are absent or they are strategically removed from the territory, made safe, intelligible on the colonizer's terms. (90)

Sarris does not himself "read" *Geronimo's Story of His Life*, but he does provide very useful questions and contexts from which to construct a reading that neither replicates the non-Indian editorial positions nor removes the Indians. Following Sarris's guidance, I propose that Geronimo's text should be read not so much as an example of more or less balanced composite authorship but rather as a text that places its two "authors" in productive and purposeful tension, violating Barrett's and, more subtly, Geronimo's senses of convention and propriety on a regular basis. In a variety of places, Geronimo articulates a continuing Apache resistance—to removal from Arizona and continued status as prisoners of war—in ways that militate against the progressive first-person conventions of Western autobiography and make Barrett, as well as various high-ranking U.S. officials, visibly uncomfortable.

In other words, rather than reading this text (as Krupat primarily does) in Euro-American historical and ethnographic contexts—"What we have, then, is Indian autobiography in the age not of Carlyle but of Hardy" (*For Those Who Come After*, 63)—it should be read more particularly in the contexts of Apache culture and experience. Geronimo's text disrupts and unsettles various Euro-American expectations as it threatens and to an impressive extent succeeds in throwing late-nineteenth- and early-twentieth-century Indian-white power relations off kilter. Apache encounters with U.S. soldiers and politicians are of course crucial to the story Geronimo tells. But, just as it is important not to overplay Barrett's role in producing the text, so is it crucial not to overproduce our own positionings of the text. As the preceding chapter argues, the Billy the Kid legend resists the stasis imposed by the Turner thesis; I will argue here that Geronimo as storyteller and historian produces what is at heart a resistance text that is, at best, only selectively concerned with the ages of Carlyle and Hardy.

Emerging in Barrett's discussion of the process of making this book, a sense of Geronimo as resisting Indian continues with Geronimo's arrangement of chapters. And it is reasonable to assume that Geronimo is responsible for the arrangement of chapters; he planned the text, he spoke it, he went over it again afterward, and perhaps most importantly, he shaped it for argumentative purposes. He has a specific end in mind; he presents his autobiography as a political tract asking and arguing for the return of the Apaches to their homelands. Krupat writes that "it seems inevitable that the final text . . . is very much the work of Daklugie and, most particularly, Barrett himself" (*For Those Who Come After*, 61–62). But Krupat does not specify what he means by "work" or by "inevitable," and as he himself makes clear, he has no evidence.[2] More to the point, Krupat's argument deflects attention from Geronimo's. Unlike Jason Betzinez in his ambiguously titled *I Fought with Geronimo* (1959), Geronimo chooses to present tribal history before personal history, or, more accurately, presents tribal history *as* personal history. Then, after introducing himself in first-person narrative form, Geronimo pointedly interweaves personal and tribal experiences in ways that counter Western notions of autobiography as a narrative of personal "progress." He also emphasizes warrior activities, in part to convey a strong point about Apache life and principles. For one thing, Indians did not simply and exclusively live to react to white U.S. government officials. They had been warring with Mexicans for years and were certainly not strangers to intertribal warfare. In fact, Geronimo's chapter titled "Coming of the White Men" is Chapter 13, which comes after over more than one hundred pages of narrative. Also Geronimo does not range far beyond war: he is a warrior and a war chief, that is what he knows, that is what he respects, and that is what he does, without apology. While some chapters, such as "Tribal Amusements, Manners, and Customs" and "The Family," deemphasize war, the book mostly details preparations for battles, battles, and aftermaths of battles. This emphasis on his responsibilities and experiences as a war chief carries over to the argumentative stance he assumes in his book as well as the alert, carefully designed contentiousness of that argument.[3]

From Chapter 13 on, Geronimo comments extensively on white Americans. He explicitly refers to wrongs: U.S. soldiers "never explained to the [U.S.] Government when an Indian was wronged, but always reported the misdeeds of the Indians" (116). However, he also refuses to read the Indian-white conflicts as simple matters of "bad" soldiers attacking "good" Apaches: "After this trouble all of the Indians agreed not to be friendly with the white man any more. There was no general engagement, but a long struggle followed. Sometimes we attacked the white men—sometimes they attacked us" (118). Geronimo makes some concessions to white religion, but his 1903 commitment to Christianity must be understood in Apache contexts, as Angie Debo explains: "He had always been religious; now he compared his old beliefs with the new, finding much common ground" (432). In other words, Christianity "supplemented" rather than replaced Apache beliefs: "It is clear that he found no discrepancy between Christian worship and his people's sacred observances such as the womanhood ceremony" (Debo, 433). More accurately, he found little discrepancy and worked out ways of strategically managing his "conversion," making selective and deliberate concessions as part of his larger argument about an Apache return to the Southwest.

Throughout the text, Geronimo abides by Apache codes, rules, and ethics to the (considerable) extent that he can. When describing his visit to the world's fair, for example, he presents himself as a careful, honest observer. While scholars such as Leah Dilworth have argued that Geronimo was exploited and stereotyped as both "a relic of a savage past" and "a celebrity" (49), Geronimo himself does not see his visit in those terms. (And in fact Dilworth herself falls into the trap of stereotyping, referring to bows and arrows as "relics of his warrior past" [150]; as is clear from Geronimo's autobiography and various other texts by and about the Warm Springs Apaches, they primarily used guns.)[4] Without overlooking his prisoner-of-war status, he emphasizes his own powers of perception and judgment. Debo writes that whenever Geronimo was "exhibited,"

> [h]is conduct . . . was a lasting demonstration of the code of courtesy and good breeding the Apaches had managed to retain even as hunted outlaws. He appeared self-possessed, alert, and not unfriendly to the people who crowded around him, and all the time he was observing, learning, marking down everything with his fresh curiosity and his active mind. At the same time, he used every opportunity he found to plead for a return to his homeland. Also, being Geronimo, he kept an eye open for business. (400)

In short, he does not appear to be—and, according to his own words, he does not see himself as—an exhibit looked at without looking back actively and critically. This is true of his experience at the world's fair, and it is also true of his autobiographical text.

Moreover, his account of the world's fair also acts as one of the most interesting and significant expressions of Geronimo's continuing resistance to the status imposed on him—not so much as exhibition but more so as prisoner of war. At first, Geronimo says, "I did not wish to go" to the fair (197). He only consents to go after the president of the United States tells him that going would be all right and that he "would receive good attention" (197). Once there, he stays for six months, making a considerable amount of money by posing for photographs and signing autographs. But he is never allowed to go anywhere without an escort: "The Government sent guards with me when I went, and I was not allowed to go anywhere without them" (198). As elsewhere in this text, Geronimo calls explicit attention to his captive status, to the conditions of his life under U.S. subjugation.

And to others'. In describing his reactions to the fair, he chooses his examples carefully: first, he recounts his amazement at a "strange-looking Negro" who magically escapes from being bound: "I do not understand how this was done. It was certainly by a miraculous power, because no man could have released himself by his own efforts" (199). Then he remembers another "good" show, which began when he and his guards entered "into a little room that was made like a cage" (203). Although he enjoyed this show, he remarks that it was "so strange and unnatural that I was glad to be on the streets again" (203). His subsequent examples include the cagelike "little house" of the Ferris wheel he rides, a woman locked up in a basket for a magic trick, and a group of captive Iggorrotes from the Philippines. Summing up, Geronimo politely remarks, "I wish all my people could have attended the Fair" (206). He says,

> I am glad I went to the Fair. I saw many interesting things and learned much of the white people. They are a very kind and peaceful people. During all the time I was at the Fair no one tried to harm me in any way. Had this been among the Mexicans I am sure I should have been compelled to defend myself often. (205–206)

But he also makes an important argumentative point about all the various spectacles of captivity at the fair. In doing so, he puts his own captivity in a larger context, thereby implicitly questioning the "kind and peaceful people" who regard such spectacles as a form of entertainment that reflects well on their culture. And he emphasizes the strangeness of these spectacles, in which a captive Apache looks at and is looked at by "captive" African Americans, women, and Iggorrotes.

Geronimo spends the entirety of *Geronimo's Story of His Life* carefully and eloquently moving toward his final point: he wants his people to be allowed to return to Arizona. His entire oration builds toward this final request, after a book's worth of evidence detailing the crucial associations between the Apaches and their home places, as well as the wrongs that have beset them since their forced removal from those locations. In the final chapter, "Hopes for the Future," he explicitly describes the Apaches as "prisoners of war," warns that their numbers are diminishing because they are being held away from their Arizona homelands, and asserts, "I want to spend my last days there, and be buried among those mountains. If this could be I might die in peace, feeling that my people, placed in their native homes, would increase in numbers, rather than diminish as at present, and that our name would not become extinct" (215). Calling direct attention to the power relations of the situation, he says, "But we can do nothing in this matter ourselves—we must wait until those in authority choose to act" (216). Most obviously, he refers to officials of the U.S. government. But what about general readers? Does Geronimo implicate them as well, reminding them of their participatory responsibilities in an ostensibly democratic society? To the extent that *Geronimo's Story of His Life* works as a sort of council or active engagement between Geronimo and his listeners/readers, the book stands as a direct address to readers and most certainly implicates them in the situation (see Lejeune). He speaks directly to us, urging us not to sympathize passively but to act as warriors against the wrongs dealt the Apaches. But—as he knows—this is its own paradox: readers pay to see the exotic man in the textual cage, asking to be let out and looking to return home.

Jason Betzinez's *I Fought with Geronimo* is much less a resistance text and much more an example of Indian assimilation to white Euro-American religion and culture. Published in 1959, when Betzinez was ninety-nine years old, the book almost overwhelms readers with its author's cheery, relentlessly optimistic attitude toward his own assimilation. He loved the Carlisle Indian School, which he entered at age twenty-seven and which he recalls in a chapter titled "Golden Days." He admires Captain Richard Pratt for "rehabilitating these primitive children" (150). He formally converts to Christianity in 1897, ten years after being enrolled at Carlisle. He frequently diminishes Apache traditions as superstitions, referring to them as "the old foolish notions" (175); he just as frequently takes a minority position in Apache tribal councils, typically urging accommodation and assimilation when most of the other members stand in favor of resistance. When the majority of Apaches wish to return to their homelands in the Southwest, Betzinez argues that they should remain in Oklahoma. He obeys Euro-American authorities with little or no questioning of either their orders or their authority. Finally, at the age of fifty-nine, he marries a white Christian missionary to the Apaches, with whom he lives happily ever after in southwestern Oklahoma. One specific moment in the text sums up his general approach: soon after the Apaches are made prisoners of war, they are transported by railroad to Florida and imprisonment; along the way, white locals gather at the railroad stations and stare at the spectacle of captive Apaches. When Betzinez remarks of this train trip, "I rather enjoyed this, my first train ride" (142), he pretty much compels his readers to conclude that he is almost pathologically good-natured.[5]

But is Betzinez's autobiography less of an Apache autobiography than Geronimo's? As Revard points out, Betzinez's circumstances differ importantly from Geronimo's: "Geronimo, born in 1829, could grow up both 'wild' and 'free,' but Betzinez, born in 1860 after the U.S. acquisition of the Southwest, was under deadly harassment from his teens outward" ("History," 87). Moreover, after leaving the Apaches for Carlisle, he "*had no homeland* unless the U.S. government would assign him one; he had no religion for his own people, no ceremonies that tied his youth to his age or self to tribe; in short, he had no *identity* unless he could recast himself" in Euro-American terms ("History," 88). But he never completely divorced himself from the Apaches, either. The ambiguity of Betzinez's title, *I Fought with Geronimo*, suggests a tension that can be detected in places throughout the text: while he at times may seem overly cooperative with Euro-American proponents of assimilation, and while he clearly denigrates particular Apache ways and actions, he also recalls and returns to other Apache beliefs, traditions, and points of view much more favorably and affectionately. However inadvertently, he leads readers to question their frustration with him and his text.

Revard aptly calls these "Apache" recollections "remnant attitudes" ("History," 88). To some extent, the remnants help market the book as a legitimate memoir of Geronimo's people and experiences; moreover, to write a narrative of conversion and assimilation, Betzinez must have something from which to convert and assimilate. But Betzinez is rarely so cynical about his memories and motives; he bases his responses and conclusions on a clearly worked out system of thought that permits him a fair amount of critical leeway, and his "remnant attitudes" continuously inform his sense of who he is and what he has accomplished. They don't disappear from the text as Betzinez tells his story about moving further and further away from an identity generally describable as "Apache." It would be a mistake to write off Betzinez's autobiography as somehow less "legitimate" than Geronimo's because it perhaps disappoints readers seeking resistance texts rather than uncomfortably comfortable Eisenhower-era accommodationist texts.

Wilbur Sturtevant Nye serves as Betzinez's S. M. Barrett, and in a brief introduction to *I Fought with Geronimo*, Nye makes no secret of the way he understands Betzinez's long life. The foreword begins,

> This is the autobiography of an Apache Indian who has been virtually a part of the Stone Age and the Atomic Era. As a boy Jason Betzinez hunted with bow and arrow within sight of the New Mexico flats where, eighty years later, the first atomic blast was fired. As savages he and his tribe fought their enemies through deserts and mountains where giant missiles are tested today. The careers of few living persons offer such striking contrasts and unique features. (n.p.)[6]

Nye further details how Betzinez made his first airplane flight, "with failing vision and hearing" and "with several changes of plane," at the age of ninety-eight. "A week later," Nye adds, Betzinez "made another transcontinental flight to New York to participate in the TV show 'I've Got a Secret'" (n.p.). Exotic both in his former identity as a "Stone Age" "savage" and in his present identity as a very mobile old man, Betzinez strikes Nye as highly exceptional *and* highly assimilated. The assimilation makes this text possible but at the same time encourages Nye to preserve or invent a Betzinez who is remarkable because of his Indian identity, remarkable not simply because he flies in airplanes at age ninety-eight but because he is an Indian who flies in airplanes at age ninety-eight.

Clearly, Betzinez's career differs from Geronimo's, as do his discussions of his Indianness, and similarly the production of Betzinez's text differs from the production of Geronimo's. Nye carefully explains,

> This is not a dialect story. Jason speaks and writes English, not pidgin English. He wrote his own account; but appreciating that his education

had been shortened, he asked that the manuscript be rigorously edited. This has been done by rearranging much of the material and by paraphrasing where necessary. It is not, however, an "as told to" type of work except where some information has been added which was furnished in conversation, correspondence, or tape recordings. (n.p.)

Nye, an experienced historian, demonstrates his familiarity with the genre of Indian autobiography. In explaining his own role as editor of the manuscript, he honors a long-standing generic convention while recognizing what this convention implies: readers can be expected to raise questions about the production of "Indian" texts, and editors bear the responsibility of anticipating and addressing these questions. These texts may not "work" without the presence of the Euro-American "guide," and so in a sense, the editor's role is to authenticate the text as "Indian" and as plausible; Nye serves this function by witnessing Betzinez's manuscript and by confirming his extraordinary binary status as both modern "civilized" man and Stone Age "savage."

Nye's emphasis on Betzinez's travels makes sense, too, as an introduction to this autobiography. In remembering his early years in the Southwest, Betzinez emphasizes the "wandering kind of life" led by the Apaches, linking these travels to the seemingly incessant warfare between Apaches and Mexicans (as well as Apaches and other tribes). Like Geronimo, Betzinez emphasizes that U.S. soldiers came later: the Apaches were active warriors long before Americans engaged them in battle. He focuses particularly on amazing, heroic journeys undertaken by Apache women captives who escaped their captors and miraculously found their way back home. He praises their stamina and desire. Of course, he also discusses the forced movements of various Apache groups, supplementing and emphasizing these movements by including several maps and photographs that stand as both illustrations and evidence.

Of the Apaches' relocation to Fort Apache, Betzinez remarks, "Some of us, perhaps most of us, didn't realize that this meant the virtual end of our old nomadic life" (125) and the beginnings of their new lives as farmers. However, the Warm Springs Apaches are sent to Florida, then Alabama, then Oklahoma; Jason himself travels from Florida to Carlisle, works at a variety of places in both Pennsylvania and New Jersey, and finally journeys back to Oklahoma to live and work, thereafter traveling to Washington, D.C., to meet with Secretary of War William Howard Taft, to the Southwest to inspect possible sites of Apache reservations, and to various other places, culminating in the journeys Nye describes in his foreword to the book. Revard argues that Betzinez "had no homeland" ("History," 88)—"How could I be homesick, when I had never had a home?" Betzinez asks in *I Fought with Geronimo* (147). But he carries with him on his travels an Apache sensibility about the act of traveling—that is, travel itself is inextricably linked to an Apache sense of self and is transferred to his later assimilated identity in such a way that he is always comfortable and, in a sense, at home when traveling. "As a matter of fact," he says of life at Fort Marion in Florida, "I doubt if any of the Apaches were homesick. They had always been wanderers, never becoming attached to any one locality" (147). While all these movements of course do not in and of themselves represent an Apache resistance, they do help to explain Apache survival in the face of constant pressure and imprisonment. As Betzinez's stories about the escapes and journeys of captive Apache women make clear, these stories of Apache travel—including Betzinez's own experiences—exemplify the stamina and the will to return to the idea if not the actuality of home.

Take for example the story of Massai, one of the captive Warm Springs Apaches on the train to Florida. Betzinez explains that when Geronimo broke out of Fort Apache in 1885, Massai went with him, joining him on the warpath. Eventually, Betzinez believes, Massai "tired of the ever-constant dodging from pursuers" (143); in any event, he returned to the fort. But "[t]his long and rough journey gave him further experience in traveling alone through relatively unknown and difficult country" (143). After establishing Massai's history of resistance and escape from captivity, Betzinez retells the story of Massai's escape from the train somewhere between Kansas City and St. Louis: "From then on for weeks no human being ever saw Massai. Traveling on foot at night, stealing food and water, and hiding by day, he succeeded in getting back to his native country in the Black Mountains of western New Mexico south of the old Warm Springs reservation" (144). Although Betzinez has long since assimilated to white Euro-American ways, he treats this escape not as the act of a misguided, unreconstructed Indian but as a genuine accomplishment. His admiration becomes even more evident as the story continues:

> To appreciate this amazing feat you should remember that this Indian could not read printed road signs, did not dare ask questions, had no map, and had never been in this country before except while on the train. Like a coyote or a wolf he lived off the country, remaining completely out of sight even while passing through a thickly settled part of the country in Missouri and Kansas. (144)

To the literate Betzinez, Massai's inability to read road signs or consult a map contributes significantly to the amazement the story inspires. Like the escaped-captive Apache women whose stories Betzinez tells earlier, Massai homes in on the places he has traveled to and through for his entire life; unlike those women, Massai does so even though the great majority of his people are headed in the opposite direction, to the Florida coast. The idea of the home place motivates him. And, as Betzinez points out near the end of the story,

> We never considered him to be outstanding as a fighter. He was just an average Apache. Yet he had demonstrated, in his long journey and his subsequent years as an outlaw, the almost superhuman power of the

Apache to find his way through unknown country and to survive great hardships. (145)

Why does Betzinez, a thoroughly assimilated man who typically distances himself from the "old" Apache ways, tell this resistance story three-quarters of the way into his autobiography? Clearly, Massai's status as an "outlaw" signifies less to Betzinez than does his status as an Apache. Massai exemplifies not the various "bad" qualities that could be attributed to him by a different teller of this story but rather "the almost superhuman power of the Apache" to find his way back home and to survive. Granted, the story of Massai as "typical" Apache hinges on the extraordinary nature of this particular escape and return: "superhuman" as his power seems to be, he is the only Apache who actually exercises it. The story also elicits a more or less conventional speculation, designed to provoke readers' romantic imaginations: speaking of the small number of Chiricahuas and San Carlos Apaches who remained in the Southwest, Betzinez ends the section by remarking, "I understand that these outlaws or their descendants are still hiding out in Old Mexico" (145). Still, though, Massai's story clearly serves as a source of ethnic pride for Betzinez, as do other moments in the text, such as his favorable comparison of Apache singers to contemporary Euro-Americans: "I doubt if modern night club entertainers can produce a more exhilarating effect" than the Apaches (176). In these moments, scattered throughout the book, Betzinez retains and reclaims "remnants," at least, of Apache identity.

Betzinez also demonstrates an engaging courtesy in a brief anecdote about his first teacher at Carlisle. The incident involves naming:

> Our first teacher was a nice little lady, Miss Flora F. Low, who gave us names and taught us to write them on the blackboard. My childhood name of Nah-delthy, which means Going-to-Run, had been changed in 1878 to Batsinas. Batsinas was an old Indian at San Carlos, a great friend of my mother who had given me his name. Miss Low now changed the spelling of this to Betzinez. I suppose she thought it was a Spanish or Mexican word though actually I think "Batsinas" was Apache. (154)

Of course, one subtext here is the enmity between Apaches and Mexicans, described in detail by both Betzinez and Geronimo. But even beyond that long-standing cultural conflict, Betzinez very politely insists on the Apache derivation of his name and, to some unspecified extent, of his sense of who he is. Even as his assimilation into white America symbolically begins with his renaming, he retains his name, which still sounds like "Batsinas." Granted, he interprets his new first name, Jason, as symbolic, in a classical Western sense, of a "search for the Golden Fleece" that "has set a pattern for my life" (154). But his last name signifies in other directions.

Although Betzinez criticizes some of the Apache leaders harshly, he generally respects Geronimo and defends him against the many scurrilous rumors and legends that circulated about him. At one of the major turning points in Betzinez's story, the "final surrender of Geronimo" (139), he sums things up in a striking way:

> Thus ended Geronimo's war campaigns. Peace could now prevail through-out Arizona, New Mexico, and northern Mexico. People could at long last enjoy peace, prosperity, and the pursuit of money. We Indians said to our-selves: "You white people can now go about your business without fear of attack by the Apaches. But you are still subject to being preyed upon. Beware of your own race, who are seeking an easy path to wealth at your expense!" (139)

For all of the moments in the text where Betzinez waxes happy about his conversion to Christianity and his conviction that Euro-American ways are the best ways of life, he also writes passages like this one, in which his tone seems much less easily identifiable. These are perhaps examples of "remnant attitudes," of places where Betzinez still identifies himself as more "Apache" than "Euro-American" ("We Indians said to ourselves"). They are perhaps ex-amples, too, of Betzinez's irony or even sarcasm, inflections lost with the pas-sage of time and the absence of a speaking voice cueing listeners as to tone.

But they also exemplify Betzinez's subtle, occasional critiques of the cul-ture he has joined; like a warning from an eighteenth-century British satirist or an Apache who has lived through the transition from sovereignty to captiv-ity and assimilation, the final sentence critiques the complacency of Euro-Americans who resist the possibility that cultural conflicts in the Southwest (and elsewhere) are more complicated than easy "Indian"-"white" binaries let on. Betzinez himself demonstrates these complexities whenever he gets into political or social difficulties with other Apaches, and he seems to chide Euro-Americans who might think otherwise when he remarks, "I suppose we are all primitive to some degree" (175). Like the "outlaw" Indian Geronimo, the "good" Indian Betzinez redefines Euro-American conceptual categories, takes textual control of his story, and actively works against being taken for either an outlaw or an icon.

4 Photography as Resistance in *Almanac of the Dead*

Far from being historically or textually contained in the late nineteenth and early twentieth centuries, Geronimo's resistance strategies remain influential and powerful. Chapter 3 examined how his autobiography, *Geronimo's Story of His Life,* combines oral tradition and military-political tactics to implicate readers in his arguments; this chapter will turn to the more specific, intertribal relationship between this Warm Springs Apache leader and a late-twentieth-century Laguna Pueblo Indian writer and photographer, Leslie Marmon Silko. Silko's *Almanac of the Dead* in particular can be read as a continuation of the work begun in *Geronimo's Story of His Life* and reflected in Geronimo's metatextual life as resistance Indian and iconic "outlaw."

Since the publication of *Storyteller* in 1981, Silko has turned and returned to Geronimo and to photography, representing both as signs and spaces in motion, sites of "collective memory" (*Yellow Woman,* 30), and agents of Indian resistance. But Geronimo never appears in her first published work "about" him, "A Geronimo Story" (first printed in *The Man to Send Rain Clouds* [1974] and later recontextualized in *Storyteller*). The story focuses mainly on Laguna scouts who "track" the skillfully elusive Geronimo for white soldiers yet take an interest in helping to preserve the Apaches' tactical absence. "A Geronimo Story," then, describes U.S. Army futility (summed up in the person of the unfortunately named Major Littlecock) as well as a subtle intertribal resistance that successfully counters threats of Indian removal and assimilation. Geronimo is absent without having been removed; the Laguna scouts "cooperate" with the army without effecting the army's goals.

These productive, strategic indirections and absences link to the narrative techniques of the narrator's uncle, Siteye, who laces silences into the stories he tells:

> It was beautiful to hear Siteye talk; his words were careful and thoughtful, but they followed each other smoothly to tell a good story. He would pause to let you get a feeling for the words; and even silence was alive in his stories. (*Storyteller,* 215)

Geronimo's absence from "A Geronimo Story" is similarly present, "alive" by design. The night before they do not find Geronimo, the narrator and

Siteye have a brief, telling exchange in which they indirectly discuss this design further:

> Before I went to sleep I said to Siteye, "You've been hunting Geronimo for a long time, haven't you? And he always gets away." "Yes," Siteye said, staring up at the stars, "but I always like to think that it's us who get away." (*Storyteller*, 222)

The rich ambiguity of Siteye's thinking raises stimulating questions: Who is "us"? The hunted Indians *and* the Indian hunters? Where do they "get away" to, and what does this getaway mean? And why does he "like to think" these thoughts? His pleasure derives from the "always" as well as the "get away": the storylike patterns of variation (each "hunt" is different in some ways) and inevitability (the story always ends the same way, with Geronimo still uncaptured), combined with an ambiguity of expression that, like Geronimo's ambiguous presence-in-absence, pleases other Indians both aesthetically and ideologically.

Silko writes, in *Yellow Woman and a Beauty of the Spirit* (1996), that she is "interested in photographic images that obscure rather than reveal . . . [and] intrigued with photographs that don't tell you what you are supposed to notice, that don't illustrate the text, that don't serve the text" (169). As in "A Geronimo Story," the most interesting images are not simply unpredictable but actively and productively evasive. She contends in another essay that verbal and visual images work similarly: "I see no reason to separate visual images from written words that are visual images themselves" (*Yellow Woman*, 14). Written words and visual images represent reality in similar ways; they also represent and exploit absences and silences in similar ways. That is, photographs for Silko do not necessarily or even primarily serve as documentary certifications or commemorations of some "authentic" representational relationship in some specifiable time and place. Photographs, like words, are certainly capable of providing evidence, but they do not necessarily do so according to Western standards of what evidence is and what it does. As many critics have noted, in the vast majority of Euro-American photographs of Indians, the person holding the camera imposes upon and in effect frames the subjects being shot. (Lucy Lippard [29] and Donna Haraway [42–46] have observed that cameras are quite capable of resembling guns and photographers hunters.) Then these images of Indians are reproduced, marketed, and entered into Western historical records as evidence for Euro-American constructions of Indian-white history. But Silko, like Geronimo, gets inside these official processes and disrupts photographic business as usual, including its political and evidentiary mystifications.

In *Almanac of the Dead* (1991), Silko says a great deal about the ways nineteenth-century Indians use photography against its inventors. Indians infiltrate this new Western technology in ways that render them more absent than present; in doing so, they resist U.S. forces who would bring about more permanent forms of absence. And, as in "A Geronimo Story," these tactics

circulate around a Geronimo who never appears in the text; Silko neither reproduces photographs of Geronimo nor identifies any one character in the
narrative as Geronimo. In particular, she describes how Yaqui and Apache
strategists work out an astonishing deception in which photographs ostensibly of the celebrated warrior are instead the pictures of various Indian men
deliberately moving in and out of the same Western-constructed, binary,
image/caption identity (see Bryant, ed., 12–14). And there is more: there is
also an ancestor, long dead, who understands the situation and intervenes,
working to ensure that all these various "Geronimos" look alike to Euro-
American spectators. This ancestor is exceptionally mobile: he crosses many
boundaries to superimpose himself on the surrogates' images, thereby developing a very persuasive meta-Geronimo who has fooled whites and fueled
Indian resistance for more than a hundred years.

In other words, the familiar, widely circulated photographs of Geronimo
are, in fact, not photographs of Geronimo—or rather, they both are and are
not photographs of a single Geronimo. There may be a single Geronimo, but
he moves outside the frames of "his" photographs, going largely unnamed (as
well as completely unpictured) in *Almanac of the Dead;* his strategies far
exceed the capabilities of Euro-American technologies to contain and interpret him. This ability to outfox Euro-American technology—to move across,
through, and against a Western machine and its products—leads toward a
strategic outfoxing of Euro-American history. Like the Geronimo discussed
but never seen in "A Geronimo Story," the Geronimos in *Almanac of the
Dead* skillfully and strategically exploit a very present absence to wage intertribal Apache–Yaqui–Laguna Pueblo Indian resistance. This resistance often
works precisely by exploiting absences, silences, and blindnesses, some of
which are identified as Euro-American perceptual shortcomings and used accordingly. In writing about these strategies, Silko links nineteenth-century,
southwestern resistances to the panoramic (spatial and temporal) range of
her novel as she herself joins these large-scale, multinational, and multidirectional intertribal resistances.

Because they seemed to make images appear in mysterious fashion, early da-
guerreotypes were at times mistaken for, or accused of, alchemy. There was
something "apparitional" (Trachtenberg, *Reading,* 13) about the technological process itself and also something witchily magical in the process of reading photographs.[1] As Lippard points out, some Indians believed—and some
continue to believe—that photography could also make people disappear:
"Photographers were called 'shadow catchers' by some tribes (the shadow referring to death, or the soul of the dead). The transfer of a black-and-white
likeness to paper meant to some that a part of their lives had been taken
away, to others that their vital power had been diminished" (30–31). To read
these likenesses, then, is to encounter not a reproduction but a diminution,

a disempowering brought about by being taken. Like the belief in photography's magical properties, "[t]hese [Indian] beliefs have never fully disappeared" (Lippard, 31).

John Tagg, writing about European and American photographic practices, insists on a different approach to photography: "The photograph is not a magical 'emanation' but a material product of a material apparatus set to work in specific contexts, by specific forces, for more or less defined purposes. It requires, therefore, not an alchemy but a history" (3). Further, "we must look not to some 'magic' of the medium, but to the conscious and unconscious processes, the practices and institutions through which the photograph can incite a phantasy, take on meaning, and exercise an effect" (4). Silko denies neither Tagg's nor Lippard's conclusions but comes closer to agreeing with Lippard as she approaches the problem from a tribal perspective: "Pueblo people may not believe that the camera steals the soul of the subject, but certainly the Pueblo people are quite aware of the intimate nature of the photographic image" (*Yellow Woman*, 176–177). To the Pueblo people, as to Silko, "the power and significance of the photographic image" must be respected; the image, with the image-taker, is capable of committing "outrages to privacy" (177). For example, Silko writes, "The more I read about the behavior of subatomic particles of light, the more confident I am that photographs are capable of registering subtle electromagnetic changes in both the subject and the photographer" (*Yellow Woman*, 180). The process itself involves uninvestigated reciprocities. She holds that "to me [photography] is still magic" (180). She marvels at photographs taken of her by a Japanese photographer, in which she herself appears to be Japanese (180–181).

In *Almanac of the Dead*, the revolutionary Maya Angelita/La Escapía struggles with this conflict between materialist and magical approaches to photography as she faces a particular photograph—not, in this instance, of Geronimo—that seems to exert magical powers over her, despite her own best efforts. She had "somehow . . . been bewitched by the photographs and writings of Engels and Marx" (521), especially "the blazing darkness of Marx's eyes" (521). The indigenous peoples camped with her in the mountains of southern Mexico "had heard stories about victims bewitched by photographs of strangers long dead, long gone from the world except for a trace of the spirit's light that remained in the photograph" (518). Angelita resists these speculations but confesses to her comrade and lover, El Feo, that "she had never entirely believed what the old-time people said about photography until she had seen the photograph of Marx" (522). This transaction is complicated: the early photograph of Marx as a young man, the photograph as a nineteenth-century European product of industrial technology, eventually brings the young, late-twentieth-century Indian woman nearer to the stories and beliefs of "old-time [Indian] people."

In *Big Falling Snow*, Albert Yava regards photographs as straightforward, reliable evidence: "If you look at those photos taken by old-time photographers in the 1890s you'll get a good idea of how big the change has been" since he was a boy (132). Angelita's suspicions about "magic" suggest a corresponding desire to see photographs as Yava sees them, to read them as historical evidence rather than as evanescences that violate cultural and historical boundaries. She is carefully shaping and controlling her emerging sense of herself as a credible revolutionary leader; she realizes that excessive attention to "magical" Euro-American images and technologies may threaten to diminish her political position in the eyes of her community. But Tagg's contentions ultimately do not diminish the force of Angelita's perceptions of "Marx, tribal man and storyteller" (520): when she sees his photograph, something happens. She weathers all the jokes about her "love affair . . . with Marx, a billy-goat-bearded, old white man. The elder sisters laughed; here was the danger of staring at a photograph. A glint of the man's soul had been captured there, in the eyes of Marx's image on the page. The elder sisters said Angelita should have been more careful" (517–518). Angelita recognizes that it is "time to clear the air" (518), and she does so by reaffirming that her great desire is not Marxist: she wants, more than anything else, to take back the land that has been stolen from the Indians. At the same time, the elder sisters as representatives of the larger tribal community circulate stories about photographs that help to resituate her tribally and to forestall bewitchings.

In other words, the storytellers remind her that there is already a place for photography within the tribe; they do not prohibit her from looking at the picture of Marx, but they do expect her to explain how and why she comes to re-place or reposition, more so than revise, the older tribal stories about photography. This she does; she clears the air, finally, by speaking in public, telling her own stories, and trying and executing her ex-teacher and ex-lover, Bartolomeo. This Cuban racist-revolutionary is convicted, in public assembly, of "crimes against the people's history" (525); his crimes come to the people's attention when he gets mixed up with photography, distributing handbills with newspaper photographs of the Mexican capitalist Menardo's corpse. The Menardo narrative exemplifies the destructive, male reign of Death-Eye Dog; the Angelita narrative links to various other woman- and Indian-centered narratives throughout *Almanac of the Dead,* narratives that set in motion political and cultural resistances toward retaking the land. Silko carefully intertwines these narratives: Tacho, for example, is Menardo's driver and the twin brother of El Feo, Angelita's lover and political ally. Together, Tacho and El Feo will follow the spirit macaws' guidance and lead the "massive human migrations" (511) from south to north. The point, though, is that Silko implicates photography in the novel's larger resistance narrative. As she intertwines the shifting textual position of photography with the shifting, transitional position of the Angelita-Bartolomeo-Marx passage, she demonstrates that the act of taking (or retaking) control of photographs links storytelling to intertribal political resistance. In redirecting attention from the photograph of Marx to the photograph of Menardo and in moving from looking at pictures in private to critiquing their power in a public forum,

Angelita—and Silko—take control of the images and help clear the way for further agitation against those who render Indians and Indian history invisible.

Throughout *Almanac of the Dead,* Silko posits such relationships between photography and Indian resistance, arguing that Indian subjects refuse to be framed, contained, and otherwise "taken" without taking themselves— and their people—back. She does so most frequently and most radically by turning to Geronimo, whom she strategically refuses to locate in a single, discrete, easily bounded physical or textual space. Instead, Silko's Geronimo is—like Geronimo's Geronimo—a migratory figure who occupies different places and positions for different characters in the narrative. For example, in a section titled "Resistance," the Yaqui Indian Calabazas remembers Geronimo stories he heard as a boy, stories told by his elders. A smuggler who is himself a proficient crosser and violator of borders, Calabazas thinks of Geronimo when he looks back over his life, reflects on growing older, and begins to make connections between his elders' remembered stories and his own emerging cultural position as an elder who is now responsible for remembering and passing on the stories. Calabazas lives in Tucson but grew up in a Mexican mountain village, and as he sits outside at night with an ice chest full of beer beside him and joints of marijuana ready at hand, he remembers a Geronimo who moves skillfully between and around a variety of southwestern places. Silko suggests that Yaqui smugglers such as Calabazas can construct their own identities because they occupy liminal spaces—or, at least, they can maintain and manipulate their own senses of who they are, not oblivious to but also not strictly determined by the decisions of others. She links Geronimo to Calabazas because for both, identity can be fluid and tactical, politically charged or inflected. Further still, "Geronimo," who slips in and out of Calabazas's night thoughts about Indianness, can be mobilized for subversive purposes that are not entirely understood and not yet entirely controllable. Similarly, while the photographs of "Geronimo" do not exactly lie, they leave their ambiguities and indirections unexplained; Indians such as Calabazas and his relations can only speculate about a process that appears to be magical yet produces material results.

In "Mistaken Identity," the section that follows "Resistance," Calabazas remembers what the elders taught him when he was a child getting sleepy by the fire: "In time there came to be at least four Apache raiders who were called by the name Geronimo, either by the Mexican soldiers or the gringos" (*Almanac,* 224). Red Clay, Big Pine, and Wide Ledge all appear in photographs identifying them as Geronimo, but someone or something else intervenes in this Euro-American technological process to produce a "Geronimo" even most Apaches and Yaquis can't identify. This turns the tables: attempting to create a "Geronimo" whom whites can't identify specifically and decisively, Yaqui and Apache strategists open or otherwise recognize a space through which a cross-cultural mystery moves. This Geronimo's power lies not in his monumental, iconic recognizability but rather in his elusive movements inside an icon that is already very much in motion and unstable by design.

Of course, the Indian strategists continue to exploit their adversaries' inability to see the world around them in a discriminating, detailed way. This Euro-American blindness dovetails with the racist conviction that "all [X] look alike": to these culturally impaired perceivers, a disabled white man like Calabazas's friend and employee Root stands out, while an Indian leader like Geronimo does not, despite (or because of) his culturally imposed, fictive role as demonized icon. For Silko, of course, this blindness involves not only people but also places:

> The elders used to argue that this was one of the most dangerous qualities of the Europeans: Europeans suffered a sort of blindness to the world. To them, a "rock" was just a "rock" wherever they found it, despite obvious differences in shape, density, color, or the position of the rock relative to all things around it. The Europeans, whether they spoke Spanish or English, could often be heard complaining in frightened tones that the hills and canyons looked the same to them. . . . To whites all Apache warriors looked alike, and no one realized that for a while, there had been three different Apache warriors called Geronimo who ranged across the Sonoran desert south of Tucson. (*Almanac*, 224–225)

Euro-American blindness to place doubles as blindness to indigenous peoples; Apache identity conversely grows out of an ability to perceive—to see and to read—a shifting southwestern land sharply, to discriminate between rocks and hills and canyons and Geronimos. Using this perceptiveness to read and respond to the blindness of the incoming soldiers and emigrants, "[s]trategists for both the Yaquis and the Apaches quickly learned to make use of the Europeans' inability to perceive unique details in the landscape" (*Almanac*, 225). As in "A Geronimo Story," Indian scouts in *Almanac of the Dead* find themselves placed in the middle, more aware than the whites of what the Indians are doing but unable (or unwilling) to persuade the whites to heed them. The "Geronimo" photographs emerge from this tangle of strategy and misperception as image-texts that exploit Euro-American inabilities to read both the connections and the differences between Indians and southwestern spaces.

The chapter titled "At War with the U.S. Government" includes Yoeme's take on these photographs. Yoeme (the Yaqui word for "the people" [see Evers, ed., 2, 190]) is Lecha and Zeta's grandmother and a keeper of the Almanac; she tells the girls a number of interesting things about "the man they called Geronimo":

> That was not his name. No wonder there has been so much confusion among white people and their historians. The man encouraged the confusion. He has been called a medicine man, but that title is misleading. He was a man who was able to perform certain feats. (*Almanac*, 129)

Again, representation entails confusion: here, attempts to encapsulate the man's identity in a name or in a title mislead. And here, the "misidentified" man encourages the misled to stay misled, fostering in the process the persistent Euro-American propensity to categorize and reduce identity. Misrepresentation is accidental and/or foolish, and it is also part of a knowing "Geronimo's" guerrilla tactics. Yoeme, out of politeness or out of not knowing but also out of a desire to keep any secrets secret, remains vague about the "certain feats" this figure can perform.

Yoeme continues,

> I have seen the photographs that are labeled "Geronimo." . . . But the Apache man identified in the photographs is not, of course, the man the U.S. Army has been chasing. He is a man who always accompanied the one who performed certain feats. He is the man who agreed to play the role for the protection of the other man. The man in the photographs had been promised safe conduct by the man he protected. The man in the photographs was a brilliant and resourceful man. (*Almanac*, 129)

In Yoeme's version of these events, both men remain nameless (though partly identified as "Geronimo"). As the name "Geronimo" gets more and more elastic, stretching as it does in *Almanac of the Dead* to comprehend many different things, Silko partially but not entirely overwrites its Western and Euro-American meaning. Her verb tenses, for example, remap the man's ability to cross and recross temporal as well as spatial and representational borders. In particular, she intervenes in the cultural construction of an American Geronimo, destabilizes all that "Geronimo" has come to represent in U.S. "outlaw" mythologies, and calls attention to the flexibility of Apache resistance as well as the instabilities of American icon formation.

Silko's Geronimo theory links to her *Almanac of the Dead* stories about the old Yupik woman who learns to manipulate air flights over Alaska and cause plane wrecks, crafting her "plane-crashing spell" (156) "with only a piece of weasel fur, a satellite weather map on a TV screen and the spirit energy of a story" (159). Like the Geronimos, this old woman skillfully manipulates "the white man's gadgets" (155); like the Geronimos, she combines old and new ways, strategically adapting the stories so that she can subvert, confuse, and "turn the destruction back on its senders" (156). And yet, because of the mysterious intervention of that ancestor "Geronimo," the one who appears in the photographs, the Geronimo phenomenon differs from the old Yupik woman's skills. He creates another layer or level or web of complication; he seems to suggest that something else is at work, outside of or beyond everyone's hands (and, perhaps, everyone's words, names, and stories). Is it that the Apaches and Yaquis have an ephemeral ally who works on his own, more metaphysically than physically, infiltrating photographs that already both represent native resistance (the Indians are rotating Geronimos) and parody Euro-American perceptual limitations (the Indians are rotating Geronimos in the knowledge that the whites lack the vision and intelligence to catch on, even to the point where they unknowingly cooperate in the rotations)? If yes, then this "Geronimo" seems both to support and to subvert the subversion.

Or maybe Calabazas's old Yaqui uncle—the only one to venture an explanation of this Apache's identity—is right when he tells Calabazas (in Silko's narrator's words):

> The face in all the photographs had belonged to an ancestor, the soul of one long dead who knew the plight of the "Geronimos." The Apaches were nervous about the dead and the activities of their souls, but the Yaquis were not. The Yaquis had extensive experiences with just such occurrences. The spirit of the ancestor had cast its light, its power, in front of the faces of the three "Geronimos." (232)

Or, as the old uncle suggests to Calabazas a little later, maybe it is a case of sorcery. In saying this, the old uncle sets in motion a whole different realm of possibilities and power relations; whatever he means, his suggestion has the effect of further muddying the tribal and intertribal waters. Things are complicated enough, he seems to say, in this Indian world; Indians don't require a Euro-American presence to qualify as complicated. In fact, especially given Silko's remarks about the ways she was consumed by writing this book, it is worth asking whether she is fully in control of "Geronimo" and whether she can be or should be: "the *Almanac* didn't want to end" (Perry, 338), and the author and publishing house had somehow to rein in its outlaw energy.[2]

This process of turning Geronimo into "Geronimo" is one way of reinventing a southwestern myth; Silko in effect claims that there are competing American Indian and competing Euro-American myths of Geronimo. At the same time, she distinguishes importantly between myth and *Almanac of the Dead* as a prophetic text that links past and future history. "Native Americans acknowledge no borders," she writes in an inset box on the five-hundred-year map; "they seek nothing less than the return of all tribal lands." Myths are certainly involved in the gradual fulfilling of this prophecy, but Silko never explicitly identifies her Geronimo stories as myths. In a sense, she presents them as simultaneously prophetic and revisionist. They may also be implicated in the revisionist prophecies of Ghost Dance power, to which she turns as *Almanac of the Dead* comes to a close. Both the Geronimo stories and ghost dancing involve transformative repetitions, recalibrations of human physiology, and rethinkings of Western and native conventions about the relationships among bodies, names, and identities. Both also serve as a sort of shorthand for Euro-American fears of Indians: one "Geronimo" is the single powerful uncatchable renegade, and the other is at the heart of a pan-Indian rebellion that moves with the force of religious belief.[3]

Near the end of the novel, the Lakota poet Wilson Weasel Tail recites Ghost Dance poetry:

> We dance because the dead love us,
> they continue to speak to us,
> they tell our hearts what must be done to survive
>
> . . . .

Spirits! Ancestors!
we have been counting the days, watching the
signs.
You are with us every minute,
you whisper to us in our dreams,
you whisper in our waking moments.
You are more powerful than memory! (722)

As the book ends, Lecha and Seese are "headed for South Dakota to the secret headquarters where Wilson Weasel Tail and the others were making preparations" (754). As the indigenous alliance led by Tacho and El Feo moves from south (Mexico) to north (Arizona), another indigenous alliance also moves from south (Tucson) to north (South Dakota). Earlier, Lecha works as a migratory television psychic, moving from studio to studio and crime scene to crime scene, "seeing" and "identifying" that which is not "there." As with the Geronimos, her photographed—filmed—presence works toward exposing disappearances and absences, except that in contemporary America, the bodies she locates have been murdered. Is Lecha predicting deaths, interpreting deaths, or imagining deaths into being? As the Geronimos do with cameras, Lecha manipulates television from the inside. The old Yupik woman uses television (and other things) to manipulate airplanes and in a larger sense to disrupt certain travels. And Silko pulls it all together, suggesting (as in *Ceremony*) that connections are complex but available and casting *Almanac of the Dead* as a participant in intertribal resistances that move across temporal, spatial, and technological borders that are sometimes clearly drawn and sometimes not.

Wide Ledge, one of the three or four "Geronimos," also investigates and reflects on photography. Like many other characters in *Almanac of the Dead*, he has some difficulty in learning how to read photographs but is very interested in getting inside the process:

> From what he had seen, Wide Ledge said, the white people had little smudges and marks like animal tracks across snow or light brown dust; these "tracks" were supposed to "represent" certain persons, places, or things. Wide Ledge explained how with a certain amount of training and time, he had been able to see the "tracks" representing a horse, a canyon, and white man. But invariably, Wide Ledge said, these traces of other beings and other places preserved on paper became confused even for the white people, who believed they understood these tracks so well. (227)

Wide Ledge does not talk about being able to see "tracks"—the routes and roots—that represent an Indian. To some extent, he naturalizes this photographic process, but again, that may be a bit less crucial than the broader issue of confused, unreliable, and suspect representations. As with Sterling's seemingly naive, deceptively savvy political sensibility, so here: the "naturalizing" of an alien process, the "simplifying," is mock simplification, a strategic breaking down of the elements of photography through which Wide Ledge can both "explain" photography to the "uninitiated" and use this explanation to render photography as something less than miraculous and rather more like an absurdity or a magic trick revealed as empty air. Photographs are difficult to read, perhaps pointlessly or dangerously so, and this difficulty differs from the tactical confusion, the sophisticated difficulty crafted by "Geronimo" as "he" exploits the technologies of taking and reading photographs. Maybe Silko is theorizing differences between reproduction (by way of photography) and distribution (the diffused, multiple Geronimos), as well as differences between Euro-American and Indian motives: photography memorializes, legitimizes, records, "proves," entertains; "Geronimos" escape, confuse, elude, fight back, survive.

All this, of course, connects to Sterling's tabloid crime magazines, *Police Gazette* and *True Detective*, with their antiseptically precise photographs of crime scenes and dead bodies. His beloved *Police Gazette* lumps Geronimo with John Dillinger, Pretty Boy Floyd, and Billy the Kid—four men problematically defined as "outlaws," four criminal heroes and heroic criminals, four bodies graphically photographed (and imagined) and at the same time mysteriously missing or absent, four bodies graphically captured in photographs and at the same time tricksterishly skilled at slipping through cracks, eluding capture, escaping, disappearing. Despite their differences, Silko speculatively links Geronimo to Dillinger through Sterling and Seese's somewhat touristy search for the Tucson places both men inhabited—the historical sites Sterling "would like very much just to stand on" (39). He would like to "have a cold beer at the same place Dillinger and his gang had been drinking beer in 1934" (29). He would like to occupy a specific physical place that allows him to "return" to 1934 and attempt both to replicate history and to gauge the differences between 1934 and the present. For Silko, though, the link between Geronimo and Dillinger probably has a lot to do with their shared commitment to being, as one chapter title calls it, "At War with the U.S. Government." Dillinger and Geronimo both, in very different ways, conducted successful and imaginative warfare against federal authorities, the soldiers and the crime stoppers, the military and the FBI.

But what of Sterling's engagement with these figures and his eagerness to share them with Seese? However unreliable and sensationalistic his tabloids may be, they also teach Sterling to be modestly streetwise, socially and politically intelligent about, for instance, the surprising similarities between "many famous criminals": "Thanks to his magazines, Sterling was aware that many famous criminals had similar grievances with the governments or communities that had failed to deliver them either protection or justice" (39–40). While Sterling is not particularly Geronimo-like and does not himself advance the Yaquis' notions of multiple, mystifying Geronimos, he occupies the "moral center" of a novel in which things and people are not necessarily what they seem.[4] To my reading, Sterling's naivete and modesty only partially mask a sophisticated political understanding culled rather undeliberately from rather modest if not altogether underwhelming sources. "Sterling thought he was probably one of the few Indians interested in famous Indian outlaws" (40); in calling attention to the oddity of the situation, he questions, however indirectly, its governing assumption about Geronimo. Gradually developing a clearer idea of what to do and where to go with his critical sensibility, Sterling first acts to involve Seese in his criminal interests. Then he moves away from the tabloids altogether, canceling his subscriptions, reengaging with the actual (and often very sensationalistic) complexities of life all around him. Finally, he chooses to return home rather than to accompany Lecha and Seese to South Dakota; he homes in to Laguna Pueblo and to the giant stone snake that also returns. In his own modest way, Sterling participates in the much broader, much more radical, migratory Indian resistances of *Almanac of the Dead.*

↙

In his self-consciously polemical recent study, *Navajo and Photography,* James C. Faris tenaciously argues that since about 1866, "Navajo have been essentially captive to photography" (23).[5] Forced to evacuate their homeland, literally held captive at Bosque Redondo, the Diné were then, in Faris's telling phrase, subjected to acts of "ethnographic predation" (23), including technological predation in the form of photography. Despite various forms of resistance, Faris suggests, Navajo were not only physically removed but also metaphysically "taken" over and over again by Euro-American photographers. These pictures both confirm and extend Navajo subjugation; each photograph reenacts and limitlessly reproduces the severe limitations imposed on Navajos by Western technologies and technicians.

Intentionally or not, these technicians significantly reinvent the longstanding American literary convention of the captivity narrative, not just replacing white women captives with Navajo captives of various genders but capturing and controlling American Indians in general. Seen as such, these Euro-American photographs of American Indians are obviously complicit in U.S. imperialism. Rather than performing as the captors, Indians are presented strategically as captives to reassure Euro-Americans that Indians have been subdued, that Indians can be contained not only inside the borders of reservations but also inside the frames of photographs, and that Euro-American technological progress can provide ways of seeing and controlling the colonized.[6] Indeed, Euro-technology can, almost ironically, "model" assimilation when it is not busy cropping to reverse-engineer it out of visible existence, as in some of Edward Curtis's romantic retro-images of Indians disguised as precolonial "noble savages" (see Lyman, *Vanishing Race*).

While Faris sees many of these photographs as captivity narratives (and, much less frequently, resistances), Silko liberates photography, in part by asserting the creative, subversive, intertribal capacity to enter into and alter processes of taking and reading photographs. In other words, Silko in *Almanac of the Dead* notably refuses to be nostalgic for some sort of precolonial tribal paradise or eager for some sort of postcolonial equivalent. Instead, she clearly sees Euro-American technology as one means of native resistance and sovereignty, part of a larger strategy of reverse-engineering set in motion by Indians and allies who expect to take back the land, in part by infiltrating and reclaiming the technologies of Euro-American colonialism. Photographic representation becomes something to talk about, not necessarily something for readers to see; the nature and status of evidence changes radically as Silko insists on a concept of "the written word as a picture of the spoken word" (*Yellow Woman*, 14–15) and a visual image as well, (re)moving images that rework, resist, and retake language itself, toward the creation and re-creation of sovereign Indian spaces. Indians, in other words, resituate this Euro-American technology by transforming it into native stories. Geronimo, a tribal collective as well as a sophisticated tactician and tactic, is one of the ephemeral and constantly moving embodiments of this spirited resistance. And Silko's practicing of both photography and novelistic forms of photographic theory intersects continually and creatively with *her* practicing of Indianness. Photography for her is a matter of family, tribe, storytelling, ideology, subversion, and resistance.

In this context, Geronimo's remark, "You never have caught me shooting" (Debo, vi, 107), like Siteye's remark about Geronimo and Silko's "a sort of prayer to the horizon or mountains I loved and desired in my photography" (*Yellow Woman*, 22), mobilizes ambiguity, a Western literary device, to contest Western efforts to control him and his people. Geronimo elides guns and cameras as the federal weaponry of captivity and regulation while indicating his ability to shoot without being caught and to confuse identities and actions—who is doing what to whom, in his six-word sentence?—thereby keeping himself elusive to a vastly greater extent than Euro-Americans previously believed. Geronimo uses both the English language and the camera to Indian advantage, as tools and weapons. Jimmie Durham observes that "even when he was 'posed' by the man behind the camera, he seems to have destroyed the pose and created his own stance. . . . Geronimo uses the photograph to 'get at' those people who imagine themselves as the 'audience' of his struggles" (56). Durham writes that "Geronimo, as an Indian 'photographic subject,' blew out the windows. On his own, he reinvented the concept of photographs of American Indians" (56). Although Silko does not see him as quite such a freelancer, she also works to take photography back and to disrupt the power relations that force Indians to adapt to Euro-American culture without encouraging a reciprocal adaptation of Euro-Americans to Indian cultures. That is, Silko argues that rather than simply and primarily "adapting"—reacting to Euro-American actions—Indians can and must also infiltrate these actions (and technologies), inducing Euro-Americans to respond to them, or, in the most brilliant strategic moves, hoodwinking Euro-Americans so much that they don't even know that Indians are "doing" anything. As Silko points out, "[t]he Indian with a camera is frightening for a number of reasons" (*Yellow Woman*, 177). But she is more than that, too. In a variety of radical ways, only a few of which I discuss here, Silko redefines the idea of assimilation and the potentiality of a migratory native resistance.

The photographs of "Geronimo," finally, depict a slippery and for the most part unidentifiable "Geronimo" who contributes to the resistance by further complicating the Indian strategists' already complex notions of identity and representation. This ancestral figure appears, seemingly of his own volition and outside of anyone's designs—neither Apache nor Yaqui, photographer nor photographed, invites or even sees this "Geronimo" until the photos are developed. As with Wide Ledge's investigation of the inside of the camera, so here; the "Geronimo" seems to enter and inhabit the "inside" of the photographs without ever materializing in the "real world outside" the photographs. He disrupts the patented, portable, and eminently repeatable technology of photography. "Geronimo" occupies a very particular border zone or liminal space, an interior space; substituting for other Indians who themselves act as "substitute" Geronimos, he also defines a blurry yet clearly sovereign Indian space. Whatever is happening here happens among Indians, in Indian space, time, and physical and metaphysical reality, and Indians remember it for the subversive and confusing phenomenon that it is.

What does Silko's Geronimo theory imply about the "real" Geronimo, the "historical" Geronimo, the Geronimo who made *Geronimo's Story of His Life*? Silko says nothing that invalidates that Geronimo or that book; on the contrary, they enter into the extraordinarily mobile conception of Geronimo that she both proposes and describes as she enters into the resistance strategies he proposes and models in his autobiography. Migration, mobility, and photography all work together; *Almanac of the Dead* appears to be simultaneously the most radical and the most typical American Indian novel in its presentation of what seems utterly new combined with what so many people have known for so long.

5 Indian Detours, or, Where the Indians Aren't

Management and Preservation in the Euro-American Southwest

As Alan Trachtenberg points out, and as has been demonstrated earlier in this book, Frederick Jackson Turner's frontier thesis "fails to acknowledge cultural multiplicity" (*Incorporation*, 16–17). Around the turn of the twentieth century, many such strong and often imperialist Euro-American arguments about western expansion either exclude the Southwest (as Turner does) or attempt to come to terms with it (as various other writers do) by regarding its indigenous cultures as disempowered, disappearing, or dead. Indian writers such as Geronimo and Jason Betzinez issue important responses to this colonial state of affairs, demonstrating clearly that the Apaches were in fact manipulated strategically and relentlessly both before and after their imprisonment. Geronimo fashions himself as an observer speaking textually against his and his people's objectification (in the eyes, for example, of the white multitudes who gathered at railroad stations across the country to stare at Apache prisoners of war as they were taken from Arizona to Florida). Even Betzinez, who has wholeheartedly joined Euro-American society, does not withhold his criticisms and complications of it; neither does he, for all his assimilationist happiness, entirely renounce Apache ethnicity. Articulating resistances and insisting on complex tribal identities, these and other Indian writers in turn influence those who come after—the contemporary Indian poets, novelists, and critics who carry on the political and textual work of their predecessors. In contrast to N. Scott Momaday, who takes up Billy the Kid as well as Kiowa ancestors, Leslie Marmon Silko turns particularly to Geronimo, regarding him as a migratory, elusive precursor to the very capable migratory Indians of *Almanac of the Dead.*

This chapter will shift attention to a different though sometimes overlapping collection of migrations and issues, focusing less on Turner's omissions or Geronimo's argumentative tactics than on the attentions given the Southwest by a variety of Euro-American tourists, artists, and politicians who sought to domesticate and publicize it as a valuable national site. One U.S. leader who turned enthusiastically to the Southwest was Theodore Roosevelt, whose tenacious global mobility linked his physical and ideological codes of athletic and interventionist vigor. Roosevelt found himself at the Grand Canyon in May 1903, where he delivered a presidential address in which he asked his listeners to "keep this great wonder of nature as it now is" (Hart and Ferleger, eds., 216). He remarked that he was "delighted to learn of the wisdom of the Santa Fe railroad people in deciding not to build their hotel on the brink of the canyon." (Their hotel, El Tovar, was in fact built on the canyon's brink during the following year and opened for business in January 1905.) He exhorted his audience, "I hope you will not have a building of any kind, not a summer cottage, a hotel, or anything else, to mar the wonderful grandeur, the sublimity, the great loneliness and beauty of the canyon. Leave it as it is" (216). To what end? "What you can do is to keep it for your children, your children's children, and for all who come after you, as one of the great sights which every American if he can travel at all should see" (216).

But how exactly, one may wonder, will the canyon stay unmarred and unmolested while generations of people stream to its rims? Particularly given that this was 1903, one phrase to highlight here is certainly "if he can travel at all": the Grand Canyon was, after all, quite remote, six hours and 128 miles (round-trip) from the nearest train stop, and much of that terrain punishing (see Hyde, 269–271). The availability of vacations and leisure time also informs Roosevelt's qualification.[1] But as the quick construction of El Tovar Hotel (and more direct, efficient train lines) implies, the site's scenic value and popularity were already being promoted. Roosevelt's benign invitation to visit the canyon contains, in fairly straightforward early form, a contradiction or paradox that remains active in the Southwest for many years: "man can only mar it," yet as many people as possible should go there. The exhortation to go contains the justification for not going. And the changeless beauty of the southwestern scene hinges on its changing status as American cultural icon: taking the upkeep of that changelessness into their own hands, Americans unwittingly risk overimproving it and marring it permanently.

Tangled up in these southwestering processes and yet also often extracted from them, American Indians undergo a corresponding, paradoxical treatment that combines elements of "overimprovement" with elements of "preservation." Some Euro-American observers liked to reinvent particular Indians as generalized or even allegorized types, as examples more than people, and it is crucial not to overlook these racist strains. In 1886, for example, Roosevelt himself presents to the American public a cartoon version of "bad" Indians:

> I don't go so far as to think that the only good Indians are the dead Indians, but I believe nine out of every ten are, and I shouldn't like to inquire too closely into the case of the tenth. The most vicious cowboy has more moral principle than the average Indian. Turn three hundred low families of New York into New Jersey, support them for fifty years in vicious idleness, and you will have some idea of what the Indians are. Reckless, revengeful, fiendishly cruel. (Hart and Ferleger, eds., 251)

Later in his career, Roosevelt modifies this anti-Indian rhetoric somewhat while continuing to mobilize it in the service of his fervid mainstream assimilationist ideology. But just as this complacent racist rhetoric fails to prevent him from traveling "Across the Navajo Desert" or presenting Geronimo as a popular spectacle during his inaugural parade in 1905, his urge to preserve American wildernesses as national parks does not forestall his strong sense that these wilderness areas should be seen and used by the American people. In other words, his dominant belief that Indians must be remade does not prevent him from also ventilating the image of a "preserved" or "conserved" noble savage or museum Indian. To address issues of wilderness preservation, though, he dissociates "native" natural places and native "unnatural" or hypernatural peoples. Stepping away from racialist issues, he implies that saving the wild places and "saving" the "wild" people are two different things done in two different kinds of places.

The increased mobility provided by railroads and automobiles, combined with the related development of southwestern tourism, lead as well to the concept of "Indian detours," begun by the Fred Harvey Company in 1926. As Leah Dilworth explains, "Harvey took tourists directly to the Indians" (91), and the tours "held the promise of even more authentic encounters with Indians" (92). In Harvey's view, commercial tourism heightens rather than compromises an authenticity predicated on something like "preservation" of Indian sites and cultures. Positioning Indians as tourist commodities in part because of their marginalization by the U.S. government, these Indian detours further redefine prevailing ideas of land use and cultural encounter without construing cultural mobility as a particularly reciprocal process. Indeed, when Roosevelt attended a Hopi Snake Dance at Walpi in 1913, he in effect took an early version of an Indian detour, visiting the culturally constructed (imposed) margins while reflecting on the "inevitable" eradication of what he elsewhere calls "pure savagery" ("Across the Navajo Desert," 224).

Dilworth reads Roosevelt's response to the Hopi Snake Dance:

> Native Americans were expected to live like white men, that is, to support themselves in a capitalist economy, but they might also preserve certain aspects of their way of life that Anglos found appealing: these included the things that seemed to Anglos most like the Western categories of art, music, and poetry. The problem with this strategy was that it overlooked the meaning to Hopis of their rituals. . . . To Roosevelt, the Snake dance did not qualify as art, music, or poetry and so was not worth preserving. (64)

Clearly, he sees such Euro-American traveling as an agent of Indian assimilation. As he puts it in "Across the Navajo Desert," "The Navajos have made long strides in advance during the last fifty years, *thanks to the presence of the white men in their neighborhood*" (217–218). To redefine both the Grand Canyon and the Indians as aesthetic spectacles, they must first be rendered accessible. "American" sites like the Grand Canyon must be kept as they are, even as they absorb the presence of increasing numbers of patriotic tourists who carry elements of their home places with them when they travel. "Indian" sites like the "Navajo desert," however, must be remade, like the

Indians themselves. In transforming the Navajo into aesthetically plausible and functional neighbors, assimilators must also transform the "Navajo desert" into an American neighborhood—a neighborhood that doubles as a reservation.

↙

Though a prolific writer, the Bull Moose was not exactly a formidable intellectual; as Richard Hofstadter concludes, "[A]nyone who today has the patience to plow through his collected writings will find there, despite an occasional insight and some ingratiating flashes of self-revelation, a tissue of philistine conventionalities, the intellectual fiber of a muscular and combative Polonius" (296). President Roosevelt's remarks at the Grand Canyon nonetheless exemplify the growing awareness among turn-of-the-century Americans that the Southwest might in fact be interesting to look at *in* the Southwest, preserved on site rather than in geographical surveys, books, and museums. Rhetorically removing Indians from the picture he paints, Roosevelt argues for the Southwest as a part of the nation and as a source of national pride. In domesticating southwestern spectacles, U.S. officials such as Roosevelt convert spatial boundaries into temporal possibilities, national monuments that connect present time to an extensive, geologically determined American "history" as well as to a far-reaching, stabilizing future. If all goes well, Roosevelt complacently suggests, generations of Americans can replicate the 1903 experience of the canyon. National boundary formation and national genealogy buttress and in a sense predict each other. But a variety of artists and writers do not entirely cooperate with Roosevelt's project, and as one result, the Southwest transforms into both a more fertile and a less complacent ground for paradoxes and contradictions.

Thirty-six years after Roosevelt's address, for example, Georgia O'Keeffe in her catalogue statement "About Myself" muses upon her painting *Cow's Skull: Red, White, and Blue:* "To me [animal bones] are as beautiful as anything I know. To me they are strangely more living than the animals walking around. . . . The bones seem to cut sharply to the center of something that is keenly alive on the desert even tho' it is vast and empty and untouchable—and knows no kindness with all its beauty" (Messinger, 72). Here the southwestern desert, though empty, contains animals and their bones; the bones are signs of death but penetrate "something that is keenly alive"; and this life force makes possible a centering on the margins, a marginal center.[2] Both Roosevelt and O'Keeffe perceive that what lures tourists or the solitary painter into these spaces is the sublime sense of vast emptiness, "the great loneliness and beauty" that fills them as they enter it. The president appeals to abstract concepts and values, posterity and patriotism, asking his listeners to preserve the canyon "in your own interest and in the interest of the country" so that it can remain available for spectators (Hart and Ferleger, eds., 216). The painter goes further in that she remakes desert sites as abstract unsentimental images. Though these places appear to be "empty and untouchable," she empties them further by abstracting bare images of death and vitality.

Roosevelt's patriotic fantasy of the canyon in national posterity changes to a decidedly untouristlike site in O'Keeffe's hands, as the aesthetic spectacle moves from spoken address to painted canvas. Both speak to a shareable, important, "American" quality inherent in the Southwest, but his idea of national history becomes, in her hands, a somewhat analogous image of natural history. O'Keeffe was after all largely unimpressed by contemporary historically inflected iconographies such as social or documentary realism, and this painting was also intended as a satire on painters and muralists such as Edward Hopper, Grant Wood, Thomas Hart Benton, and John Steuart Curry: "Just the thought of" a Curry mural "makes me tired," O'Keeffe said (Robinson, 351). She also remarked, "To [those painters], the American scene was a dilapidated house with a broken-down buckboard out front and a horse that looked like a skeleton. . . . For goodness' sake, I thought, the people who talk about the American scene don't know anything about it. So, in a way, that cow's skull was my joke on the American scene, and it gave me pleasure to make it in red, white and blue" (Messinger, 76). The cow's skull does the skeletal horse one better as it stares down the social realists' images of quaint American poverty. And the white skull, framed by red and blue, marks the center of the painting and makes the focal point of the national colors bareboned death, thereby manipulating their more familiar abstract implications.

Very different from her catalogue statement remarks about this painting, these words nonetheless combine with "About Myself" to capture paradoxes of biology, art, and time if not of history, paradoxes that double, both verbally and visually, as challenges. The differences between Roosevelt's and O'Keeffe's statements help measure the ways perceptions of an aestheticized Southwest change. O'Keeffe's formidable desert, intensely personal and intensely purposeful, is leaner yet denser than Roosevelt's scenic and (aesthetically) rather platitudinous Grand Canyon. It is also more difficult, as it is more radically remade. Finally, its aesthetic claims rest, paradoxically, on its capacity to be both an arresting and a defiant image; while Roosevelt's aesthetic is first and foremost inviting, O'Keeffe's both invites and distances. While his expects to be sustained by posterity, hers rests its case in a satirical reproduction of a single generation's America. His looks from the outside into the Southwest; hers stares from the inside out. Finally, hers assumes more about the artist's intimacy with her subject and asks more of the viewer, and hers surely challenges and darkens his assumptions about the beauty and worth of a symbolically charged southwestern space as "American scene."

As both O'Keeffe and Roosevelt recognize, attempts to read the Southwest aesthetically are often crowded out by other approaches to the region. Indeed, throughout the late-nineteenth- and early-twentieth-century West, questions and issues of land use overlap with U.S. Indian policy while often taking precedence over the creation and reception of art. These concerns about conservation, management, and land value often, as in both Roosevelt's and O'Keeffe's careers, generate contradictions, paradoxes, and ambiguities. When Gifford Pinchot became, under Roosevelt, director of the National Forest Service, he set in motion a bureaucratic federal conservation program that intervened in, among other things, economic interests; as Patricia Limerick explains, "In Pinchot's time in office, the conflict seemed to lie between those engaged in quick, wasteful extraction for short-term profit and those committed to careful, long-term use" (*Legacy*, 301). Pinchot's aphorism, "Wilderness is waste," points this conflict up; according to Richard White, it

> exemplified the dilemma faced by advocates of nonutilitarian preservation of the public lands in the National Parks. The National Parks came under federal management not because progressives or western interest groups thought the government could make the lands more productive, but because they believed those lands to be useless in terms of the extractive economy of the West. (410)

Blocking out American Indian affiliations with their home places and in general the possibility of productive, unextracted cultural encounters, this tangle of environmental and economic concerns tends to obstruct or diminish aesthetic ones; indeed, as Limerick remarks, those "committed [solely] to the preservation of pristine wilderness . . . seemed at first to be an eccentric and ineffective minority" (*Legacy*, 301).

When in 1916 commercial uselessness, not environmentalism, helped persuade Congress to establish the National Parks Service, the parks' administrators were directed to "provide for the enjoyment of same in such manner and by such means as will leave them unimpaired for the enjoyment of future generations" (Abbey, *Desert Solitaire*, 48). Limerick, Edward Abbey, and many others point out that this language is riddled with ambiguities; as Abbey explains, "The Developers, the dominant faction, place their emphasis on the words '*provide for the enjoyment*.' The Preservers, a minority but also strong, emphasize the words '*leave them unimpaired*'" (48). Limerick adds, "Most confusing was the matter of timing: what limits had to be placed on present-day 'enjoyment' in order to leave the parks 'unimpaired' for future enjoyment?" (*Legacy*, 308). Moreover, national parks administrators'

> [s]uccess in recruiting visitors earned the usual paradoxical results of Western history. Park supporters got what they wanted, then had to cope with the consequences. As crowds flooded the parks, Americans demonstrated their substantial fondness for nature—and their ability, in Roderick Nash's phrase, to "love it to death." If the parks were to be showcases of nature, an uncontrolled stream of automotive tourists wore away at the very basis of the parks. (Limerick, *Legacy*, 308–309)

For westernizers like Pinchot, untroubled by aesthetic concerns and unsatisfied with passive appreciation, the Forest Service entails not simply preservation but strong management. But even those who prefer leaving nature to its own devices face the problems of "managing" its meanings, of constructing public appreciation grounded in places, things, and (sometimes) peoples not generally understood as aesthetic.

Limerick retells a story about one early aesthetic experience in the Southwest:

> In 1891, Gifford Pinchot—then a self-confessed "tenderfoot"—first saw the Grand Canyon. He was speechless, but his arbitrarily acquired traveling companion, an office boy named Doran, was not. While Pinchot "strove to grasp the vastness and the beauty of the greatest sight this world has to offer," Doran "kept repeating, 'My, ain't it pretty?'" Pinchot remembered, "I wanted to throw him in." (*Legacy*, 293)

Hierarchically, silent struggling in the face of sublime natural beauty outranks repetitive statements of the obvious without ruling out the turn to physical comedy (as well as the play on "Wilderness is waste"). Pinchot's reading of the Grand Canyon as a site of humorous class conflict does not differ markedly from Roosevelt's remarks at the canyon in 1903; both men set out to preserve both the natural spectacle and a particular version of the social order, and both regard these projects as connectable if not already connected. Along the way, Roosevelt's response to the canyon also reveals cross-purposes similar to those expressed in the 1916 National Parks Service mandate; as suggested above, the attempt to legislate consensus produces instead a contradiction-laden packaging of a southwestern place as both an eternally reusable, reproducible aesthetic spectacle and a national monument that is, finally, bounded in both time and space.

Roosevelt's presidential program included the setting aside of spectacular western regions as national parks. Reserving 800,000 acres of Arizona Territory, he in fact created Grand Canyon National Monument in 1908, the last year of his presidency (Richard White, 411). But the railroad and the hotels got there sooner, certifying the scenic value of the place and making possible the arrivals of tourists in greater and greater numbers. Paradoxes and other assorted complications followed close at their heels. A "more accessible" canyon is a canyon at once more popular, more endangered, and less immediate, less menacing physically, and more safely and comfortably distanced. One could look at the desert from a train window, observation deck, automobile or, as early as 1910, a seat in a movie theater rather than struggling in and through it. One could stay at El Tovar Hotel on the edge of the Grand Canyon's south rim and enjoy not only its rustic elements and motifs but also

> a solarium, a music room, and a ladies' lounge. These rooms had fully plastered walls, wallpaper, oriental carpets, French lace curtains, and velvet upholstered furniture. . . . The guest rooms offered visitors a choice. Some were "tinted in Nile green, buff, and cream colors," with Wilton carpets imported from England. Others presented "colonial style" accommodations or "weathered oak, old mission style." (Hyde, 275)

Advertisements for the hotel asserted that it was "highly modern throughout": "money has here summoned the beneficent genii who minister to our
bodily comfort" (quoted in Hyde, 276). And El Tovar's upper-class modernity
has a distinctly cosmopolitan flavor. One would encounter the Southwest not
as an unavoidable obstacle to be endured while en route to a more westerly
destination, not as a multicultural area experienced as a series of encounters
with "others," but as a place to visit and sample at one's choice and leisure,
all the while comfortably surrounded by familiar social procedures, ameni-
ties, and companions. To appreciate the place firsthand, one would of course
have to go there, but to make casual, recreational visits possible and appealing, engineers and businesspeople would have to change the nature of the
place, building roads, hotels, and the like. Such changes compromise the already fraught goal of seeing "it" directly.

As more and more Americans look southwestward, they tend, all in all,
to transplant familiar trappings and thereby to convert by domesticating unfamiliar sites; to the considerable extent that travelers and migrants carry
things with them, they change the terms in and of the Southwest, reducing if
not eliminating the possibilities of complex contact with its various topographies and peoples. In other words, entrepreneurs and travelers import and
promptly construct relatively impermeable boundaries. Pinchot links wilderness and waste, and El Tovar, which not only showcases but also competes
with the natural spectacle, reveals both wilderness and waste conspicuously.

Many of the Euro-American explorers, surveyors, tourists, and emigrants who
traveled to the American Southwest in the late nineteenth and early twentieth centuries encountered and gradually domesticated the cultural geography
of the region, broadly defined. But again and again, they also faced the particular challenges of American deserts head on. Some travelers sought out this
difficult terrain; others worked hard to avoid it but in the process defined their
southwestering experiences in relation to it. Many converted their desert
crossings into narrative, textual form. These physical and textual encounters
with southwestern deserts provide useful examples of the gradual processes
by which a variety of travelers invented a variety of Southwests; the aesthetic
desert emerges only gradually out of a series of compromises involving Euro-
American perceptions of both topographies and indigenous cultures.

In the mid–nineteenth century, a trail of bones lined many sections of the
overland trails; Limerick writes,

> Draft animals, worn down by the preceding months of travel, collapsed
> under the pressure of heat, thirst, and the effort of pulling through heavy
> sand. Their deaths not only left their owners in a precarious position,
> they left the trail littered with carcasses. "Did not see anything but
> bones and dead animals" was a frequent comment. The effect was more

than visual; travelers also commented on the "most obnoxious hideous gases . . . arising from the many dead animals around."

(*Desert Passages,* 18)

Around the middle of the twentieth century, O'Keeffe not only paints bones in oil, on canvas, she also moves to the desert and settles there. That she makes relatively little of the forbidding and potentially lethal qualities of the landscape and climate suggests that its very real dangers, while never entirely overcome, no longer demand the desert traveler or inhabitant's undivided attention. Her access to the desert is in a number of important ways easier than that of nineteenth-century migrants; though it may at first seem monolithically powerful, the American desert is no less subject to historical and cultural change than any other American region.

Indeed, as Limerick explains in *Desert Passages,* Euro-American attitudes toward their desert encounters have changed and developed over time and can be usefully organized into three distinct but sometimes overlapping categories, touching on first biological, then economic, and finally aesthetic concerns. These categories help gauge how and why O'Keeffe's desert is for various reasons safer and thus more accessible than, for example, Frank Norris's; they also underscore the ways in which perceptions of a bounded, unpeopled terrain often overwhelm and overrule the possibility of less bounded, transcultural desert places. Ansel Adams catches something of this accessibility and safety when he remembers O'Keeffe "painting in her station wagon, protected from the hot summer sun. She had folded down the back seats and was comfortably seated before an easel, working away at a luminous painting of fantastic cliffs and a beautifully gestured dead piñon tree" (Adams, 225). She herself wrote of "that famous Ford that I now drive very well—attempting to paint landscapes—I must think it important or I wouldn't work so hard at it" (Cowart, Hamilton, and Greenough, 203). The homey car makes for a sort of surrogate living room, a mobile studio, from which O'Keeffe can transform "dead" and "fantastic" physical places into gestures.

But O'Keeffe is not therefore automatically beyond problems and questions of survival. As Limerick puts it, "Let the car break down in the desert, or let the Indians file a lawsuit to reassert an old land claim, and the quaint appeal of nature and native can abruptly vanish. The frontier is suddenly reopened" (*Legacy,* 25). In other words, the protective, regulatory boundary or frame between the self and the place can still splinter or be splintered; marginalized Indians can reappear in unsettling ways, moving inside the frame by filing a lawsuit or adapting the Western literary form of the autobiography, to give but two examples. In the Southwest, of course, such reopenings often happen textually, particularly when different cultures come into contact; these reopenings can lead to redefinitions of conceptual categories (such as "virgin land" or "tribal secrets"), setting in motion "frontier" encounters both abstract and concrete, both retrograde and very new. These are difficult encounters, and their conversions into texts must be read critically, whether these conversions be in the form of mid-nineteenth-century diaries or late-twentieth-century television documentaries. The process of moving the Southwest toward the status of aesthetic spectacle remains gradual, punctuated, unfinished; the cultural and artistic mix is often surprised into new—and old, sometimes ancient, "reopening," or reappearing—problems and possibilities. Meanwhile, romantic narratives and solutions are usually all too close at hand.[3]

To Euro-American fur trappers in the 1820s and, later, to travelers on the overland trails, the desert was first and foremost a dangerous "biological reality" laying bare their "vulnerability to hunger, thirst, injury, disease, and death" (Limerick, *Desert Passages*, 6). True, as early as 1843, the explorer John C. Frémont "noted the fact that would preoccupy twentieth-century desert admirers: for a land so easy to characterize as sterile and barren, the desert is oddly life-filled, stocked with its own adapted flora and fauna" (ibid., 41). For most Euro-American travelers in Frémont's time, the desert was first and foremost a terrible ordeal involving, among other things, heat, thirst, desolate landscapes, Indian attacks, and dangerous rumors of delusory shortcuts. Indeed, as Limerick ominously notes, "Not all of the emigrants knew the Spanish phrase for a desert crossing, but the term *jornada del muerto* conveyed the essence of their impressions. Consensus on this issue was no surprise" (ibid., 19). But, as Jason Betzinez remarks of *jornada del muerto*, "The Indians knew where to find water in such country where others would perish. When their enemies were in hot pursuit these Apaches simply withdrew into this apparently waterless country" (52). More generally, the "oddity" or paradox of a life-filled desert is fundamentally Euro-American. Indian autobiographers such as Geronimo and Sarah Winnemucca detail the uses of the flora and fauna Frémont describes, and while the Apaches and Paiutes acknowledge the difficulties of desert terrain, they do know how to survive there. In fact, Winnemucca and Betzinez explicitly demonstrate that Indians can cross deserts relatively safely unless they are menaced by other people (see, e.g., Chapters 2 and 3 of Betzinez's *I Fought with Geronimo*). Again, it is crucial to keep cultural contexts in mind when reading "desert" texts. As Euro-Americans begin to travel to and through deserts, they enter into a space that Indians have been traversing for centuries; as Euro-Americans begin to identify aesthetic possibilities in deserts, they must also come to terms with—or, as Roosevelt often does, change the terms of—Indian occupations of these same places.

Though it remained a threat to life and an ordeal to Euro-Americans throughout most of the nineteenth century, the desert gradually came to be seen as valuable, commercially useful, an "economic resource," indeed, "a container of treasures awaiting extraction or development" (Limerick, *Desert Passages*, 6). This Euro-American economic perception of the desert begins, according to Limerick, with either the boom economy of Nevada silver mines from 1859 or the introduction of irrigated farming in Utah, Arizona, and other territories at approximately the same time; with it, the word "waste" acquires broader economic meaning, coming to suggest inability to turn the desert to productive and profitable use (see ibid., 20–24). Thus the 1856 preliminary report on the Pacific Railroad Survey concluded that America's "rich possessions west of the 99th meridian have turned out to be worthless. . . . Whatever route is selected for a railroad to the Pacific, it must wind the greater portion of its length through a . . . dreary waste" (quoted in Hyde, 61). The train trip in question would not be physically threatening for passengers—railroads took pains to secure and guarantee the safety of train travel through deserts—but it also would not be particularly attractive (and, consequently, profitable).

This "waste," considered economically, could be altered and "improved" by irrigation or rationalized by emphasizing the buried minerals and other riches beneath a dismal geographical surface. But by and large the Southwest as a part of a national economy signifies a formidable barrier characterized by commodity exchange rather than a permeable boundary characterized by broader cultural exchange. Though it usually frequents a somewhat different context, Pinchot's "Wilderness is waste" enters into these not-so-conservationist debates as well: that is, sheer wilderness, lacking the shaping hand of man the manager and provider, is worth nothing (Richard White, 409). But from the railroad's point of view, the physically "dreary waste" might detract too strongly from even the powerful lure of California and the spectacular scenery of the "wild" Northwest. As a result, railroad advertisements worked hard to diminish or doctor their images of desert passages, slandering them as grassy, tree-filled, and river-watered plains or simply stacking the deck in favor of the more attractive or spectacular scenery, such as the Sierra Nevada, that the railroads passed through after the desert. For example, as Anne Farrar Hyde reports, in 1870 a San Francisco stereograph retailer "advertised a series on the Central Pacific Railroad. It contained 135 stereographs, all of railroad tracks, tunnels, cars, or mountain scenery. No views of the Nevada deserts or mountain ranges, Indian tribes, or even California farmland appeared in the collection" (87). While nineteenth-century photographs of spectacular western beauty—such as is found, for example, in Yosemite National Park, San Francisco, or the California mountains and "Big Trees"—were very popular, "[i]mages of unfruitful deserts and unsettled plains seemed to be a marketing risk" (Hyde, 87). To some extent, the burgeoning businesses of western travel and pulp fiction clash: dime novels make exaggerated depictions of the "Wild West" very much available, while railroad promoters elect to cover up the wildness of particular western and southwestern locations.

As it turned out, railroads to and from the major far western cities, San Francisco and Los Angeles, could not be constructed around deserts. The Central Pacific Railroad line, completed in 1869, cut through the northern Nevada desert, and by 1887, as Hyde demonstrates, railroads took passengers across northern and southern Arizona, New Mexico Territory, and southeastern California. These first passengers were not immediately enamored of the desert; however, "[d]isappointed tourists did get some pleasure out of denouncing the Great Basin region; and this soon became a tradition on the transcontinental trip, just as it had for earlier travelers. Despising the desert seemed to be part of the package for tourists" (ibid., 140). For many, the desert did not yet qualify as a legitimate spectacle; in the words of one tourist, it was "a fortunate thing that the length of the journey admits of a degree of intimacy between the passengers, and the outward ugliness may be forgotten in social intercourse" (ibid.). Others less fortunate remembered what they had seen:

> Words like "waste," "barrenness," "nothing," "forlorn," and "sterile" characterize most of the descriptions of the journey across Utah and Nevada. One disgruntled tourist explained quite simply, "On the route I found nothing to note . . . until we arrive at a station called Reno." "Weary are the hours as we pass over an arid waste of sand and dust," commented another frustrated observer. Others noted the ubiquitous presence of the sagebrush, a plant they found particularly unattractive. "I became deeply imbued," wrote one man of his desert crossing, "with an undying hatred for the everlasting sagebrush." (ibid., 138)

Though the desert qualifies for some as a spectacle, it is not a pleasant one, in part because the topographies fail the economic test: they are "waste" because they are arid, sterile, seemingly unworkable. But they are also woefully unpicturesque. The railroads cross them only because they must. Falling short on both economic and aesthetic grounds, the desert at best calls forth energetic catalogues of its shortcomings; notes one tourist, it had "no smooth, level lawn, no pleasant field or rolling meadow-land, no friendly habitation, no house of any kind, not a tree or a shrub,—in a word, NO GREEN THING WHATEVER" (quoted in Hyde, 138). Nothing, either natural or man-made, arrests the eye; nothing attracts.

But, as Roosevelt's enthusiastic 1903 response to the Grand Canyon, Stephen Crane's journalistic excursion to the Southwest and Mexico, Charles Lummis's and Mary Austin's published efforts to make the region accessible to the nation, and the aesthetically minded southwestern work of white anthropologists like Frank Hamilton Cushing and Adolf Bandelier suggest, the general perception of the Southwest was changing and with it the attitude toward deserts.[4] Of course, as Hector Calderón and José David Saldívar point out, "Lummis had a conservative and patronizing side, intent on writing about the most folkloric and romantic elements of Native American and *mestizo* culture. Through his first books Lummis reveals his attractions for courtly dons, beautiful señoritas, innocent Indian children, kind Mexican peons, witches, and penitents" (3). Mary Austin, as I discuss in Chapter 7, also betrayed her own self-proclaimed status as an Indian expert by stereotyping and romanticizing the peoples she undertook to promote. My point is simply that the Southwest began to look intensely interesting to a wide variety of Euro-Americans with a relatively narrow range of motives and inclinations, not least because of its potentially iconographic spectacles (the Grand Canyon as a sort of western Niagara Falls) and newly sublime desert landscapes.

As early as 1886, tourists remarked, as O'Keeffe does more than fifty years later, on the range and brilliance of color that "transformed the desert waste into such a scene that would delight an artist to reproduce" (quoted in Hyde, 239). And for all their passengers' critical sniping about deserts, the railroads also helped draw attention and positive regard to these ungreen landscapes. Hyde credits 1870s railroad surveys for their important role in provoking interest in things western:

> With the triple revelations of ancient civilizations in the Southwest, the Grand Canyon, and Yellowstone as centerpieces, the elaborate surveys of the 1870s served to awaken public interest in previously unknown or abhorred regions of the Far West. The attention given the surveys reflected the new interest in incorporating the West into national culture. (203)

While it is difficult to see the first of these "revelations" as particularly surprising given the historical context of the U.S.-Apache wars, the discourses of the West and Southwest were certainly changing, appearing as relatively exotic and inconsistently nationalized at approximately the same time.

Limerick makes a similar point, arguing that the railroads, along with "the proliferation of automobiles and roads," eventually cleared the way for the third general attitude toward the desert:

> With the ordeal of travel eased, and with the installation of the technology and equipment of a hydraulic society dependent on the large-scale manipulation of water, more and more Americans found themselves in a position to think of the desert as interesting and even beautiful. . . . [I]n the twentieth century, with a margin of safety established, the desert by its very novelty qualified as a site worth seeing. The more that Americans felt themselves insulated and protected from the desert, the more they felt safe to appreciate the desert for, as many of them put it, its "reality."

(*Desert Passages*, 91–92)

Before the desert could be remade artistically, it had to be remade economically; from its inception, the notion of desert as aesthetic spectacle was a mixed breed of careful management and less bounded (but often "private," even iconoclastic) imaginings. Notions of an exotic Southwest are handled very carefully as well, to stimulate tourists' interest without frightening them away; in this mainstream Euro-American discourse, Indians by the 1920s have a place—the "Indian detour"—that promises exactly the "right" sort of planned deviation. Mobility, once the birthright of American Indians in the Southwest, ironically becomes part of a Euro-American business strategy that positions and fixes Indians in place—and this place remains both on and off the new beaten tracks of temporary sightseers.

Meanwhile, Euro-Americans who produce desert texts never quite let go of the idea that the terrain is terrifyingly autonomous: mostly emptied of indigenous peoples and scarcely inhabited by anybody else, the desert is an isolated, relentless, formidable, altogether alien place. But as the excerpt from O'Keeffe's catalogue statement suggests, these southwestern deserts and, increasingly, peoples also take on broader and more confident national (and sometimes, as in John Ford's westerns and the iconology of Billy the Kid, mythic) meanings. They begin to look good in public, that is, and they enter into national and even international circulation; desert texts range widely, appearing in a variety of discourses and disciplines including American novels and poems, a Sherlock Holmes narrative, American paintings, western historiography, anthropology, and various elements of popular culture.[5] Domesticated and nationalized, these deserts even begin to seem lovable. Writes Limerick, "Is the war really over, the desert really conquered? Stay among the parks, lawns, golf courses, fountains, faucets, and flush toilets of Phoenix or Tucson, and the answer seemed clear: yes, the humans had won—won solidly enough to indulge in the exercise of admiring their conquered enemy" ("Second Views," 48). But the untamed power of the desert never quite vanishes, and at various times and places, efforts to control and contain it textually tangle with elements less controllable. To quote Limerick again, "Move outside the towns and cities, though, and the balance of power wobbles. Beyond the reach of the sprinklers, the desert seems to be holding its ground, and the roads and ditches 'dominating' the landscape bear a distinct resemblance to the irritating tangle of little ropes and cords with which the Lilliputians temporarily tied up Gulliver" ("Second Views," 48). As Limerick's literary metaphor suggests, the desert—Gulliver, the satirized traveler—somehow does not quite seem of its place. The desert is, strangely if at times subtly, another country, a country difficult to tie down securely, a not-so-welcome and a not-so-controllable alien.

Despite these difficulties, textual management of the desert and of the Southwest at large—be it narrative, historiographical, modernist, or otherwise—gradually helps secure the region's place as part of the nation, even when the southwestern writer or artist explicitly stakes out a highly personal territorial position and resists the company of the country. This book has already begun to suggest some of the problems involved in these textualizing and nationalizing processes; there are many more. At least at first, southwestern topographies—especially corporately designated natural spectacles—attract closer attention than do indigenous peoples.[6] Later, of course, the "Indian detours" direct attention to particular southwestern tribes deemed aesthetically interesting in large part because they have been decisively marginalized; neither "Indian" nor "detour" would be as attractive separately. As discussed elsewhere in this book, it is important not to overlook the various misrepresentations and erasures of the people—including the misrepresentations that justify the processes of constructing artificial, impermeable boundaries between "Americans," "Indians," and particular, contested southwestern places.

All in all, late-nineteenth- and twentieth-century Euro-American constructions of the Southwest as aesthetic source and spectacle are reflected in paradoxical texts adaptable to a range of western conventions and disciplines. The often-permeable boundaries of these texts variously erase, sanitize, and (less often) critically unsettle points of contact between disparate peoples and places. By the time we get to Roswell in 1947, the Indian detours of the 1920s have perhaps mutated into a more general exoticism, a vested interest in playing out alien dramas and seeking out alien spectacles. The Southwest remains to a significant extent interchangeably alienated and aesthetically charged, a place to pass through and to situate in relation to a long national history of migrations and displacements.

6 Driven to Extraction

McTeague in the Desert

In describing the cultural geography of the American Southwest, this book has thus far emphasized American Indian literatures and, secondarily, American historiographical narratives. Part of the point in deferring Euro-American literature is to read writers such as Frank Norris, Mary Austin, and Willa Cather in Indian contexts for the simple yet often overlooked reason that the Southwest is first and foremost Indian country. As I have already argued, a rich variety of native cultures has circulated through and across this region for centuries, since long before the arrivals of migratory Europeans and Euro-Americans; these Indian migrations have been purposeful, creative, and complex. Moreover, the practice of migration has proven its adaptability; as Euro-American colonials have constructed impermeable boundaries around and across a variety of Indian spaces and cultures, Indians have responded in strategic and often subversive migratory ways. Geronimo, both as he constructs himself and as he is constructed by contemporary Indian writers such as Leslie Marmon Silko, actively resists Euro-American attempts to assimilate, eradicate, or exhibit "preserved" and neutralized versions of himself and the Warm Springs Apaches. Beginning with this chapter, I turn to a handful of Euro-American literary texts grounded in the Southwest and more nebulously associated with southwestern Indians; I read them with Indian migration narratives and strategies in mind. *McTeague, The Land of Little Rain,* and *The Professor's House* speak in powerful, fraught ways to James Clifford's observation that roots and routes intertwine to construct both personal and cultural identities and to keep those identities in process.

Patricia Limerick in *Desert Passages* argues that, for most Euro-Americans, the notion that the desert might yield aesthetic raw materials and values first takes hold around the beginning of the twentieth century. She acknowledges that such processes do not easily fit inside systematic readings of how the West works; she pays close attention to various ways in which these processes are disrupted. Similarly, this book has suggested that as a result especially of scientific and commercial photography, topographies once simply endured by travelers or laborers could now be perceived as framed spectacles—not necessarily beautiful to the eye but "safe" to look at, to reproduce, and to circulate culturally. As Chapter 2 details, dime novelists use the Southwest (and at times the desert) as a dramatic backdrop to adventure stories. In both contexts, the place carries an element of danger; it needs to be framed, and it suits outlaw narratives. Yet both the pulp fiction and the packaged spectacles participate in a cultural process of boundary formation that contains Indian migration while situating the Southwest as a distant "last frontier" that is nonetheless attached in an increasing number of ways to an imperial nation. A little later, writers of "literature" begin to frame the region, sometimes working up interestingly crude representations of desert topographies as well as of the characters who migrate across and (less often) through them. In the process, disruptions less often noted by historians are set violently in motion, while in other ways these disruptions also reinscribe rather than dismantle cultural and national boundaries.

Near the end of *McTeague* (1899), for example, Death Valley overpowers the physically powerful dentist with overwhelming heat, brightness, and space. It is a brutal, punishing, inescapable place, captured in crudely powerful prose. Some critics see this setting as an awkward disruption of the realistic urban class-based narrative; others argue for lurking continuities between the city and desert sections of the novel. I work against any critical orientation toward linear, temporally measured causality, emphasizing instead the discontinuous disruptions that characterize, in different ways, both the unhistorical brute and the desert spaces he moves across. Disruptiveness is a narrative strategy in *McTeague*, but Norris mobilizes it unpredictably throughout the book and dramatizes it spatially much more so than he measures it temporally. He does not entirely refuse to link the city and the desert to each other, but these comparisons typically hinge on the emptinesses and disruptions that characterize McTeague himself, traveling from place to place and externalizing psychic turbulences. The city and the desert differ, that is, except that they both work well as sites for uncontainable, portable eruptions of brutality.

But the desert Norris represents should also be read in the cultural contexts described in the previous chapter; in finding a place for the desert in *McTeague* and a place for McTeague in the desert, he participates in a larger turn-of-the-century American movement toward cautiously aesthetic deserts. Another way to phrase this point is that Death Valley inhabits a novel well versed in several turn-of-the-century artistic styles; the desert is artistically usable as a postimpressionist canvas, a naturalist case in point, an appropriate setting for melodrama, a place where lone Indians are both literally and figuratively left behind by passing trains, and (less directly) a place patently and potently unhistorical, a terrifying magnification of the genealogically challenged dentist's plight. Norris's graphic translations, reflections, and exaggerations of the California desert reaffirm the place's isolation at the expense of the place's inhabitants and, conversely, underscore that the desert is by 1899 in circulation as a cultural and textual American space.

It is appropriate to begin with one of the more disorienting moments in *McTeague*. Exactly once in this 442-page novel, an American Indian character briefly enters the narrative. As he encounters the novel's main character, a dentist on the lam, this Indian man participates in a striking moment that points to the problems of language and history in cross-cultural conversation. The Indian remains speechless and subsumed, though acknowledged:

> [O]nce in the northern part of Inyo County, while [the train and its crew and passengers] were halted at a water tank, an immense Indian buck, blanketed to the ground, approached McTeague as he stood on the road-bed stretching his legs, and without a word presented to him a filthy, crumpled letter. The letter was to the effect that the buck Big Jim was a good Indian and deserving of charity; the signature was illegible. The dentist stared at the letter, returned it to the buck, and regained the train just as it started. Neither had spoken; the buck did not move from his position, and fully five minutes afterward, when the slow-moving freight was miles away, the dentist looked back and saw him still standing motionless between the rails, a forlorn and solitary point of red, lost in the immensity of the surrounding white blur of the desert. (393)

The silence here is mutual, as is the odd, almost surreal passivity of both the animalized "buck" and the lurking animal McTeague. Striking, too, is the narrator's insistence on animalizing Jim; captivated by the highly charged reflections of Indian in dentist and dentist in Indian, Norris nonetheless appears unreflectively racist in his hypersexualized "buck." Big Jim stands both literally and figuratively between the lines, standing stock still as the lines—marks of "progress," of Western industrial technology, of mobility—both contain him and leave him behind. McTeague and the train look back at the vanishing red point as it recedes into the "white blur of the desert," made accessible by the "white blur" of manifest destiny but attributed mostly to the sheer nature of perception in a blinding desert rather than to any humanly constructed determinist paradigm. Still, the ideological links between ways of seeing and ways of not seeing overwhelm both Jim and McTeague.

The process of making Big Jim invisible and of watching him literally vanish from sight in the book as he vanishes from the book enacts with remarkable efficiency the actual political plans of most turn-of-the-century Indian fighters, military, governmental, missionary, or otherwise. This process is perhaps best encapsulated in the illegible signature on the letter Big Jim carries; the signature has been marked on him, presumably by a white authority, as a way of recommending him as a "good" Indian to other whites who, one assumes, imagine a world full of "bad" Indians but remain unable to differentiate between "good" or "bad" without the help of written documents. Here, though, the signature itself is illegible—white in at least two senses—

and its absence efficiently and quickly renders Big Jim invisible as well, a process probably begun when he was first "marked," written on, interpreted, caricatured. Yet a similar fate awaits McTeague as well; all that he sees around him in Death Valley is predicated on all that he has *not* seen throughout the novel, and his repeatedly emphasized activity in the final scene of the novel—his looking up, down, and all around him—looks very much like a prelude to his own fading away out of sight (see Eric Gary Anderson).

The process of becoming invisible is of course not simply self-induced, but in *McTeague,* such a washing out and paring down of visual perception makes, finally, for an emptying out that both literally and figuratively freezes the life history of the brutal male object—McTeague predominantly, but also Big Jim—in its tracks. Norris both erases and reconfigures various sorts of abstract and physical borders—temporal, historical, psychological, generic— throughout the narrative, but like his main character, he also insists on boundaries, even as he leaves people and things behind while moving closer to the attractive yet repulsive southwestern American desert. Toward the end of the novel, these naturalist reconfigurations of borders increasingly appear to be at odds with the process of approaching and entering a place very different from San Francisco and Placer County—the California desert. The increased attention to McTeague's physical mobility (as distinct from his enormous physicality) also unsettles readers who first see the dentist as altogether sluggish, "crop-full, stupid, and warm" (1). While the relentlessness of these processes makes an odd sort of naturalist sense, it also isolates both the main character and the final setting of the narrative, and it does so in ways that continue to frustrate and mystify readers already deeply enmeshed in the paradoxes and problems of reading naturalistically.

Burdened with a criminal history he doesn't fully remember and an "animal cunning" he doesn't fully understand, McTeague toward the end of the novel is driven by vague yet pressing instincts to escape something he senses but cannot identify: "'I don' know, I don' know,' muttered the dentist, lowering the rifle. 'There was something . . . I don' know. Something—something or other" (409). It seems to be less something he has left behind in San Francisco than something that follows him all the way from the city to the vast, formidable desert, where

> [o]nce more the rowel was in his flanks, once more an unseen hand reined him toward the east. After all the miles of that dreadful day's flight he was no better off than when he started. If anything, he was worse, for never had that mysterious instinct in him been more insistent than now; never had the impulse toward precipitate flight been stronger; never had the spur bit deeper. (422)

Alone and unable to see anyone or anything in the surrounding miles of desert, the dentist falls victim to his overcompensating imagination: he is perhaps lonely, guilt ridden, bewildered, frightened, melodramatized, and his "mysterious instinct" plays out what he cannot otherwise articulate.

Yet as the narrator makes clear, McTeague faces not merely a vague apprehension, a "something or other," but a specific, persuasive physical threat. It pricks and shoves and spurs him. It chases and in chasing bewilders him into the desert, where it then keeps after him, hounding him into a wilderness, the "openly and unreservedly iniquitous and malignant" stretches of Death Valley (425), that is both extreme and increasingly familiar to readers of American desert texts (see Limerick, *Desert Passages*, Hyde, Teague[1]). Clearly, he imagines or intuits this "unseen hand" as a force external to him, a force that makes inroads into his mind by doing violence (actual or imagined) to his body. It blurs the line, in other words, between the effects of the punishing desert topography and the workings of his uncharted mental topography. Most egregiously, whatever its actual psychic and physical dimensions, it animalizes him, so that what once lurked latent within him, "the animal in the man . . . the evil instincts that in him were so close to the surface" (30), now attacks and overtakes his instincts from outside. Where once "the sudden panther leap of the animal, lips drawn, fangs aflash, hideous, monstrous, not to be resisted" (30) came from deep inside the dentist, now the "horrible wilderness where even the beasts were afraid" (424) animalizes him in a different way, not as predator but as prey, "[t]racked and harried" relentlessly (424). Or it exaggerates what he has resembled pretty much all along, a beast of burden: "Altogether he suggested the draught horse, immensely strong, stupid, docile, obedient" (3). It treats him like a horse to be reined and spurred at its pleasure and in so doing compels him to imagine responding by moving like a horse—"It seemed to him that on the next instant he *must* perforce wheel sharply eastward and rush away headlong in a clumsy, lumbering gallop" (413)—and even to dream horse nightmares: "his rest was broken; between waking and sleeping, all manner of troublous images galloped through his brain" (426).

Clearly, what Norris dramatizes in the closing, desert passages of *McTeague* happens between the brute dentist and the brutal terrain that occupies him as he occupies it. Certainly these intersections of dehumanized character and humanized place set in motion complicated exchanges of identities and volitions, border exchanges worked out by the naturalist novelist according to the peculiar, not-entirely-logical logic of determinism. "Determined fictions," as Lee Clark Mitchell calls them, presuppose the inevitable workings of powerful forces mostly beyond human design and control, though, as Mark Seltzer argues in *Bodies and Machines*, "the naturalist machine" (whether figured as human body, industrial technology, or turn-of-the-century novel) is made and remade and put to various uses by human design. Indeed, determined fictions are invented, arranged, and narrated by writers and narrators who are not, or who imagine that they are not, themselves subject to these forces "out there." What June Howard claims about "the characteristically naturalist tension between spectatorship and participation" (*Form and History*, 151) is true of *McTeague* and Norris: "[O]ne cannot appreciate the significance of naturalism's philosophical determinism without also recognizing the perspective from which those characters are viewed, that of the observant and articulate naturalist in close conference with his reader" (ibid., x). Most contemporary critics agree that naturalist texts construct what Seltzer calls a "double discourse" (4) and Walter Benn Michaels terms a "double logic" (*The Gold Standard*, 174) wherein, as Michaels argues, the "consistency—indeed, the identity—of naturalism resides in the logics and in their antithetical relation to one another, not necessarily in any individual, any text, or even any single sentence." (ibid., 173). Posing, violating, and exemplifying conflicts and contradictions, these doublings suggest, among other things, that an important question to keep in mind when reading naturalist fictions is not so much "who is doing what to whom?" as "who knows what?" or its corollary "who doesn't know what?"

Knowledge, memory, history: one thing the dentist does not remember, let alone agonize over, in all his agonizing time in the desert, is the record of his own past acts of brutality. That these eastern California landscapes remind McTeague of *something*, despite his hereditary amnesia, seems implicit in the novel's final section as well as psychologically likely. That the desert, in surrounding and finally overwhelming him, also reflects and exaggerates certain of his characteristics seems more explicitly to be so. Like the dentist's mental geography and physical power, the desert's terrible combination of monotonous, empty space and aggressive, overwhelming climate makes for sites and experiences repetitive yet seemingly "illimitable," vacant and "primeval" yet powerfully present, dangerously brutal yet cautiously approachable and even, at times, genuinely impressive. Just as Norris early in the novel "outlandishly turns McTeague into a field for the play of sexual desire" (Cain, 206), so the closing chapters of the book turn the geographical "field" into McTeague. The oft-noted melodrama of the book's final chapters involves not simply this desert "field" the dentist enters and the strenuous physical adventures that ensue but also the psychological commotion, the interior melodrama that redoubles as the desert invades him.

But this agitation typically does not seem interior to McTeague; rather than taking the form of an insidious interior monologue, it attacks his imagination as though attacking his body and in the process convinces him that the danger is immediate, territorial, and outside: "It seemed as though he were bitted and ridden; as if some unseen hand were turning him toward the east; some unseen heel spurring him to precipitate and instant flight" (412). Relentlessly dramatized by the desert and also (apparently) by his own agitated mind, the condition of brutality yet remains insistently for him a present-tense physical experience; similarly, the causes of this brutality float somewhere indistinctly and inarticulately apart from himself. He neither connects that brutal self to any past experiences nor formulates from it any expectations of either doom or deliverance. He can and does react to his fearsome pursuer(s) physically and instinctively, but he cannot for the life of him interpret, name, or even see them. Even the omniscient narrator of *McTeague* describes the dentist's instinct not as mental but as physical, not as interior (voice, conscience) but as exterior (hand, heel). The narrator, in other words, accumulates these details and events as if gathering up clues to a mystery or data for a psychological case study but never delivers an interpretation, solution, or moral, choosing instead to leave these outside as well.[2]

As a result, this narrator demonstrates that the limited mentality of the main character limits the range of the omniscient narration and that the dentist does not connect these desert occurrences to any prior, urban sequences of events. McTeague notices that the desert warnings recur, but he responds to these recurrences one at a time, as necessary: "If I could only *see* something—somebody," he frets (413); "ah, show yourself, will you? . . . Come on, show yourself. Come on a little, all of you. I ain't afraid of you; but don't skulk this way" (414). Maybe one of the characteristics of a brute, for Norris, is precisely the absence of personal let alone broader historical consciousness, an absence that in the geographical and psychological terrains of this novel is represented most often as changelessness: "There was no change in the character of the desert" (429) and no change in the character in the desert.

Two points, in any event, are clear: McTeague cannot escape his latent (and the desert's thoroughly manifest) brutal nature; he is shackled to it as tightly as he is shackled, at the end of the novel, to Marcus Schouler's dead wrist. And the history of his prior acts of brutal violence—his frenzies of maniacal rage, culminating in the vicious murder of his avaricious wife, Trina—escapes him completely. Instinctively aware that he is being pursued through eastern California, from the Big Dipper mine (Placer County) through Panamint Valley and down into Death Valley, he demonstrates no remorse for the violent crimes that cause the pursuit and indeed no recollection of them. Finally, the linear narrative available to readers remains invisible and foreign to him. He inhabits a narrative that is paradoxically out of character for him, for in patching together a sequence of events, it also makes explanations of them possible. And the disjunctions between McTeague and *McTeague*, like the disjunctions between McTeague and his readers, point up the importance of reading both how it is and how it is not.

Near the end of the narrative, the dentist sees only the endless, undifferentiated, vacant space, the "emptiness of primeval desolation" (411); he hears only the "gigantic silence" (411) that "vast, illimitable, enfolded him like an immeasurable tide" (419). "All the world was one gigantic blinding glare, silent, motionless" (420). Seemingly without measure, certainly without signs of (other) human presence, the desert not only lacks but also eradicates the materials of Western linear history: human occupation, measurable units of time and space, ideological motives and strategies. Here Norris's persistence in calling McTeague "the dentist" becomes noticeable, odd, even anachronistic—and not because McTeague has lost his license to practice dentistry.[3] Death Valley, as Norris sees it, overwhelms the unhistorical brute but it also complicates a more general sense of history, a more general practicing of historical mindedness. No one—dentist, narrator, novelist, reader—can take its measure, fill its space, incorporate it. It is empty not only spatially but temporally, except for the fugitive dentist, himself a more or less empty "field" outside of history and, for one of the first times in the book, dwarfed. Its emptiness is "unbroken by so much as a rock or cactus stump" (418), as if it out-deserts even the desert. It is "primeval," "primordial" and "infinite" (424); its "illimitable stretch of alkali . . . stretched out forever and forever" (401), as if stretching beyond the capabilities of language to describe it without simply yielding to repetition; as if in some ultimate act of limitless stretching, it stretches into both subject and verb and keeps stretching.

And it is dramatically, remarkably unlike the cityscapes that fill much of *McTeague*, whose subtitle is, after all, *A Story of San Francisco*. Removing McTeague from the urban, documentary-style realism of Polk Street, San Francisco, with its carefully researched particular details and memorably eccentric cast of characters, Norris in his last few chapters gives the dentist a sort of extended soliloquy broken into only by an ineffective Marcus Schouler and (finally, lethally) by the "vast, interminable . . . measureless leagues of Death Valley" (442). In Norris's account of what happens when McTeague's former friend finally tracks him down, the pursuing sheriff's posse is now only this lone man from the dentist's past, and Norris renders their reencounter as if it has nothing to do with either man's motives for being in the middle of Death Valley:

> For a few seconds, McTeague looked at the man stupidly, bewildered, confused, as yet without definite thought. Then he noticed that the man was singularly like Marcus Schouler. It *was* Marcus Schouler. How in the world did Marcus Schouler come to be in that desert? What did he mean by pointing a pistol at him that way? (435)

To the brute without historical orientation, faced with a past friend who suddenly materializes as an enemy in an ahistorical, brutal, monotonous, yet disorienting space, all is puzzling. Norris, not helping much, melodramatically interrupts Marcus's melodramatic announcement—"Hands up. By damn, I got the drop on you!" (429)—with a backward, expository glance at what Marcus has been up to since his last appearance in the novel, some eight chapters earlier. But in so catching his readers up at the start of Chapter 22, Norris again diverts his characters' attention from the reason they find themselves face to face in the middle of Death Valley; the explanation, given for the benefit of readers, also calls attention to what doesn't get explained. Repetitions of Marcus's full name play out the dentist's slowly dawning recognition of Mark in the flesh. The sheer act of recognition crowds out any further response, such as remembering their past friendship or deducing why Mark might be "pointing a pistol at him that way." Moreover, in this final face-to-face encounter with another human being, McTeague's past, represented incompletely by Marcus, confronts him from the outside in a desert terrain where thinking and remembering give way to sheer physical efforts to endure, to survive. No longer psychologically compatible with McTeague, no longer a monstrous reflection of him, the desert confronts him with stark enormity as, simply and threateningly, a formidable space outside and all around him. Just as he eliminates the immediate threat of pursuit by "the law," he sees, as if for the first time, the absolute clarity of the land and of his long-range chances in it. It looms, more than ever before, as an utterly alien place, for McTeague but also for Norris, for whom its aesthetic usefulness never quite supplants the terror and fascination of blank, desolate spaces.

Norris's critics have often remarked the disjunctions in *McTeague* between wilderness and city or between melodrama and realism. Occasionally they link the change in setting to the perceived shift in genre, so that the open spaces of the desert become the appropriate place for "western" action and adventure, while the city provides what Donald Pizer, for example, sees as a workmanlike "world of concrete actuality . . . [a] texture of the ordered and routine . . . rendered with a detail and repetitiousness which suggest the commonplace and unexceptional" (79–80) while witnessing, at rare intervals, the truly sensational. These critics have worked hard to explain ways in which these seeming disjunctions in fact maintain thematic and structural continuities, but they generally work less hard on the implications of these continuities.[4] As a result, their pursuit of unity does credit to Norris's many real consistencies but does violence to the already simmering, often subterranean turbulence that dislocates his main character in time and space. To Pizer, for example, the "reappearance" of McTeague's animal nature, this time as his "sixth sense," does the trick: "[E]ven in this guise [it] links the closing section firmly with the rest of the novel" (82). Pizer's evaluation of the novel's ending is not harsh, finally, though he notes flaws, inconsistencies, and a shift in genres:

> To most readers, however, the effect of the last three chapters is less that of thematic or structural relevance than of narrative adventure. We are involved most of all in a good melodramatic chase, with McTeague's sixth sense more interesting as a narrative device which allows him to keep one jump ahead of his pursuers than as a thematic link. There are a number of glaring errors in plot, plausibility, and fact in this section. Norris suddenly shifts from December to May; he broadens Death Valley to over three times its width; and few canaries could survive the hegira McTeague's bird experiences. Moreover, in a novel which contains a rich supply of diseased and neurotic minds, it is perhaps too much to have McTeague's mule go mad from loco weed in the last chapter. Yet ultimately these are all quibbles. The close of *McTeague* is melodrama, but it is effective melodrama convincingly related to the rest of the novel. (82)

Pizer alternately forgives and defends Norris for perpetrating melodrama and for permitting this melodrama to run off without directly heeding the demands of "thematic or structural relevance" and "plausibility." He expects a unified linear narrative rather than, say, a narrator's attempt to evoke how "diseased and neurotic" minds might perceive things. A longtime proponent of the argument that Norris is not merely a clumsy, unfinished naturalist stylist, Pizer nonetheless sets limited goals for him. Might not the novel's continuities sustain multiple levels by enacting McTeague's limitations as perceiver and interpreter while implying that different participants (readers, narrator, other characters) discover different continuities?

In a study published three years after Pizer's, William B. Dillingham meticulously and persuasively mobilizes Norris himself to contravene William Dean Howells's judgment that "'the death in the desert' business" just doesn't work, except as "anticlimax" not sufficiently prepared for earlier in the novel. "I am sure," wrote Norris, "that [this anticlimax] has its place" (quoted in Dillingham, 138), and Dillingham agrees in copious and specific detail, locating various foreshadowings, narrative and thematic patterns, and other correspondences between earlier sections of the book and its beleaguered desert passages. His discussion of the novel's ending also assumes that it needs not merely explicating but also defending: "Although some later critics have agreed with Howells on the 'death in the desert business,' it can be defended" (138). Dillingham undertakes this defense by tracking down various ways Norris "foreshadows" the ending and carefully works out a "progression . . . always away from the more civilized to the more primitive" (138), so that McTeague's desert surroundings act as "a counterpart to McTeague's personal movement toward bestiality" (138).

But how can McTeague move toward something so clearly lodged inside him from the very beginning of the novel, his unfortunate genetic map or, as Norris more graphically puts it, "the foul stream of hereditary evil" that runs below his surface "like a sewer" (32)? And as such, how linear and orderly is this deterioration? Are the dentist's periodic brutal rages themselves "orderly"? The beast always latent in the dentist leaps to the surface as early as Chapter 2 and falls most steadily under control around the middle of the novel, during what Dillingham himself calls the "somewhat dull courtship" (135) of McTeague and Trina, through the bland domestic scenes between the newlyweds, before greed and miserliness insinuate themselves thoroughly. *McTeague* does not, as *Sister Carrie* does, plot a more or less symmetrical chiasmus, where one character's fall contrasts and complements another's rise and where the economic affairs of both Carrie and Hurstwood change much more dramatically across class borders than Trina and McTeague's ever do. A distinction must also be made between the urban deterioration—the gradually widening gap between the amount of money Trina has saved and the poverty level of their lodgings and neighborhoods until the couple, mostly under her miserly direction, move toward and finally into slum housing—and the later, more "rural" scenes, set in "untamed" landscapes that the dentist enters as a fugitive *from,* among other things, that deterioration. (Though he doesn't remember it once he leaves San Francisco, he rails noisily against what he sees as needless poverty when in it and avenges Trina in part because of it.) And when he plunges into the desert, he is in some ways at his sharpest and most alert. Though still bewildered, he hardly seems "crop-full, stupid, and warm," as Norris describes him in the second paragraph of the book. Instead, McTeague proves himself to be capable of some alertness and vigilance: at one point, for example, the dentist "slowly turned his head and looked over one shoulder, then over the other. Suddenly he wheeled sharply about, cocking the Winchester and tossing it to his shoulder" (409). Though not really in control of these vague yet insistent forces that urge him to keep moving, he responds to them actively and energetically. And as he moves overland through brutal terrain, his "bestial" instincts point toward self-preservation, not toward the more brutal acts of sexual assault, battery, robbery, and murder he commits earlier in the book. Focusing on McTeague running for his life, Norris in fact modestly expands the dentist's range of mental activity, showing him planning, reflecting, dreaming, and suffering. All in all, though, he remains if anything fundamentally unchanged throughout the novel, particularly in his stunted historical relations—and as such, the "plot of decline" and its punitive implications do not strongly apply.

The empirically derived New Critical continuities urged by Dillingham, Pizer, and others assume that *McTeague*'s characters, like those in a great many naturalist works of fiction, inhabit a literary narrative constructed by an observer who does not fully participate in the characters' world. Often this naturalist narrator winks, like one of Stephen Crane's sardonic spectators, across the vast gulf between his relatively sophisticated perceptions and the cruder conduct of the folk he describes. In other words, the narrator and the critics are allies seeking to unify the text, while Norris's naturalist characters, much more turbulently and uncontrollably obsessive, do not domesticate as readily. (In a way, the critics are more determinist than the determinist.) Still, as the "double logic" or "double discourse" posits, the disjunctive, dislocated experiences of these characters can also be understood as disruptive continuities, made up of what the characters typically don't see, do, or know. As such, take McTeague's tendency to behave as though outside of anything resembling a historical consciousness. That is, he rarely remembers things on the strength of his own volition, and his links to the past are instead passive, the result of genealogical imperatives and uncontrollable brute instincts. This continuity is, paradoxically, the sum total of numerous absences and emptinesses, compounded by McTeague's various occupations in the novel—dentist, prospector, miner, thief, murderer, fugitive—all of which involve extraction. He is both consistently removing and consistently removed. Placed in a documentary-style setting throughout much of the novel, surrounded by particular details painstakingly researched and realistically observed, the dentist alternately shatters and forgets this time frame and in so doing reminds us, quite by accident, of its fragility but also of its consequences. Thus, the closing chapters of the novel are both disjunctive and continuous, as they exemplify by magnifying McTeague's fundamental, continuous emptiness. He is of course not a vacuum, but he is, especially in the perverse sublimity of Death

Valley, "the empty spirit in vacant space," the empty container unaware of the possibility of being filled, for better or worse, by the demands, problems, and recognitions of history.

How, then, does a New Historicist critic fare with *McTeague?* Michaels emphasizes that McTeague carries the stolen gold with him into Death Valley and that eventually, somewhere beyond the final page of the novel, he dies there: "What then is the real point of McTeague's dying in the desert with his five thousand gold dollars?" (*The Gold Standard*, 150). Keeping his eyes on this gold, Michaels plays up an element that certainly figures throughout much of the novel. The best critical catalogue of the novel's gildedness is Dillingham's:

> McTeague wants a huge gold tooth to advertise his "dental parlors." . . .
> He has the canary in the gilt cage. Maria Macapa continually babbles about the hundred-piece gold service and steals gold foil from McTeague. Zerkow is crazy for gold. Trina has gold fillings in her teeth and counts gold pieces until they are smooth, sometimes sleeping with them, wallowing in them like a pig in its mud. McTeague grew up at a gold mine; he goes back to it, and later he discovers gold near places called Gold Gulch and Gold Mountain. Even the sun streaming into Trina's room looks like gold coins. "The wonder is," wrote Vernon Louis Parrington, that Norris "didn't give Trina gold hair instead of black." (118–119)

The wonder, too, is that Norris does give McTeague yellow hair. But, as a narrative, thematic, or figurative detail, gold all but disappears from the novel after McTeague, obeying his instincts, forgoes the gold strike he makes with his fellow prospector, Cribbens. Michaels speculates, "Perhaps, instead, reading Death Valley as the last stage in gold's disappearance from circulation, we should understand it as a kind of ironic alternative to the coffers of the Wall Street Misers" (*The Gold Standard*, 150). Perhaps. But wouldn't it be just as well to read Death Valley as a desert space that is, around the turn of the century, beginning to be incorporated into a new yet bounded construction of a transcontinental, colonial America? That is, Death Valley may be less an alternative to Wall Street than a linked co-conspirator with it. As Alan Trachtenberg argues, the "desert regions of the West" acquire "a look of prehistoric enchantment" precisely though paradoxically because "[w]ays of interpreting the land tend to become equivalents to acting upon it, consuming it as an aesthetic object, as a resource" (*Incorporation*, 18).

Michaels knows full well that the gold disappears from the book—but why not complement this vanishing with closer attention to what remains or to what else vanishes? His reading of this doggedly unironic novel, despite his strong analysis of contemporary debates over free silver and the gold standard, lacks a sense of migratory processes of coming and going as these processes are registered in novelistic time and, more so, geography. The closing sections of *McTeague* gradually abandon the notion of history that Michaels's New Historicist reading circulates around and through, as Norris explores extraction metaphorically, and radically, as a manifestation of a much wilder, much less domesticated sort of history, perhaps even an emptying out of history: the extraction of history from the "timeless," seemingly "infinite" setting; from the main character in the setting; and from the novel. In other words, the desert subsumes the gold as it subsumes all else. Or the narrator systematically abstracts from the documentary realism of San Francisco to the "vast, interminable," empty closing tableau. Michaels does observe what "the point of McTeague's dying in the desert with his five thousand gold pieces" is not: "In what might be called the Erich von Stroheim interpretation, the point is that greed kills. But it isn't exactly greed that gets McTeague into Death Valley" (*The Gold Standard*, 150). Indeed, it isn't greed at all, unless perhaps a greed for sheer physical survival. How can it be greed for gold, when the dentist is perfectly happy, even with all the stolen gold, to work in a dank, stale mine, "in the midst of the play of crude and simple forces" (387): "The life pleased the dentist beyond words" (387)? Being beyond words, after all, is more basic and potentially more unsettling than being beyond gold or the market for gold.

The point of McTeague's entire passage into the desert is described more accurately by David Wyatt:

> Norris ends *McTeague* by representing his hero's story as a picture. Although the content of this picture invites analysis (it is a pure reduction of "The American Sublime," "The empty spirit in vacant space"), the fact of the closing tableau has the most significance for Norris's career. *McTeague* has dealt with steady devolution in time, but it registers that process as failed transcendence in space. Attention to the self in landscape diverts us from the fate of the self in history, and the strategy of the ending, as of the whole, is to imagine human actors as bodies "in space." (107)

The problem of the ending is that it shifts McTeague's fundamentally destructive, hereditary brutality from latent (interior and usually hidden, leaping from inside him to the surface and attacking outward) to manifest (exterior and thoroughly obvious, magnifying his traits and attacking him from outside). At the same time, Norris complicates that binary construction of his main character by emphasizing, more powerfully than anywhere else in the novel, the ramifications of its stark vertical/horizontal axes or, in other words, the consequences of abstracting history ("real" people, concrete details, "turning points") into "time," "space," "figure," and "ground." As Wyatt puts it:

> Norris's effort is to raise a figure up above the ground. It is as if his characters struggle with a gravity pulling them back into the earth. His word for this resisted process might be "devolution," and his novels and stories take as their subject the threat to human stature posed by our career on an evolutionary ladder. . . . The paradox of his work is that although its theme is motion throughout time, its plots appear to measure man

within a space. Actions he initiates as dramas of development attempt to convert themselves, through his insistence on making fate visible, into dramas of position.

Two images recur in Norris's work with uncanny force: an isolated vertical figure and a vast, empty, horizontal space. (98)

Punctuating time, these violent extractions bring the primeval and the "modern" into harsh and often confusing contact. And, as Wyatt suggests, this confusion or diversion of large historical forces tends to diminish not only "the fate of the self" but the self in general, so that "beyond words" and beyond historical consciousness, characters become figures, objects visible in space but not really articulated in time.

From the crowded and densely detailed city to the colossal masses of mountains (the earthiness of Placer County, both surface and subterranean, and always alive) to the gorgeous Panamint Valley, McTeague moves by degrees toward a very different, very empty desert terrain, a place that perhaps most grimly figures his interior wastelands. Norris draws the line very distinctly:

> By noon [McTeague and Cribbens] were climbing the eastern slope of the Panamint Range. Long since they had abandoned the road; vegetation ceased. . . . The motionless air was like the mouth of a furnace. . . . Behind them was the beautiful green Panamint Valley, but before and below them for miles and miles, as far as the eye could reach, a flat, white desert, empty even of sage-brush, unrolled toward the horizon. In the immediate foreground a broken system of arroyos, and little cañons tumbled down to meet it. To the north faint blue hills shouldered themselves above the horizon. (400)

In McTeague's first face-to-face encounter with this desert, the vast emptiness and barrenness begin to be peopled figuratively as well as literally. Writing several decades later, Edward Abbey explains that personification is almost impossible to avoid or resist when writing about deserts, even though the act of imaginatively peopling the desert seems somehow inappropriate, a bad human habit of imposing on the place and reshaping it (*Desert Solitaire*, 6). Personification, however problematic, may work as a sort of linguistic pathway into an alien place. In a somewhat distorted way, the narrator of *McTeague* personifies this landscape in ways that paradoxically convey the difficulty of imagining it in human terms, of aestheticizing it. The narrator, that is, establishes that a landscape difficult to personify promises to be a place at least as difficult for the dentist (or anyone else) to inhabit. Here the personification mostly appears in the verbs and (like McTeague) mostly has to do with physical actions: cañons "tumble" down to meet arroyos, the desert "unrolls," the distant hills "shoulder" themselves toward the horizon. Indeed, some of this personification works indirectly; the desert is linked not to human traits or actions but to human products: the unrolling (carpet? canvas?), the air like a furnace. As the eye reaches out into this formidable topography, nothing reaches back; in fact, personified elements within the place move away from the spectator, unrolling and tumbling and shouldering in the opposite direction.

That the desert appears to be both connected to and dislocated from things human complicates its positions in space and time. Like the dentist himself, who keeps crossing and recrossing the line between the manifest human being and the usually latent brute, the desert blurs and distorts a similar line between the knowable and the unknowable. Its spatial and temporal coordinates may be detectable but may just as well be impossible to see, let alone measure:

> "What do you call the desert out yonder?" McTeague's eyes wandered over the illimitable stretch of alkali that stretched out forever and forever to the east, to the north, and to the south.
>
> "That," said Cribbens, "that's Death Valley."
>
> There was a long pause. The horses panted irregularly, the sweat dripping from their heaving bellies. Cribbens and the dentist sat motionless in their saddles, looking out over that abominable desolation, silent, troubled.
>
> "God!" ejaculated Cribbens at length, under his breath, with a shake of his head. Then he seemed to rouse himself. "Well," he remarked, "first thing we got to do now is to find water." (401)

Here the prospectors' plans and their ability to locate themselves in relation to three of the four cardinal directions come up against a much more daunting because immeasurable place; "illimitable," stretching out "forever and forever," Death Valley first induces "motionless" and "silent" mesmerization. In the face of such a place, the effect of McTeague's question is to highlight even further the tendency of humans to name and by implication to know and to take such places for their own, a process that here seems largely out of the question. McTeague's question is saved from being pointless, even, by the effect of the answer, which is to underscore once again the desert's links to the unknown and the unchartable. The desert can be named, that is, but naming it does not guarantee or facilitate access, use, ownership, familiarity, anything at all.

Entering and attempting to cross it, then, becomes at best an extremely risky proposition. And when McTeague finally makes the turn into Death Valley, Norris most powerfully empties his narrative of time. Wyatt's observation that "[t]wo images recur in Norris's work with uncanny force: an isolated vertical figure and a vast, empty, horizontal space" (98) is worth repeating here. What is especially pertinent is Wyatt's sense that the main human character becomes merely an "image" or an "isolated vertical figure." McTeague has of course throughout the novel crossed and recrossed a line between human and brute, but these crossings are more than just an evolutionary case study, a modern instance of reversion. The important point is the point of interaction between this human "image" or "figure" (itself pared down or emptied out to the extent that it seems only an image, perhaps a hollow structure or an illusion, like a mirage or a metaphor) and a fundamentally unhuman space, within which even evolution would be too historical, too measurable. "Attention to the self in landscape diverts us from the fate of the self in history, and the strategy of the ending, as of the whole, is to imagine human actors as bodies 'in space'" (Wyatt, 107). Again the visual image of the bodily effaces all but what can be seen of the human figure:

> He hastened on furtively, his head and shoulders bent. At times one could almost say he crouched as he pushed forward with long strides; now and then he even looked over his shoulder. Sweat rolled from him, he lost his hat, and the matted mane of thick yellow hair swept over his forehead and shaded his small, twinkling eyes. At times, with a vague, nearly automatic gesture, he reached his hand forward, the fingers prehensile, and directed towards the horizon, as if he would clutch it and draw it nearer; and at intervals he muttered, "Hurry, hurry, hurry on, hurry on." (*McTeague*, 416)

> On he went, straight on, chasing the receding horizon; flagellated with heat; tortured with thirst; crouching over; looking furtively behind, and at times reaching his hand forward, the fingers prehensile, grasping, as it were, toward the horizon, that always fled before him. (*McTeague*, 428)

Clearly, evolution is not entirely out of Norris's head here; his language is loaded with Darwinian imagery and powerfully conveys reversion ("prehensile") reflected in McTeague's physical descent ("crouching over"). But, as Norris's characteristic and here entirely pertinent repetition indicates, any sense that the vertical character is descending in humanity is contravened by the utter fixity of the horizon and more generally of the vast open space. The drama of character and desert, figure and ground, vertical and horizontal in fact tends, with the help of such repetitions, to erase any evolutionary imagination of events occurring and developing in and over time.

Thus, rather than seeing a Darwinian reversion in the already brutish dentist, I find something closer to an abstraction, an extraction, an emptying out of space and time, so that "empty" character and empty place come together, in these basic, stark "figures." Certainly McTeague's sixth sense seems to communicate with him from outside, suggesting some sort of connection between his inner workings and his surroundings—perhaps a projection. In the mountains of Placer County, "he yielded to their influence—their immensity, their enormous power, crude and blind, reflecting themselves in his own nature, huge, strong, brutal in its simplicity" (387). And in Death Valley, McTeague's is not the only hand in sight:

> Here, in these desolate barren hills . . . [t]he emptiness of primeval desolation stretched from him leagues and leagues upon either hand. The gigantic silence of the night lay close over everything, like a muffling Titanic palm. (411)

As he reaches out to it, it reaches toward and stifles him beneath its synes-thetic "gigantic silence." Or, "It seemed as though he were bitted and ridden; as if some unseen hand were turning him toward the east" (412); "once more an unseen hand reined him toward the east" (422). The narrator personifies the desert, again, in a selective and predominantly physical way (though this physicality is perhaps hallucinatory); the humanized desert animalizes Mc-Teague, though McTeague perhaps externalizes basic qualities of himself here in the blank measureless spaces of the desert and in this sense makes mani-fest and unleashes the animal latent within him. In any event, the psycho-logical and the physical/topographical conflicts merge. But this play of hands, one prehensile and the other invisible, never becomes a handshake, as the lines between brute and dentist, dentist and terrain, terrain and aesthetics all remain tricky—odd combinations of the very murky and the painfully clear. And in a place where "[c]haotic desolation stretched from them on either hand" (439), where Marcus's first words upon encountering McTeague are "Hands up" (429), and where McTeague finally finds himself literally hand-cuffed to Mark's dead wrist and figuratively in the hands of the desert, one set of hands is conspicuously absent and conspicuously irrelevant: the hands of time.

The desert enables Norris to undertake a remarkably complex investigation of a variety of borders configured and dismantled in a variety of ways. Focus-ing so intensely on Norris's desert serves not to cast aside but rather to re-situate critical debates about narrative continuity or discontinuity. As tex-tualized in this 1899 novel, the desert plays aesthetic as well as synesthetic tricks on its readers as well as its main character; it is clearly more compli-cated than a mere site for generic melodrama and more ambivalent than its seemingly absolute emptiness and deadliness at first promise. It is clearly im-plicated in, rather than tacked onto, the narrative as it is discussed here; the migration from city to desert clearly reflects the increasing late-nineteenth-century Euro-American interest in migrations between cultural "centers" and a paradoxically expanding late-nineteenth-century sense of cultural "margins." Norris relates the desert most closely to his most brutal and un-historical character, yet suggests more interestingly that it bears little rela-tion to measurable space and less to time; it reaches far beyond the coordi-nates and concepts of time and space that make history possible. It entertains but finally dismisses personification as it contains but finally kills off those persons who enter it. (It is also, as my language here displays, very difficult to write about without resorting to personification.)

Most probably, Norris's favorite phrase for the desert is "abominable deso-lation," and in certain scenes in *McTeague,* such as the description of the dentist's night terrors, the place seems a positively malevolent host:

McTeague saw himself as another man, striding along over the sand and sage-brush. At once he saw himself stop and wheel sharply about, peering back suspiciously. There was something behind him; something was following him. He looked, as it were, over the shoulder of this other McTeague, and saw down there, in the half light of the cañon, something dark crawling upon the ground, an indistinct gray figure, man or brute, he did not know. Then he saw another, and another; then another. A score of black, crawling objects were following him, crawling from bush to bush, converging upon him. *"They"* were after him, were closing in upon him, were within touch of his hand, were at his feet—*were at his throat.*

McTeague jumped up with a shout, oversetting the blanket. There was nothing in sight. For miles around, the alkali was empty, solitary, quivering and shimmering under the pelting fire of the afternoon's sun. (426–427)

With gestures to Edgar Allan Poe, Norris permits McTeague to watch himself as readers much earlier watched him, watching Polk Street from his Dental Parlors window, "over the shoulder." And what we see, with (and inside) him, is both a splitting into two ("this other McTeague") and a blurry melding together ("man or brute," attacker and attacked) of his most salient qualities. The "other McTeague" being pursued in the dream probably also contributes to the "indistinct gray figure," also known as "something dark crawling upon the ground." Thus Norris not only italicizes but puts quotation marks around *"They." "They"* distorts and reflects "us" (or "him") but is also inseparable from "him." In this scene, which comes closer than any other to reenacting McTeague's murder of Trina, the terrifying drama takes place in, and in a twisted way urbanizes, both Death Valley and the dentist. It is as if the desert has some hand in not only facilitating but also producing the nightmare, as if his mind collaborates with the physical terrain to create the particular horrors and suspicions of the scene.

But conversely, the "abominable desolation" remains just that, its emptiness providing an important backdrop and coda to the nightmare. For the nightmare becomes a nightmare precisely at the moment when "black, crawling objects" accumulate, filling up the vast emptiness of the space. In fact, all of the horror of the dream enters not with the desert but with things that it does not ordinarily feature, nonindigenous creatures that populate it only in nightmares imported from the mountains and the mines and the crowded city; as a result, the solitary actual desert he sees upon waking becomes, at least for a moment, more comforting than punishing. Moreover, this desert offered, two days earlier, a morning of genuine, if paradoxical, beauty:

The day was magnificent. From horizon to horizon was one vast span of blue, whitening as it dipped earthward. . . . In the distance it assumed all manner of faint colors, pink, purple, and pale orange. To the west rose the Panamint Range, sparsely sprinkled with gray sage-brush; here the earths and sands were yellow, ochre, and rich, deep red, the hollows and cañons

picked out with intense blue shadows. It seemed strange that such barrenness could exhibit this radiance of color, but nothing could have been
more beautiful than the deep red of the higher bluffs and ridges, seamed
with purple shadows, standing sharply out against the pale-blue whiteness of the horizon. (418)

This is not McTeague talking but Norris, the former art student, though with
a departure: as Dillingham points out, Norris's Parisian academic training in-
culcated in him the ideal that subdued colors were superior to impressionist
color explosions. Norris's Harvard writing instructor, Lewis E. Gates, however, was a theorist and proponent of impressionism, and Norris's dedication
of *McTeague* to Gates perhaps suggests a breaking free from Ingres, Gérôme,
Hippolyte Taine, and company.[5] Spectacular colors are very much inhabitants
of the desert Norris describes, and in their presence the dentist significantly
disappears from the picture and does not in any way manipulate its beauty.
As ever, the desert ultimately seems more than indifferent to McTeague; beyond all the questions of personification, projection, devolution, and, for that
matter, beauty, Death Valley is motiveless toward him. For Norris, the desert more often repels than fascinates, though his use of it reflects something
deeper than a mere stage set. Perhaps the best way to describe his complex attitude toward it is to call it sublime, for this "abominable desolation" means
more than just a vast emptiness, potentially lethal and occasionally sprinkled
with beautiful colors: it overpowers measurable space and stretches beyond
the count of time. As such, immeasurable and illimitable, it tricks infinity
and looms spectacularly threatening:

> [T]he stars burned slowly into the cool dark purple of the sky. The gigan-
> tic sink of white alkali glowed like snow. (428)

> The air was quivering and palpitating like that in the stoke-hold of a
> steamship. The sun, small and contracted, swam molten overhead. (426)

> The sun was a disk of molten brass swimming in the burnt-out blue of
> the sky. (419)

> The stars winked out, and the dawn whitened. The air became warmer.
> The whole east, clean of clouds, flamed opalescent from horizon to ze-
> nith, crimson at the base, where the earth blackened against it; at the top
> fading from pink to pale yellow, to green, to light blue, to the turquoise
> iridescence of the desert sky. The long, thin shadows of the early hours
> drew backward like receding serpents, then suddenly the sun looked over
> the shoulder of the world, and it was day. (414)

A poetics of naturalism? If the poetic, or the sublime for that matter, slums
with naturalism and Norris but rarely enters the minds of their critics, it does
so in large part because the brute remains, for all the attention given it, largely
an untapped metaphor. McTeague, like most naturalist brutes, is not often
described metaphorically; such brutes, the argument goes, crudely resist and

destroy such schemes and tropes and the vast possibilities figurative language implies, as they so easily destroy so much else in and around them. But the uneven relations between this brute and this desert make him seem just a bit closer to the human side and more significantly make a strong case for comparing (rather than, for example, defending) brute and desert—for his extractions play off of it in interesting ways. As this metaphor suggests, genealogy and something near to abstract art (language, that is, that attempts to come as near as it possibly can to "purely" visual images) combine to do violence to time and history. And the fundamentally discontinuous nature of McTeague, in both time and space, is paradoxically reflected in the overwhelming vastness of a desert so continuous that it too blows up rather than sustains those continuities. Time and (especially) history often appear to be not merely linear but horizontal. The "time line" spreads out from left to right, past to present; this visual metaphor of passage through space represents and helps organize the passing of time. *McTeague*, in its powerful attention to the vertical as well as its prehensile grasping after a horizon forever out of reach, offers in its unevenly beautiful desert passages something just as figurative yet tantalizingly (in part because incompletely) different.

7 Mary Austin, Sarah Winnemucca, and the Problems of Authority

Mary Austin begins *The Land of Little Rain* (1903) by promising "the better word" for "desert." Especially in 1903, and especially out West, after well over half a century of intense military, political, and psychological warfare between Indians and whites, Austin's direct announcement of her preference— "the Indian's is the better word"—seems designed to be provocative. U.S.-Indian warfare was often complicated, compounded, and confounded by the general unreliability of anyone's word, be the speaker or writer white or Indian, "savage" or "civilized," "unschooled" or "literary." As Theodore Roosevelt wrote in 1885, "The [U.S.] government makes promises impossible to perform, and then fails to do even what it might toward their fulfillment" (Hart and Ferleger, eds., 249); as historian Robert M. Utley explains one hundred years later,

> When vital interests were involved, neither Congress nor the executive branch felt the same scruples about violating Indian treaties as they did in honoring treaties with foreign nations, especially when the Indians seemed equally adept at violations. And indeed they were, with good reason. Chiefs who signed treaties did not always understand what they had agreed to. . . . Furthermore, chiefs rarely represented their people as fully as white officials assumed, nor could they enforce compliance if the people did not want to comply. And chiefs and people alike sometimes failed to see compelling reason to keep promises when the other party to the agreement so often broke promises. (*Indian Frontier*, 43–44)

Austin's decisive alliance with an Indian perspective at the turn into the twentieth century must not be underestimated. Neither should it be overpraised: Karen S. Langlois details how Austin relentlessly pursued her "unique myth of the self as Indian expert" (154), appearing rather foolish to readers and associates who distrusted her intuitive methods, her stereotyping of Indians, and her self-promotions.

By claiming to take the Indian's word for this desert landscape, then, Austin assumes a strong but also a controversial position. For example, why doesn't she, for all her conviction, actually transcribe the Indian word itself, untranslated? Why does she introduce her position in a passage that, as Marjorie Pryse puts it, "deliberately disorients her readers and gets us lost" (xxi)? Austin hints at a potentially useful irony: that nonnatives might not be schooled or "civilized" enough to find their way through "Indian" spaces—geographical, cultural, and textual—much more intricate and sophisticated than most white Americans expect. But is Austin confused as well as confusing, more an "Indian savant" (Langlois, 158) than the Indian expert and expert Indian she claimed to be? And, anyway, who is Austin to attempt to speak for these "Ute, Paiute, Mojave, and Shoshone" (*Land*, 9)? In returning to Austin's work as part of the larger effort to open and revitalize the American literary canon, several recent critics have found themselves agreeing with her early-twentieth-century detractors, even as the issues she raises continue to be energetically debated (see T. M. Pearce, 126–128; Castro, 42–45; Pryse). Austin's interventions into American Indian cultures were enormously problematic; according to her critics, including Elizabeth Ammons (see *Conflicting Stories*, 101–102), Helen Carr (see 218–222), and Karen S. Langlois, Austin frequently conducted herself in a disrespectful and irresponsible manner. Her "reexpressions" of "Amerind poetry," published in *The American Rhythm* (1923), are difficult to take seriously. Austin represents Seyavi, a Paiute woman basket maker, as a creative yet fairly limited, even immobile, figure, particularly when Austin's Paiute is read in relation to the autobiography of Northern Paiute Sarah Winnemucca, who travels across regions and cultures fluidly and fluently. But, at least in *The Land of Little Rain*, Austin attempts to represent, rather than denying or sensationalizing, the physical and textual difficulties of entering the desert. As both a regionalist and a cultural critic, Austin is interested, as Lois Rudnick argues, "in generating a myth of the Southwest that revised traditional Anglo male perceptions" of the region by redefining it in the larger context of the American nation as "a New World whose terrain, climate, and indigenous peoples offered a model of ecological, spiritual, and artistic integration to an alienated and decadent Western civilization" (10).

Austin is complex for just such reasons. Accused of pretensions and racism, she is also lauded for trying to comprehend, respect, and promote Indian points of view, although, as Carr points out, her cultural pluralism was highly selective: she was an exclusive "Indianist"—"quite racist, deeply antisemitic, and suspicious of Black Americans and their culture" (221). Ammons concludes that

> if it is possible for a member of the dominant [racial] group honestly to cross cultural boundaries, then Mary Austin may have succeeded better than most. She was hardly perfect in her relationships with Native Americans . . . [but] she also campaigned for Indian rights and worked hard to understand Native American lifeways and values. She did not assume it would or should be easy for her to enter into the lives and belief systems of other people. (*Conflicting Stories*, 102)

Austin got nearer and went farther than almost any other Euro-American literary figure of her day, farther than all but a few folklorists, anthropologists, traders, and other migratory non-Indian visitors. Explicitly presenting herself as an exceptional woman, forcefully affiliating herself with regional places and indigenous peoples, she reworks the prevailing conception that western and southwestern traveling is (and should be) a predominantly male activity, full of adventure but not troubled by alternative forms of gendered conflict and aggression. Her early books bear some surface resemblance to nature writings grounded in other parts of the country, writings by (among others) Henry David Thoreau, John Burroughs, John Muir, and even her sometime friend Roosevelt. But her turns to the California desert "Country of Lost Borders," to Native Americans, and especially to Native American women artists distinguish her unmistakably from Roosevelt, Muir, and other contemporary male writers. In other words, what is new about her project is the combination of what she reveals to the nation (a "new" region, "new" cultures, and an emphasis on strong women) and what she overlooks (principally the multicultural complexity of the Southwest and of America). In these ways her work both revises and resembles the "alienated and decadent Western civilization" Rudnick discusses.

Whatever Austin's intentions or political effectiveness, her Southwest comes as though upon compulsion; in her dramatically rhetorical performances, she describes, evokes, and enacts what she sees as the most compelling processes of making southwestern spaces and indigenous Americans newly visible to the nation. Moreover, *The Land of Little Rain* is her first book, and throughout it she works carefully and confidently at making herself visible, too. Ammons suggests in linking Austin to her contemporary, Gertrude Stein, that like the American in Paris, the Illinoisan in the Southwest invents herself as an artist and maverick literary figure: "Operating on opposite sides of the Atlantic, each presented herself to the world as a complete original and a sage, a kind of modern-day Sibyl who lived her life as she pleased and created art in brilliant defiance of traditional white western literary theory and practice" (*Conflicting Stories*, 88). As Ammons immediately points out, "In one way these rebellions were utterly conventional" (88). Yet in other ways Austin's audacity, however conventional or unconventional it may now seem, is of real interest, combining as it does performance, authority, and energetic transformations of selves into various sorts of texts and contexts, most notably (in printed form) Stein's language experiments and Austin's "Amerind" and desert passages. In the process Austin both loosens and reinscribes a variety of boundaries as she attempts to present a complex Southwest to a national readership.

In *The Land of Little Rain*, such visible persuasions—the rhetorical strategies she musters to bring this alliance of the land, its inhabitants, and the figure of herself as writer into public view for the first time—include her attempts literally to reproduce, and thereby to privilege, her own perceptions in writing. Throughout the book Austin evokes the California desert, a place with which she expects most readers to be unfamiliar, by showing them the processes through which she sees, understands, and represents it and its Indians aesthetically. The Country of Lost Borders is not a wasteland but rather is particularly beautiful—and readers know it because Austin tells them so. Clearly, Austin does not deny or mitigate her own centrality, her managerial role; further, her self-imposed, self-celebrating rhetorical stance combines with a willingness, at times perhaps a necessity, to argue her tastes, sympathies, and ideas. She actively presents herself as an authority and strongly demonstrates that this authority derives from her abilities as a traveler, observer, and advocate. Her writings often focus on characters and places in motion: "Water Trails of the Ceriso," "The Pocket Hunter," "The Mesa Trail," "The Streets of the Mountains," "The Return of Mr. Wills," and "The Walking Woman." While she does not necessarily argue that readers should join her in the desert country, her books do model ways of traveling and ways of understanding travel, implying in the process that travel has not simply personal value but national cultural significance as well. In other words, she advocates a migratory sensibility that dislodges and rearranges previously fixed personal and cultural identities.

Austin, as various critics remark, liked to aggress (see Ammons, *Conflicting Stories*, 87–89). She aggressed in person, on acquaintances and strangers, and she aggresses on paper. At the same time (or near enough to signify together), she works at preserving the Country of Lost Borders, discovering this place of great beauty and artistic potential to her readers while managing to keep it in vital ways lost. In this cautiousness about losing it in the finding, the desert comes to seem an active partner, indeed, an autonomous force capable of protecting itself. And here is where paradoxes similar to Georgia O'Keeffe's and Patricia Nelson Limerick's—discussed earlier in this book—mobilize. Early in the opening chapter of *The Land of Little Rain*, Austin insists on one cardinal rule—"Not the law, but the land sets the limit"—and in so establishing the land's authority, she presumably weakens her own. Though not acting maliciously or capriciously, she undercuts the writer's and for that matter anyone else's authority in the presence of such a masterfully authoritative, self-maintaining yet salutary and sometimes very beautiful land. Conversely, this leveling of everyone including herself is in its own right an act of authority, a sign of power. It is a rhetorical strategy that enables her to speak knowledgeably and persuasively, to demonstrate her own capabilities, without appearing to be anything but equal to her audience in the presence of a desert that is subject, she says, to no one. Her point is not simply to stake textual claims where no man or woman has staked them before; rather, she aggresses more interestingly, playing the "autonomous" subject and the deep aesthetic response and the urge (or rhetorical necessity) to argue off of each other, toward an original, powerful, and paradoxically self-containing sense of desertness. Thus, at the turn into the twentieth century, the Southwest is in no way self-evident. Its deserts and Indians can be described, as Austin describes them, aesthetically. Their beauty and power can be reported, displayed, evoked, but they must also in 1903 be explained, reckoned with, debated, wrenched into an American aesthetic realm quite new to most readers, though unevenly adapted (at least in Austin's treatment) from a purportedly American Indian worldview. They must, in short, be argued from within and argued out.

When Austin begins *The Land of Little Rain* by getting her readers lost, she sets up her argument about lostness as a political and cultural situation, complicating the prevailing idea that Americans travel to find selves or things.[1] Even though she gives the coordinates east and south twice in the first sentence, she quickly and efficiently directs readers away from landmarks, "east and south many an uncounted [and uncountable?] mile" (9), so that they end up arriving both geographically and syntactically at this distantly situated Country of Lost Borders. Already the jostling prose acts as a sort of surrogate for the place, a textual version of lostness that conveys a sense of the place's power. In the important second paragraph, Austin secures her readers' entrance into this country by opening up her language, by blurring and loosening the connections between words and things so that she may show them not only how to travel through but also how to read the desert. Here, where the Indians are, at the places Austin knowingly describes as unknowable, she makes an often-discussed, enigmatic statement: "Not the law, but the land sets the limit" (9). Both skeptical and celebratory, these words transfer authority from the law to the land and at the same time undermine or at least mystify the nature of that authority and suggest the authority of the writer as guru. What, after all, is "the law?" Which law? And what is "the limit?" Is it restrictive, limiting? Or does it offer the promise of immeasurable limitless possibilities?

As the play of words suggests, "The Land of Little Rain," the first chapter, introduces the place and a self-consciously evasive though authoritative style of writing more or less simultaneously. Indeed, in dramatizing this desert as a place suffused with death as well as life, sublime annihilation as well as mysterious renewal, Austin also dramatizes the literary or stylistic process involved in wording such a place: "Desert is the name it wears upon the maps, but the Indian's is the better word. Desert is a loose term to indicate land that supports no man" (9). The preferable name, the "Country of Lost Borders," fits better because it admits its own inability to define or otherwise demarcate the desert; "lost" is, to the extent that it is possible, found. Here too, in the epigrammatic "Not the law, but the land sets the limit" and in the next three sentences, another of Austin's characteristic rhetorical strategies, the "not this, but that" antithesis, further contributes to the text's strategic contentiousness. In a variety of ways, Austin's construction of dramatic contrasts and tensions establishes and maintains an important contrariness, a sense that the desert is constantly being explained, debated, and argued out. For her, the place's formidable ability to "make the poor world-fret of no account" is a global version of the *word*-fret she reveals throughout, the desert's powerful unmoorings of terms attempting to describe and represent it. Austin's first book, then, begins not with a simple declaration of her own authority but with a dramatic engagement between the writer and the place, each of which claims aesthetic coherence and a powerful authority.

Even so, writing the desert—telling stories, making and partaking of fables, romances, adventures, lyric descriptions, silences—comes to seem an ephemeral business, indeed. Obvious as the place may at first seem, it quickly grows elusive and difficult to capture, let alone to sustain in writing. As Austin makes plain, in the desert, coming and going, making and unmaking, accounts and no account are difficult to separate, to distinguish. Yet the desert is throughout a text, and to appreciate (as well as to survive in) this place, the traveler must be able to read it alertly and imaginatively. For instance,

> In the broad wastes open to the wind the sand drifts in hummocks about the stubby shrubs, and between them the soil shows saline traces. The sculpture of the hills here is more wind than water work, though the quick storms do sometimes scar them past many a year's redeeming. In all the Western desert edges there are essays in miniature at the famed, terrible Grand Cañon, to which, if you keep on long enough in this country, you will come at last. (9–10)

And

> Around dry lakes and marshes the herbage preserves a set and orderly arrangement. Most species have well-defined areas of growth, the best index the voiceless land can give the traveler of his whereabouts. (12)

These are unsurprising frames of reference for a writer positioning herself as a literary figure and finding self-reflexive texts in all sorts of things, as if by predilection. She seems at first blush to fit her prose securely into various styles and genres: romantic lyric, nonfiction travel and nature writing, regionalism. But Austin's ever-present concern with orientation paradoxically serves as a reminder that she is not so easy to categorize; the desert even as text remains a dangerous place, a place where it is very easy to lose one's way and very difficult to read one's way out or, for that matter, in. The signs she notes in the first passage—"wastes," "traces," "sculpture," "storm scars, "essays in miniature"—conjure up terror and endurance, not happiness, and the ostensibly more legible landmarks of the second passage are quickly qualified by the land's voicelessness, the traveler's potential disorientation, and the overarching sense that this particular "index" is the best and the most the desert can manage.

These darker undercurrents and lurking dangers come nearer to the surface in a quietly horrifying paragraph about water and thirst:

> There are many areas in the desert where drinkable water lies within a few feet of the surface, indicated by the mesquite and the bunch grass (*Sporobolus airoides*). It is this nearness of unimagined help that makes the tragedy of desert deaths. It is related that the final breakdown of that hapless party that gave Death Valley its forbidding name occurred in a

locality where shallow wells would have saved them. But how were they
to know that? Properly equipped it is possible to go safely across that
ghastly sink, yet every year it takes its toll of death, and yet men find
there sun-dried mummies, of whom no trace or recollection is preserved.
To underestimate one's thirst, to pass a given landmark to the right or
left, to find a dry spring where one looked for running water—there is no
help for any of these things. (11–12)

Immediately following a paragraph about the surprising fertility and vitality
of desert flora, this passage offers what is for the most part a dramatic moral
exemplum about the consequences of reading the desert badly. On the one
hand, Austin crafts a narrative about helplessness, inevitability, a shrugging
of shoulders; the final clause, "there is no help for any of these things," relaxes
the didactic pressure of the paragraph as a whole. An earlier question, "But
how were they to know that?," also appears to sympathize with "that hapless
party." On the other hand, she applies with considerable force an argument
about the life-or-death connections between smart desert traveling, instruc-
tive stories, and sharp capable reading. The story of the "hapless party" and
the naming of Death Valley; the "sun-dried mummies" both preserved and
unpreserved, both unstoried and (thanks to Austin) storied; the mesquite
and bunch grass as, literally, signs of life; the misreadings of these signs, of
landmarks, of one's own body—all these and more make a powerful argument
for the desert's textuality and the importance of being "properly equipped" to
read it. Unable to locate, let alone read, the desert's traces, one risks mum-
mification into something unreadable in turn, traceless and untraceable. The
real problem, indeed, the real "tragedy of desert deaths," is not that potential
help is "hidden" but that it is unimagined. And the unimagined is but one
short step away from the unimaginable.

The final three paragraphs of the opening chapter flamboyantly rehearse
the pleasures and pains of writing, telling, and reading desertness. In flourish
after flourish, Austin relentlessly outperforms herself again and again, at the
same time thoroughly playing up the ephemeral nature of both her topic and
her text. Indeed, each succeeding sentence has the rhetorical effect of extin-
guishing its predecessor. Here, her lyric aggression supplants her earlier argumentative aggression. The transitions between sentences are sometimes
just a bit oblique; the prose still disorients as it urges readers beyond itself.
Meanwhile, Austin turns her attention to an ephemerality visible in the desert's features and temperaments and also reflected back at all who would
travel and read the Country of Lost Borders, this place surprisingly abundant
and various with life but always haunted by death and always haunting. What
the desert produces (and what Austin, writing of desertness, makes) is just
such ephemerality, whether in fables, lyrics, tragic keys, "the color of romance," fragile expectations, or "deep breaths, deep sleep"—life and death
themselves. Similarly, when Austin remarks that her account is "of no account," she seems to turn against or at least to unsettle her previous claims
of authority.

But the closing passage of the chapter is a spectacularly decisive, masterful statement about being mastered by the desert:

> For all the toll the desert takes of a man it gives compensations, deep breaths, deep sleep, and the communion of the stars. It comes upon one with new force in the pauses of the night that the Chaldeans were a desert-bred people. It is hard to escape the sense of mastery as the stars move in the wide clear heavens to risings and settings unobscured. They look large and near and palpitant; as if they moved on some stately service not needful to declare. Wheeling to their stations in the sky, they make the poor world-fret of no account. Of no account you who lie out there watching, nor the lean coyote that stands off in the scrub from you and howls and howls. (17)

Falling perhaps "into the tragic key in writing of desertness," trying perhaps "to satisfy expectation," Austin suspends expectations as she asserts with great courage that something very significant about desertness lies beyond signification, "not needful to declare" and not possible to touch. Turning to the sublime lyric authority of these stars, she sees them as desertlike in the ways they overwhelm a viewer who is, interestingly, first identified as male and then blurred into an unidentified second-person figure. But she refuses to appeal, finally, to a sort of lyric erasure of the self, to literary impressionism, or to intuition alone, taken as authority. Significantly, the piece ends with the voice of the coyote (Coyote?) as he "stands off in the scrub from you and howls and howls." In vaulting "the poor world-fret" into a perspective simultaneously cosmic and coyotean, Austin argues for a salutary distance not motiveless but also not accountable to simple-minded (and/or lethal) misreadings or trivializations. For a first chapter of a first book about an American topography more often than not still perceived as anything but arresting, Austin makes and unmakes a mark as dazzling stylistically as it is daring professionally.

This mix of strong contention, close observation, and oracular didacticism, all working in conjunction with a powerful insistence on the desert's beauty, informs *The Land of Little Rain* throughout, and, combined with her "Indianist" persuasions, makes a fair summary of Austin's literary career in all of its self-fashioned theatricality and "authority." As Ammons, Langlois, Carr, Leah Dilworth, and others have argued, this mix is not always persuasive, particularly when Austin's self-promotional tendencies railroad her efforts to reinvent American myths and recenter American culture. Because the aesthetic she embraces smacks of the unconventional, argument is expedient (though sometimes counterproductive), not only as a means of buttressing and defending her work but also as a necessary strategy for situating her perceptions along with making them manageable and marketable. Aggressing, she sharpens the edges of selected, toughened lyric passages; aestheticizing, she softens and blurs particular prohibitive borders. And all the while she keeps in mind the conviction that the desert is to a significant extent language; though not entirely translatable or knowable, this place as text reflects and in the process justifies the various turns, counterturns, and mysteries of Austin's text as place. Reexpressing what she somewhat paradoxically sees as the desert's autonomy, she implicitly lays claim to her own.

And yet in writing of desertness, Austin discovers and emphasizes reciprocal, if not perfectly symmetrical, exchanges between artists and texts. Both the desert and the book are, after all, lands of little rain, alike in more than name only. Taken as a whole, her book urges both the language of the place and the place as language, toward a demonstration that the desert is like many other aesthetically charged landscapes in that it can be made and remade imaginatively and problematically, compromising, at least to an extent, its particular native (and in this instance Native American) features and traditions. David Wyatt is therefore not quite right when he remarks that the place Austin writes about is "a landscape out of hell. . . . Sustained attention to such a place measures one's power to nurture an unsponsored thing. Austin adopts this landscape because it is empty, unclaimed, unstoried" (81). The place is no more an adopted child than Austin is an adoptive mother. In fact, as Austin sees it, it is a powerful repository of stories, stories of place beings and spiritual nourishments; she writes of animals in general as "the little people" (21), specifies accordingly when discussing rabbit people (25), remembers a cougar "crying a very human woe" (136), anthropomorphizes coyotes and badgers, critiques the sociability of scavenger birds, and imagines "birds, squirrels, and red deer" as "children crying small wares and playing in the street" (109). Turning in a central chapter to Native American women artists, she focuses particularly on Seyavi, an old Paiute woman who makes baskets "for the satisfaction of desire" (96) and the creation of beauty and who understands basketry as part of the stories and storytelling that constitute who she is. And throughout *The Land of Little Rain*, Austin retells the stories she so abundantly finds in the desert; she does not have to invent these stories, she suggests, because they are already there. Each example given above, each personification, each metaphor—and there are many others—condenses and at the same time provides a story. "You see in me a mere recorder," she writes with typically oracular self-assurance, "for I know what is best for you; you shall blow out this bubble from your own breath" (68).

Wyatt hits closer to the mark when he describes *The Land of Little Rain* as "a book that reconceived autobiography as lexicography" (83) without, as Austin's "I know what is best for you" makes absolutely clear, losing or hiding the self in the lexicographical self-narration. As Ammons explains,

> To the extent that it is repetitive, fluid, and aggregative, Austin's narrative guides western-trained readers to see things we have not been taught to see, to find life where we have not assumed it to be. The earth, for example, becomes language. In "Water Trails of the Ceriso," we learn to read strange squiggly lines in the dust. We are taught to decipher and comprehend elaborate surface patterns and deep underlying meanings

where, prior to being initiated into this borderless space, we would have thought there was only blankness, silence. (*Conflicting Stories*, 93)

Seeking to bring the southwestern desert to a national audience, Austin uses a pedagogical approach, guiding readers through strange territories by teaching them to read not only these water trails but also the western skies, "the language of the hills" (71), and "The Streets of the Mountains" (103–109): "There is always an amount of local history to be read in the names of mountain highways where one touches the successive waves of occupation or discovery" (103). She describes the numerous and subtle animal trails, the voices of the outdoors, the water borders, the clouds—"one sees from the valley only the blank wall of their tents stretched along the ranges" (134)—and even sometimes the witchery of a developing storm: "Out over meadow or lake region begins a little darkling of the sky,—no cloud, no wind, just a smokiness such as spirits materialize from in witch stories" (135). In teaching readers how to observe and read these trails and traces, Austin connects the desert to active creative work, potentially and preferably done in partnerships between writer, readers, and texts, texts in and of the earth and the sky as well as the printed page. As much as Austin presents herself as an expert, she is also clearly a collaborator. Through readers reading deserts, in other words, Austin teaches and argues the aesthetic processes and possibilities of desertness.

Other arguments pertain too, of course. In *The Land of Little Rain* and in another collection of desert writings, *Lost Borders* (1909), Austin purposefully distances herself from the prevailing "Wild West" narratives of manly adventure and heroic conquests, turning instead toward a version of the American Southwest that romanticizes in its own right but also challenges the romantically idealized Wests of Roosevelt, Frederick Jackson Turner, Frederic Remington, and a host of dime novelists. Turner in "The Significance of the Frontier in American History" (1893) homogenizes and familiarizes western experience, particularly by locating it in essentialized conflicts between (for example) white settlers and "primitive savages," evolving civilization and devolving barbarism, heroic individualists and "virgin land." For Turner, the frontier closes around 1890 yet remains alive in the sturdy, independent, "American" character it helped produce; as the frontier line recedes into nostalgia, it also makes way for hope bred from the long legacy of western exploration and conquest. And for Turner's audiences, both academic and popular, the frontier thesis celebrates strengths of character as national resources that memorialize a great, heroic past and betoken a powerful, promising future.

For Austin, the valued frontiering traits comprehended by Turner's "dominant individualism"—the "acuteness and inquisitiveness," the "practical, inventive turn of mind," the "masterful grasp of material things, lacking in the artistic but powerful to effect great ends" (Turner, 37)—fall short of representing, comprehending, and generally coming to satisfactory terms with both the affirmative and the destructive elements of southwestern character, territory, and experience. In *The Land of Little Rain,* Austin respects and tries to avoid idealizing the harsh, elusive, beautiful desert and its native inhabitants; she also writes skeptically not only about the means of coming to (literary, historical) terms with the American Southwest but also about any assumption that such terms are obvious or even available. While Turner helps create an image of the West as scene for strenuous activity and progressing Anglo-Saxon civilization, the image itself remains fixed and stable; his language, so willing to fall into conventional narrative and rhetorical form, tames and controls precisely the troubling racial, ethnic, sexual, and artistic diversity that Austin celebrates in her own selective way. His frontier is not a place rich with tribal cultures and arresting topographies but a thesis. Her desert is much richer, with all sorts of human, animal, plant, and climactic vitality; it is a place of great beauty, subtle textuality, and borders more flexible than any invoked by Turner.

As such, Austin's acutely complex sense of the diversity and difficulty of the California desert can be understood as an alternative to the Turner thesis. Seen as metaphors, for example, the closed frontier and the land of lost borders move in different directions as they are argued out in the service of different narratives predicated on different ways of seeing. Even though Austin sometimes idealizes and excludes, *The Land of Little Rain* stresses the presence of American Indian men and women, white pocket hunters (Edward Abbey with mischievous ambiguity calls them "single-blanket jackass prospectors" [introduction, ix]),[2] indigenous animal "folk," pious Mexican villagers, and the land itself, sometimes mingling uncompetitively and sometimes colliding disruptively. This land she sees as trickster, tempter, killer, breeder, and open book. It creates, mystifies, transforms, and annihilates. To return to Austin's opening maxim, "Not the law, but the land sets the limit" for those who live, work, travel, write, and read there, and in saying so she differs from Turner while demonstrating a kind of respect for the unheroic, the undramatic, and the unbound. "The rainbow hills, the tender bluish mists, the luminous radiance of the spring, have the lotus charm. They trick the sense of time" (*Land,* 15), the sense of linear time that helps measure and at times impose notions of historical "progress" and expansion.

In "The Basket Maker," the chapter both Ammons and Pryse see as the spiritual, artistic heart of the book, Austin says more about time:

> The Paiute fashion of counting time appeals to me more than any other calendar. They have no stamp of heathen gods nor great ones, nor any succession of moons as have red men of the East and North, but count forward and back by the progress of the season; the time of *taboose,* before the trout begin to leap, the end of the piñon harvest, about the beginning of deep snows. So they get nearer the sense of the season, which runs early or late according as the rains are forward or delayed. But whenever Seyavi cut willows for baskets was always a golden time, and the soul of the weather went into the wood. (96)

Austin's description of Paiute temporality is vague. Indeed, the extent of her involvement with Paiute culture is unclear from this passage. Clearly, though, she interests herself in the connections between Seyavi and natural, seasonal processes—the concreteness of time, "the soul of the weather." Finding the materials of her basket-weaving art in the earth and making these materials into something beautiful without unmaking the beauty that resides there, Seyavi inspires and informs *The Land of Little Rain:* "The weaver and the warp lived next to the earth and were saturated with the same elements" (95). Ammons offers that "Seyavi's aesthetic as Austin describes it—earthbound, erotic, generated by women, productive of multiple pieces, each of which is different and yet the same, and expressive of an elastic concept of time—is the aesthetic of *The Land of Little Rain*" (*Conflicting Stories*, 94).[3]

But Austin's contentiousness influences these aesthetics, too. In *The Land of Little Rain*, she offers a counterargument to the likes of Turner's frontier thesis and its paradoxical "dominant individualism": while Turner sees the frontier, the West, and its peopling as metaphors located inside a larger narrative about national progress and the American character strictly defined, Austin has a clearer, though problematic sense that the land is already peopled and already powerfully charged. The problem for Austin is not that the region is precolonial but that it is postcolonial—and misread and undervalued as such. Simply by including Seyavi in the book, Austin opens a great deal of what Turner closes. Unlike "the historian and his pioneers," Richard Drinnon writes, "Mary Austin took the trouble to enter Indian lives, found therein the reverse of 'primitive' simplicity . . . [and] brought to the West more than conventionally blinding assumptions and attitudes" (231). In her hands as in Seyavi's, reading, writing, and resituating desertness are collectively a way of participating in a great and necessary beauty. The process is not simple, particularly when Austin resituates the Country of Lost Borders— "the better word"—in bound form as a published book. But on the other hand, this turn-of-the-century book reaffirms connections very old as it teaches a word, a text, a place very richly new.

To echo comments made by some of her contemporaries, then, Austin at her best was an extremely capable prose writer. But Carr's point about Austin's racism and Langlois's detailed demonstration of her often crass self-promoting lead to troubling conclusions; for example, Austin invents rather than earns her expertise, sometimes at the expense of the Indians with whom she professes sympathetic and collaborative alliances. Beyond the strength of the textual bonds she, not Seyavi, claims between Seyavi and herself, Austin's career from its inception raises questions and arguments still very much relevant: is it really possible to forge and sustain a mutually cooperative and productive community of Euro-Americans and Native Americans? If *The Land of Little Rain* is another in a long line of unsuccessful American artists' colonies, communities much easier to write about than to live in, how should American Indians respond to being recolonized in ways that represent them as utopian and romantic? What can be done about wanna-bes? As Langlois writes, "Obviously Austin was self-taught, but how much did she know? Had she exploited her intuitive understanding of Indians, a superficial acquaintance with their culture, and the borrowed expertise of more knowledgeable people to develop a career as an Indian savant?" (158).

Clearly, the act of building a professional literary career on or around Indians creates all sorts of opportunities for manipulation and exploitation. To her credit, Austin does not set out to create an easeful desert utopia, nor does she offer large authoritative prescriptions about Indian policy. (These would come later; see Dilworth, 14, 67, 189; Weigle and White, 443.) But she still exercises power relations in ways that directly say "I know what is best for you," even as she works at "producing and aggressively promoting a highly marketable image" (Langlois, 160). To point specifically to just one of the difficulties: acquiring, possessing, and marketing Indian "artifacts" becomes tangled up with professedly "nobler" motives such as learning about and helping to preserve indigenous cultures. Austin freely acknowledges commercial status: "If you had ever owned one of Seyavi's golden russet cooking bowls with the pattern of plumed quail, you would understand all this without saying anything" (*Land*, 96). Without saying anything? Here, Austin implies that ownership purchases intuitive understanding and that intuition justifies a potentially unexamined silence. Yet a few paragraphs later, the acquisitive impulse is undercut:

> "What good will your dead get, Seyavi, of the baskets you burn?" said I, coveting them for my own collection.
> Thus Seyavi, "As much good as yours of the flowers you strew." (97)

Then, after admitting to her own covetousness, Austin discusses Paiute ownership of the earth—or, more accurately, the dispossession of a Paiute trust or stewardship. She writes of "the clans who owned the earth, fallen into the deplorable condition of hangers-on" (98) but immediately idealizes and sentimentalizes this "condition":

> Yet you hear them laughing at the hour when they draw in to the campoodie after labor, when there is a smell of meat and the steam of the cooking pots goes up against the sun. Then the children lie with their toes in the ashes to hear tales; then they are merry, and have the joys of repletion and the nearness of their kind. They have their hills, and though jostled are sufficiently free to get some fortitude for what will come. (98)

To describe Indians under early-twentieth-century U.S. Indian policy as "jostled" is to throw the rest of the statement, and the writer's authority, under suspicion.

In general terms, the Euro-American "discovery" of Native American arts and artists begins in earnest only after the vast majority of Indians have been killed off or penned up on reservations. According to Utley, "the Indian Wars of the United States" ended at a specific time and place—September 4, 1886, at Skeleton Canyon, Arizona. Here Geronimo and a small group of Apache fugitives, "the last holdouts" in the long and bitter armed Indian resistance to the reservation system, surrendered to General Nelson A. Miles of the U.S. Army (*Indian Frontier*, 201). Three years earlier, in 1883, a Northern Paiute woman, Sarah Winnemucca, published *Life among the Piutes: Their Wrongs and Claims*, an autobiographical text filled almost entirely with accounts of troubled Indian-U.S. relations through large portions of the western United States, including Nevada, Oregon, and Washington. Carr, Dilworth, and Langlois have written useful accounts of Austin's careers as a woman artist in the Southwest and as a self-proclaimed Indian expert; to build on their work, this chapter will now turn to this Paiute autobiography, drawing contrasts between the writings of Winnemucca and Austin. Both writers demonstrate extraordinary social and geographical mobility, and both argue toward a re-making of national identity, but Austin uses her mobility to interpret her relatively immobile construction of Indians such as the Paiute woman, Seyavi, while Winnemucca's traveling across regions and cultures is a personal and tribal survival tactic with which she positions herself as a highly flexible cultural intermediary.

Though it is difficult to say for certain, *Life among the Piutes* is believed to be the first autobiography published by a Native American woman,[4] and it differs markedly from *The Land of Little Rain*. The book is mediated to some (probably indeterminate) extent by an "editor," the white Boston humanitarian Mary Mann, who copied and presumably corrected the original manuscript since her preface describes Winnemucca "fighting with her literary deficiencies" and thereby losing "some of the fervid eloquence which her extraordinary colloquial command of the English language enables her to utter" (2). Despite Mann's efforts to tidy up her Indian friend's spelling, grammar, and perhaps "literary" decorum, the finished product preserves Winnemucca's authoritative and still unsettling arguments about white, federal, Christian misdealings with the Paiute people. Unlike Austin's texts, then, Winnemucca's text conveys authority despite its announced fallibilities in manuscript form. But the book's somewhat florid, highly theatrical rhetoric and more or less linear, more or less chronological narration do not in any significant way disguise her much more apparent separation, as an American Indian and as a woman, from such literary conventions and the people who maintain them. In fact, the narrative power of her rhetorical, political, and cultural performances—including her ability to outmoralize the moralists and outcivilize the "civilizers"—dramatizes the irony as well as the disruptiveness of that well-lubricated binary racism and sexism.

Ammons's insights about women writers such as Humishuma (Mourning Dove) and Sui Sin Far come into play here: as one of the first American Indian women novelists and the first Chinese-American woman writer, respectively, each found that "there was absolutely no history of women writers like herself in the United States, no forebears and almost no contemporary context," and therefore for each "the invention of herself as a writer was a literal, not a symbolic, act" (Ammons, *Conflicting Stories*, 11). Likewise, as the first

American Indian woman known to write her life, Winnemucca must literally create as well as imaginatively re-create herself autobiographically. As David Brumble argues, she does of course know and adapt indigenous ways of seeing the world and the people: "In many ways, *Life among the Piutes* assumes an audience with Paiute habits of mind, not Christian. She is what she has accomplished; like White Bull and Two Leggings . . . she is the sum of her reputation. And so the maintenance of her reputation is of great importance to Winnemucca" (66). But she must also make herself legible as well as sympathetic to a late-nineteenth-century nonindigenous American culture for the most part demonstrably unable and unwilling to comprehend native cultures in all or even some of their depth and complexity. The rhetorical problem resembles Harriet Jacobs's in *Incidents in the Life of a Slave Girl* (1861): how can a doubly, perhaps trebly othered writer find, let alone establish, the common ground necessary to meet the powers that be face to face or text to text; how can she persuade any of them to consider salient political action?[5] For both, the "conventions" by which their texts will be evaluated are not so much literary as more broadly cultural; for both, the task of positioning themselves as Americans involves a sort of layered self-fashioning in which they demonstrate that they both are and are not like their non-Indian, non–African American, nonslave, non-reservation-bound readers. Remaking themselves as writers, that is, involves them in the double act of changing and not changing who they already are.

In *Life among the Piutes*, Winnemucca in effect constructs a collage of rhetorical strategies, some—chronological arrangement, anecdotal examples, discussion of family relationships—familiar to her non-Indian readers. But she must also bring to bear stories and situations previously unimaginable as nonfiction, as documentary evidence demanding to be taken and acted upon as contemporary actuality. For example, the conventions direct her to recollect and represent tranquil, happy domestic scenes. Thus in Chapter 2 of *Life among the Piutes*, "Domestic and Social Moralities," Winnemucca reinforces Paiute familial bonds and loyalties, and she does not do so by falling back on romantic imaginings as Austin does: "Our children are very carefully taught to be good," Winnemucca writes. "We are taught to love everybody. We don't need to be taught to love our fathers and mothers. We love them without being told to. Our tenth cousin is as near to us as our first cousin; and we don't marry into our relations" (45). Further, "We have a republic as well as you. The council-tent is our Congress, and anybody can speak who has anything to say, women and all" (53). Her pedagogical remarks implicitly critique American culture, while, as the comment about inbreeding suggests, her cross-cultural comparisons also enable Winnemucca to reverse prevailing binaries hinging on the cultural categories of "civilization" and "savagery": "There is nothing cruel about our people," she observes; "They never scalped a human being" (54). And since, as geographical proximity would have it, one of the Paiutes' first encounters with whites involved the Donner party, Winnemucca cannot resist pointing out that the Paiutes never did what whites did:

"'Surely [the whites] don't eat people?' 'Yes, they do eat people, because they ate each other up in the mountains last winter'" (15). In writing of her own family and tribal community, then, Winnemucca scrambles prevailing Euro-American racialized categories by establishing important contrasts between loving, "civilized" Indians and mean-spirited, racist, cannibalistic white people. She delivers deserved reproofs to the violations of various self-styled and U.S. government–styled "Great Fathers," white patriarchs like Indian Agents W. V. Rinehart and Reverend James H. Wilbur, to name no more, while remaining all the while in clear sight of Paiute traditions grounded in family (as well as tribal) love.

As this account of the early, pedagogical chapters of *Life among the Piutes* indicates, Winnemucca hopes to convey the moral soundness and authority of the Paiute people by demonstrating that they do in fact practice what could be seen by Euro-American readers as a recognizably Western system of secular ethics, proper "civilization," and even at times effective sentimentality. This is not to say that she happily and easily gives way to Euro-American systems of culture but rather that she attempts to use her status as a mediator between the Paiutes and the U.S. government strategically, toward securing Paiute rights and desires. In addition, as Brumble and Gae Whitney Canfield point out, Winnemucca had been performing on stage and on the lecture platform for nearly twenty years before she performed *Life among the Piutes* on paper (see Canfield, 36–43, 162–171, 201–203, 222–228). Brumble usefully discusses how skillful Winnemucca was "at adapting Paiute oral conventions to the uses of the pen and to the entertainment and persuasion of white audiences" (69). Much of the book, he continues,

> must have had its original in one of her lectures. By the time she came to write it down, she would have delivered her tale, in parts, on many occasions, and she would have had a lively sense of how white audiences had responded to this version of a particular episode, and how they had responded to the other version of the same episode. (70–71)

Winnemucca's textual performance shows as well a deft ability to reproduce different voices: she collages together "official" documents—letters of recommendation from military authorities and from her editor and sponsor, Mann, for example—while transcribing her own authoritative ventriloquizings and reworkings of many different, often male, voices of tribal, federal, military, political, and literary authority.[6] She does, for example, her father, Chief Winnemucca, and a generally reprehensible sampling of Bureau of Indian Affairs lowlifes—most notably Indian agents and their wives—as well as a range of male military figures both kind and unkind. Austin may seem to be undertaking a similar strategy when she writes, "You see in me a mere recorder," but her characteristic second-person address and her follow-up sentence, "for I know what is best for you" (68), suggest a more manipulative, more univocal relationship with both her audience and perhaps her subject. In contrast, Winnemucca actively reproduces a diverse mixture of voices and does so with a sense more of what is best for American Indians than for Euro-American readers.

Still, in a gesture Austin might have tried herself, Winnemucca sometimes speaks through or as somebody else so that she may record praise for her own heroic actions. She speaks as her father, for instance, demonstrating in the process a flexible, purposeful sense of gender: "Now hereafter we will look on her as our chieftain, for none of us are worthy of being chief but her, and all I can say to you is to send her to the wars and you stay and do women's work, and talk as women do" (193). Winnemucca holds gender-based divisions of labor and social function up to scrutiny and questions their usefulness in a time of crisis; she also knows, as she prepares her book, that the Paiutes did in fact "send her to the wars" and elevate her to a controversial position of tribal leadership. Of speeches such as this one, Brumble makes the interesting observation that Winnemucca performs the literary equivalent of a coup tale, a tale told and retold, ordinarily by male warriors, as a way of celebrating and commemorating their own glorious deeds. In this way, he suggests, she transforms a fundamental Native American cultural process of storytelling and reflects those Paiute habits of mind that so strongly influence her self-presentation throughout *Life among the Piutes* (Brumble, 65–66). In addition, the speech subverts not only gender roles but also Euro-American cultural assumptions: in effect, Winnemucca maintains and insists on Paiute cultural codes and practices, even as she speaks as a male Paiute chief and warrior and suggests a radical reversal of Paiute social organization. Her speech may to some extent be self-serving, but it is also constructed in the service of the tribe. It may upset tribal traditions, but it does so in the hopes of preserving them.

Despite these daring and authoritative performances, Winnemucca often inserts apologies for her perceived literary and social deficiencies; she performs in brilliantly inverse proportion to the frequency and seeming conviction of her many textual disclaimers. Like Jacobs in *Incidents in the Life of a Slave Girl*, Winnemucca apologizes often, referring to herself as "only an Indian woman" (164): "I am powerless, being a woman, and yet you come to me for help" (139). These statements sometimes precede accounts of her heroic attempts to take action for the Paiutes, but at other times she erases her Indian identity: "A citizen came in and reported Indians close by. The General [O. O. Howard] asked me what I thought about it. I told him I did not think there were any Indians within ten hundred miles of us" (166–167). Perhaps these expressions of self-doubt, inability, inferiority, and non-Indian identity are rhetorical ploys, but more likely they are deeply ingrained self- and cultural perceptions. Sometimes, though, Winnemucca's best method of attack is a good defensiveness: "It is the way we savages do when we meet each other; we cry with joy and gladness" (101). She reverses binaries energetically maintained by white Euro-Americans and their institutions, particularly those binaries that define the victims of savagery as savages. Winnemucca specializes in exposing the hypocrisy of so-called Christian Indian agents and their wives: "She had a Bible with her. Ah! ah! What do you think the Bible was? Why it was a pack of cards. . . . She was an Indian agent's wife" (223). She repudiates Agent Wilbur to his face: "[H]ell is full of just such Christians as you are" (239). And she demonstrates, even as she condemns or regrets her own perceived weaknesses as both reader and writer, that her empowerment is closely connected to language: "Mr. Wilbur, you will not get off as easily as you think you will," she declares. "I will go to Yakima City and lecture" (240).

All in all, many of Winnemucca's battles are fought in language. There are many more examples. Paiutes implore her to help them: "We know our sister can write on paper to our good father in Washington if she will" (140). She is constantly valued for her ability to "talk on paper," but, as the narrative develops, the Paiutes learn to trust U.S. writings less and less: Secretary of the Interior Carl Schurz tells her that government leaders "would grant all I asked of them for my people, which they did; yes, in their minds, I mean in writing, promises which, like the wind, were heard no more" (221). And, of her closely chaperoned visit to Washington, D.C., she informs her readers that Schurz basically allowed her to do everything *but* lecture; she archly remarks, "The Soldiers' Home is the only place we did *not* see while we were in Washington" (222), and she knows full well that her government-assigned chaperone "was with us every minute, for fear I would say something" (219).

As a performer, lecturer, interpreter, and writer of enough repute to be feared by ranking cabinet officials, Winnemucca upholds a strong sense of Paiute culture while adapting and making that culture and her experiences accessible to a larger American culture. Her rhetorical performances and her textual construction of authority can be spectacularly persuasive, as when she presents and dismantles the white voices of authority that she has so powerfully mastered. But *Life among the Piutes* articulates a more tenuous and more powerful authority as well, an authority Winnemucca works toward as a woman othered to the extent that she has no literary ancestors, has few or no models within either Paiute or U.S. culture, and feels constrained nonetheless to apologize for her uncertainties as a writer. The Paiute woman narrator must find ways to articulate a self that is both inviolately Paiute and irreproachably "civilized" according to Euro-American standards; she must also situate that self in the context of all the various other selves she encounters. Sometimes she can't resist tipping sacred cows, or sacred presidents, as the case may be; reacting to one of Rutherford B. Hayes's less favorable decisions, she confesses, "Every night I imagined I could see the thing called President. He had long ears, he had big eyes and long legs, and a head like a bull-frog or something like that" (205). But, much more often, Winnemucca cobbles together a performance text that is authoritative to the extent that it demonstrates a complex awareness of the shapes, forms, and sad limitations of power-laden cultural encounters. Her text is authoritative to the extent that it refuses to regard itself, its author, or its collaborative production as any sort of simple solution. And it is authoritative, finally, to the extent that it questions and redefines the concept of authority without ever forgetting to urge respect.

Clearly, Winnemucca refuses to fall into the key of the noble savage,

while Austin, who begins her book by turning to an ostensibly Indian seman-
tic authority and who celebrates a Paiute woman basket maker, Seyavi, in-
vests much more deeply in a romantic, stereotypical image of natives elemen-
tally and nobly involved with the earth. Winnemucca, busy fighting for the
basic human rights of her people, simply does not have time to behave like
Austin's postwar traditionals. Fighting corrupt Indian agents, spiriting her
people from danger during wartime, warding off would-be rapists, serving as
an interpreter between Indians and U.S. soldiers, she makes not pottery or
baskets but rather arguments, rhetorical appeals to political, military, and
tribal authorities. And, far from waxing poetic about the Land, her bare mentions of natural topographies—usually as sites of battles, barren reservations,
or risky pursuits—obliquely demonstrate the Paiutes' forced and wrenching
dislocation from their specific homelands.

Austin, for all her self-proclaimed sensitivity and intelligence about Indians, was more than capable of losing her cultural equilibrium, with the result that her "reexpression" of a "Sioux Song at Parting" sounds like this:

> Breaks now, breaks now my heart,
> Thinking, from thee I part.
> Hear thou what says my heart:
> Keep me,
> Keep me in thine alway!
>
> Dreams now, dreams now my heart.
> Weeping, awake I start,
> Thinking, again we part.
> Dream thou,
> Perchance thy dream will stay!
>
> (*American Rhythm,* 97)

The quality of the work notwithstanding, Austin's "claim that Indian poetry
had immediate relevance to the concerns and direction of modern American
verse" (Castro, 22) directs attention as well to the desert's aesthetic potential
and circulates a new idea of the Southwest as a place where "Americans could
reinvigorate their culture" (Norwood and Monk, eds., 1). But this reinvigora-
tion does not comprehend already vigorous indigenous cultures such as the
Paiutes as described by Winnemucca. Austin and others undertake a resource-
ful, at times promotional, usually optimistic reclaiming of the American
Southwest and of selected American Indian cultures. Their project reaches
outside the slender forms of imagist-Indian poetry; in fact, the most interesting Euro-American artists to take up desertness in the 1910s and 1920s—
Willa Cather, Georgia O'Keeffe, and George Herriman—specialize in fiction,
painting, and comic strips, respectively. Their works are all the more modernist in that they try, not always successfully, to avoid blanket notions of primitivism; instead, they take it upon themselves to celebrate deeply personal,
spiritualized perceptions shaped to a significant extent by the topographies,

the peoples, and the cultural intersections they find freshly and uniquely active in the American Southwest. But the considerable abilities and complex textual performances of actual, contemporary Indians like Winnemucca do not significantly influence these twentieth-century artists. In this sense, Austin's checkered and highly problematic version of "the Indian" prevails over Indian voices and texts themselves. Austin's self-proclaimed authority supersedes Winnemucca's hard-earned knowledge.

Austin participates in a modernist redefining of "the primitive," a project in which genuine respect and crass appropriation often conflate. Ammons states the case strongly: "Modernism is rooted in repeated raids by the twentieth-century west, for its own psychic and artistic purposes, on cultures it has defined as less 'civilized' or more 'primitive'" (*Conflicting Stories*, 101). In addition to poaching, of course, there is the widespread overlooking of Indian texts such as *Life among the Piutes* and *Geronimo's Story of His Life*. However, the condition of lost borders does not necessarily imply or facilitate appropriation, and, as Ammons concludes, perhaps it is wisest to say that Austin did the best she could and created new imaginative possibilities for modernists, many of whom meant well. Consider the following passage from Austin's tract on "Amerind" and American poetry, *The American Rhythm*:

> The exigencies of what we call civilization have forced upon us moderns a selective intensity of observation such as rarely occurs in primitive experience. An Amerind, no doubt, if he had to cross Fifth Avenue in the midst of traffic, in the absence of a traffic manager, would be constrained to the same concentration of passage which keeps us largely unaware of the color, the majesty, the multiplying rhythms of our streets. (28–29)

The ability to recontextualize, the mild logical vertigo, the absence of actual American Indian testimony, the attempt to imagine reciprocal cultural experiences—all of these and more epitomize Austin.

To sum up, then, the turn-of-the-century desert and Southwest, often conflated, meet the American public eye as both potentially aesthetic sites and arguments variously about the southwestern land itself, its indigenous cultures, and a whole range of national issues and preoccupations, including women's rights, technological encroachment, conservation, urban development, and immigration. As exemplified in Austin's complex weavings, this combination of spectacular beauty and visible persuasion is in turn part of a complex larger rhetoric of modern American desertness, a rhetoric that again in the work of O'Keeffe and Cather, twenty-plus years after *The Land of Little Rain*, moves toward making desert places and women artists aesthetically visible.

But these intersections of aesthetics and rhetoric, of beauty and argument, often seem jarring; in simplest terms, the desert as described may not sound very attractive. Much trickier are the motives of these modernist desert writers as they inevitably "use" or overlook while often trying to respect American Indian cultures in their aesthetic and political dimensions as both are constantly renewed in a variety of contemporary forms and styles, some of which are predominantly Euro-American. Austin, it seems, would rather speak for a Paiute woman, Seyavi, than read the testimony of a Paiute activist, Winnemucca. Winnemucca's public and textual claiming of Indian authority is as complex as Austin's and ultimately much more grounded in actual, "inside" knowledge and experience. At the same time, Winnemucca's book, like the work of the later writers and painters in question, typically urges quite complicated things in quite complicated ways, and as a result, the place, its people, and the texts themselves can seem somehow incomplete, ephemeral, fragile, and at the same time overwhelming, relentless, monumental, dazzling. Perhaps Austin understands the Southwest, and especially the desert, as more autonomous both geographically and historically than other American regions and therefore difficult to transform into, let alone to conserve in, language expecting to be treated as literary convention and national historical truth. Perhaps she believes that these regions should be nationalized precisely because of this edgy autonomy. Perhaps her argument about the Country of Lost Borders, the Indians who give it "the better word," and the woman writer who begins her literary career with the Indians and the land of little rain rests on such an idea, or ideal, of autonomy unbound. Still, though, contrasted with the cultural work of Winnemucca, Austin's interests in marketing herself as an expert in American Indian cultures look far less urgent and far less authoritative than they so strongly wish to be.

8 Cleaning out the House

Tom Outland, Dead Indians, and the First World War

"Tom Outland's Story" is a first-person narrative written by a dead man about a dead culture, or so the story says. Famously situated in between two long sections set in the narrative present of Willa Cather's *The Professor's House* (1925), Outland's retrospective story of discovery and exploitation in the Southwest pushes on both sides against the larger narrative's subtler midwestern turbulences and tales of exploitation. Hermione Lee writes, "The insertion of [Tom's] memory into the house of the Professor's thoughts makes the most startling dislocation in the whole of Cather's work" (232), but it does not do so because Cather tucks a coherent, unsplintered 75-page narrative into a coherent 180-page narrative broken into two unequal yet connected parts. More jarring than the novel's structure is the way "Tom Outland's Story" turns away from both the modern "present" and the indigenous past, casting both as marketable ruins liable to vanish into "natural history" museums and other encroaching modernizations.

Lee argues that "Outland's story . . . is a record of exploration and disclosure, loss and repossession, which could stand on its own as a metaphor for the writer's process of finding, losing, and recreating experience. So the novel provides two different, split models of writing-as-memory" (230). But Cather's sense of history, like her novelistic migrations to and from the Southwest, makes a problematic romantic claim for such writing and the emptying out that it both reports and practices; extracting, Cather seems to suggest, is integral to any literary-historical process of re-creating, even when extraction reenacts or urges cultural dispossession. Walter Benn Michaels argues, "It is because the Indian's sun was perceived as setting that he could become . . . a kind of paradigm for increasingly powerful American notions of ethnic identity and eventually for the idea of an ethnicity that could be threatened or defended, repudiated or reclaimed" (*Our America*, 38). In turning to an Indian culture not dying but dead—or at least gone—for more than six hundred years, Cather perhaps intensifies Michaels's paradigm to the extent that depatriation (of Indians) purchases a sort of repatriation (of white men whose houses are unstable and contested). For Cather, the interconnections of routes and roots—her own, her characters', and perhaps even "her" Indians'—seem somehow to be at once deferred and exploited. More powerfully still, though, her turns to the Southwest in the 1920s describe ironic intersections of things turned away from and things not named: modernism and Native America in all their complex, entangled cultural vitality. Elizabeth Ammons puts the case more strongly: "Even as Cather wrote about white women's struggles against discrimination, including those of immigrants, she ignored living Native Americans in favor of celebrating dead ones. . . . Like most privileged white women at the time, she did not use her own situation to understand the situations of people of color in the United States" ("Gender and Fiction," 280).

"Tom Outland's Story" worries the issue of Indian "relics" and remains—who "owns" them, what should be done with them—but the story itself, and its teller, ironically displace Indians as the novel's most persistent and troublesome relics. From very early on in *The Professor's House*, memories of Tom's vitality underscore his death, and consequences of his death alternately profit and discomfit St. Peter and his family. It is tempting, in fact, to see this novel as Cather's better war novel, perhaps a rethinking of the weaker *One of Ours* (1922), which was a popular success but a critical embarrassment.[1] Tom, an appropriately noble and glorious youth before the war, thinks like a brighter Theodore Roosevelt, writes like Ernest Hemingway, and insinuates his dead self into an ironic postwar narrative of disillusionment and displacement. His absence, and thus the war's long-term influence, may be, for Cather, the single most important circumstance in the book. Despite his inescapable presence-in-absentia throughout, though, Cather puts off his first-person story for approximately 165 pages; similarly, Tom when first seen alive spends his first three years with the St. Peters warding off and stalling their requests that he tell his story. The Southwest, and Mesa Verde Indian culture, therefore come into view by way of a more or less inexplicable, or at least unexplained, delayed reaction that suggests that the significance of both the Indians and the region is inseparable from Tom, determined by Tom, and ultimately not quite as important as Tom.[2] Somewhat jarring in light of the professor's own writing project, a monumental eight-volume history euphemistically titled *Spanish Adventurers in North America*, the form of Cather's narrative confers precedence to Tom in a way that cuts against the precedence Tom himself ultimately gives to the Blue Mesa and its vanished Pueblo culture.

Upon finally introducing "Tom Outland's Story," both Tom and the novel's other narrator buffer it with disclaimers and apologies. Closing Book 1 of *The Professor's House*, the third-person narrator modulates to a minor key as she finally introduces Outland's story:

> It was on one of those rainy nights, before the fire in the dining-room, that Tom at last told the story he had always kept back. It was nothing very incriminating, nothing very remarkable; a story of youthful defeat, the sort of thing a boy is sensitive about—until he grows older. (176)

This somewhat nostalgic manner of presentation both deflects and ironically underscores two painful removes from the narrative present: the occasion of Tom's first-person oral narration some ten years earlier and the fact of Tom's premature death in Flanders some five years after he tells his story. As if working in concert with the third-person voice that introduces his tale, Tom opens by diminishing the burden of his memory: "The thing that side-tracked me and made me so late coming to college was a somewhat unusual accident, or string of accidents" (179). Clearly the abrupt shift in time, place, and person makes for a narrative tour de force all the more impressive for its being so downplayed and cushioned. But conversely, the connection between Books 1 and 2 of the novel is made quite clear in that very cushioning, taking the nebulous form of an attitude both narrators share. At the same time, catastrophic historical "accidents"—the destruction and disappearance of the cliff city's inhabitants, the cataclysmic world war—bracket this recent Southwest and serve as cultural analogues to more specific, personal disruptions and losses: Tom's quarrel with Roddy Blake, the professor's struggles with his advancing age and new house, Tom's death. So the return to Tom's past as it is most powerfully recaptured—by his story—links that past to disruptions in cultural history and narrative form and in so doing underscores the process by which vitality swiftly fades from memory and falls into relic.

Throughout the novel, St. Peter acts as the custodian of Tom's memory, keeping alive both the image of his gifted friend and the memories that form and sustain the oral narrative Tom tells. Immediately after the close of "Tom Outland's Story," though, the third-person narrator sums up the professor's overarching sense that for him, too, history records not certainties but accidents: "Tom Outland had been a stroke of chance he couldn't possibly have imagined; his strange coming, his strange story, his devotion, his early death and posthumous fame—it was all fantastic" (257). In these words, the hint of self-promotion as well as the sense of Tom as fantasy, accident, or modernist found object broaches once again the question of possession. Because it was told orally, it cannot "now" in the narrative present be retold verbatim as Tom Outland's story; because it engineers the "startling dislocation" inside Cather's narrative, it recedes further away from the tight control Tom exercised over it. So who "owns" Tom? Cather invites readers to reject the racialized "foreigner" Louie Marcellus and his wife, Rosamond's, "vulgar" profiteering off of Tom's patent, but are Professor St. Peter and for that matter Willa Cather any less implicated?[3] St. Peter intends to edit Tom's diary for publication; Cather already has worked up the boy's larger narrative. The professor, acting as a sort of literary executor–critic, is well along in the process of interpreting and thus reshaping a diary that now sounds like a Hemingway original:

> To St. Peter this plain account was almost beautiful, because of the stupidities it avoided and the things it did not say. If words had cost money, Tom couldn't have used them more sparingly. The adjectives were purely

descriptive, relating to form and colour, and were used to present the objects under consideration, not the young explorer's emotions. (262)

With characteristically introspective expressions of his affection for Tom and with controlled admiration for the dead man's frugal prose style ("this plain account was *almost* beautiful"), the professor will nonetheless make that account's careful ransacking of the cliff city available as a commodity. Though St. Peter resists and at times deplores the way his daughter and her husband transform Outland's name and legacy into extremely conspicuous consumption, and though Tom at one point buried his diary inside a cliff dwelling, claiming that a return to the journal's factual account "would have been going backward" (252), the professor does not finally prevent it from undergoing a commercial process similar to the one the Indian relics themselves, much to Tom's eventual regret, underwent. As an ironic result, "his" story about relics changing hands will also change hands, moving from the domestic house to the marketplace.

In other words, the important fact about "Tom Outland's Story" is not that it belongs to and helps illuminate the all-wonderful Tom Outland. Rather, it opens discussion of the cultural processes that inhabit and surround "Tom Outland's Story" every step of the way while also pressing outside the covers of *The Professor's House*. Outland as both southwestern place and professorial, narrative memory is characterized by extraction—removal or emptying out of Indian "artifacts" as well as transformations of friendships into losses—and possession, which throughout the novel involves jealous guardings of the spaces between private domains and public sectors, in addition to repeated failures to prevent appropriation and depatriation of American Indian remains. Yet the related processes of selling the relics, emptying the mesa of artifacts, and losing his companions (Roddy Blake and Henry Atkins) enable Tom ultimately to purchase what he sees as a spiritual "possession" of Mesa Verde.

By his own admission, Tom never really finds the right key in speaking of the cliff city, in translating its silence and stillness into articulate speech:

> I wish I could tell you what I saw there, just *as* I saw it, on that first morning, through a veil of lightly falling snow. . . . I saw a little city of stone, asleep. It was as still as sculpture—and something like that. It all hung together, seemed to have a kind of composition. . . . [The round tower] was beautifully proportioned. . . . The tower was the fine thing that held all the jumble of houses together and made them mean something. (201)

A little later, he reiterates, "I can't describe it. It was more like sculpture than anything else" (202). He sees the cliff city as a coherent, cohesive, aesthetic, built structure; somebody made it and made it "mean something." As Lee and a host of others have noted, "The cliff-city, Tom's find, is an art-work waiting for readers." It is "[v]ery like Keats's Grecian urn" (245) and, particularly when viewed as a composition, it takes its place in the larger, classicizing pattern Cather develops throughout the book. Lee argues that Father Duchene's interpretation of the cliff city "presents the culture as the American classical age" and elaborates on the point as follows:

> Tom reads his Virgil on the mesa, and, in his memory, superimposes the scenes from the *Aeneid* onto the cliff-city. . . . The book is full of illustrations of this history. Tom reads his *Caesar* while he is minding cattle; when he walks into the Professor's garden, he starts to recite Aeneas's account of the sack of Troy to prove his knowledge of Latin. . . . St. Peter's concealed first name, Napoleon, is derived from the great-great-grandfather who "came out to the Canadian wilderness to forget the chagrin of his Emperor's defeat." (247–248)

On the one hand, this is a handy, available paradigm, wrapping the romantic sensation of a tragic or at least poignantly lifeless immortality around the theory of an ancient global classicism surging restlessly westward. On the other hand, Tom's perceptions of fine pueblo compositions by ancient indigenous craftspeople are darkly complicated by the visible evidence of loss, death, destruction, and extinction. One mummy's "mouth was open as if she were screaming, and her face, through all those years, had kept a look of terrible agony" (Cather, 214). Lee suggests that Cather "provides a paradigm for a history of the world seen as a succession of tribal conflicts" (247), but this global paradigm of history as recurring conquest by tribal imperialists points up the fragility and emptiness as well as the beauty discoverable in what a culture leaves behind. Cultural invention and destruction, composition and decomposition, autonomy and imperialist takeover all tangle together.

As a result, Tom Outland stumbles upon much more than a simple Indian ruin, and his story's mixture of firsthand experience and reflective memory, of foresight and hindsight, indeed, of vision and blindness, works toward reconstructing the process through which he first complicates then simplifies and spiritualizes the mesa and its absent Indian presence. From almost the beginning, the situation exerts a considerable amount of pressure on Tom. He first responds to the cliff city not only by noting how difficult it is to describe his first sighting in words but also by seriously entertaining the possibility of healthy silence: "As I stood looking up at it, I wondered whether I ought to tell even Blake about it." The wisest course may be to "keep that secret as the mesa had kept it" (202). Of course he does share his Christmas Eve find with Roddy and Henry; he simply cannot contain himself. Besides, Roddy seems sympathetic to Tom's initial concerns. As Tom recalls, "We didn't want to make our discovery any more public than necessary. We were reluctant to expose those silent and beautiful places to vulgar curiosity" (205). By this point in Tom's narrative, though, these memories of early caution and respect themselves begin to be displaced and replaced; Tom as storyteller on a rainy midwestern summer night in 1910 obviously knows all too well how this 1905 expedition into Mesa Verde turns out. Of course he rarely jumps ahead of himself to the extent that he gives away the story; having learned his lesson about giving things away, he guards the narrative like he never guarded the relics, storing it up for years before telling it and then telling it in a carefully measured step-by-step manner. But Cather closely juxtaposes his second statement about circumspection ("We went about softly, tried not to disturb anything—even the silence" [208]) with various narrative hints to the contrary: "Beside this spring stood some of the most beautifully shaped water jars we ever found—I gave Mrs. St. Peter one of them" (209). And their second excursion into the cliff city persuades them to "fix" the "road" up the mesa, build a cabin on the mesa top, and begin "what we called excavating" (211). "We numbered each specimen," Tom reports, and they removed the "smaller articles" from their resting places (212); at the end of each day he would write up his careful factual accounts in what St. Peter later cherishes as his friend's diary. As Susan J. Rosowski asserts, "a troubling undercurrent of human values betrayed runs through the story" Outland tells (133).[4]

Tom's modulation from "silent and beautiful places" to "specimen" makes clear sense within the confines of his narrative and has often figured in the critical responses to *The Professor's House*; less visible to most critics, however, is the broader ideological impetus of Cather's narrative. For all her awareness of the relentless push of cultural imperialism, she takes part in the colonial act of removing Indian cultural "relics," including bodies, from the places where they are found. A recognizably modernist strain of appropriation and commodification appears here, in the midst of what is ostensibly an antimodernist turn to a less "corrupt" native aesthetic and a less "contaminated" American space.[5] The pueblo artifacts must belong to someone, Cather seems to suggest; they must be recorded somewhere and stored someplace, preferably in the hands of a living culture able and willing to exploit them instead of leaving them undisturbed or at least less disturbed.

Such issues lead directly to the Belgian priest, Latinist, and amateur archaeologist, Father Duchene. Tom's teacher and adviser, Duchene has been widely and generously praised by a number of Cather critics and taken to task by remarkably few.[6] E. K. Brown admires "the sensitive and civilized Belgian priest" (245). Lee respects and draws on "Father Duchene's authoritative commentary" (246), seeing it as a "formal, reasoned, elegiac celebration of their civilization" (247). Kathleen Wheeler likes his "insight" (38). Cather presents his credentials: "Father Duchene had been among the Indians nearly twenty years then, he had seventeen Indian pueblos in his parish, and he spoke several Indian dialects" (218). Delivering himself of his findings, he ventures a handful of deductions, mostly about the functions of various pueblo structures; in attempting to retrieve the native culture as a living whole, however, he reveals more about himself than he does about the Indians. An imaginative and to some extent a sympathetic character, Duchene nonetheless exemplifies the difficulties involved in even a well-intentioned effort to recover and describe an indigenous American cultural inheritance. First, in attempting to praise the civilization of the dead pueblo people, he condescends to some of the living tribes he (presumably) encounters in New Mexico: "They had an appreciation of comfort, and went even further than that. Their life, compared to that of our roving Navajos, must have been quite complex" (219). Moreover, the relative complexity of this particular Indian pueblo proves very difficult to read. Limited to speculation colored by hindsight, Duchene tries to organize and make sense of a cultural encounter that really only moves in one direction:

> "You must go to the Director of the Smithsonian Institution," he said. "He will send us an archaeologist who will interpret all that is obscure to us. He will revive this civilization in a scholarly work. It may be that you will have thrown light on some important points in the history of your country." (222)

The working assumption here is that America should be the beneficiary of an assimilation that is primarily textual. Overseeing this process of cultural revival, the federal government transforms a dead Indian civilization into a self-illuminating text and in the process overlooks more recent official acts of Indian removal and forced assimilation. However well intentioned, the priest still sanctions versions of removal (excavation) and assimilation (nationalistic archaeological interpretations); though hardly an imperialist, his point of view reflects and reinscribes a more or less tacit assumption of American technological and all-around cultural superiority.

Along these lines, the priest expresses functionalist astonishment not that the cliff city is beautiful but that it was built by Indians: "There is unquestionably a distinct feeling for design in what you call the Cliff City. Buildings are not grouped like that by pure accident, though convenience probably had much to do with it" (219). The subtext here implies that at best, the cliff city was flung up by a sort of happy intuition; the architect is Nature, not native, and the architecture follows no significant cultural form.[7] (Recent critics such as Wheeler comply fully with such a reading; Wheeler cannot get beyond the idea that the cliff dwellings are "nature.")[8] Furthermore, Father Duchene familiarly confers ownership of the pueblo and its dead inhabitants to Tom and Roddy, speaking of "your tribe" (220) and "[y]our people" (221). This ascription of possession works as low-impact dramatic irony, but it is also of a piece with Duchene's easy general assumption that the mesa is theirs to manage and excavate. Additionally, a tricky Darwinian logic troubles his worldview. Again measuring progress by hindsight, judging the achievements and status of a particular people at a particular time on the basis of things they could not yet know or do, the priest invents a narrative in which admirable and heroic Indians nonetheless come from a "lower" condition and then overreach themselves. On both ends of their history, as Duchene constructs it, there is something lacking:

> I see them here, isolated, cut off from other tribes, working out their destiny, making their mesa more and more worthy to be a home for man, purifying life by religious ceremonies and observances, caring respectfully for their dead, protecting the children, doubtless entertaining some

feelings of affection and sentiment for this stronghold where they were at once so safe and so comfortable, where they had practically overcome the worst hardships that primitive man had to fear. They were, perhaps, too far advanced for their time and environment. (220–221)

Unfamiliarity with sacred geography and architecture forgives Duchene his speculations about the Indians' qualified and altogether rather Anglicized "feelings of affection and sentiment" for their home. More importantly, however, the conclusion of the passage both applies the at-best anachronistic word "primitive" to the pueblos and suggests that their builders and inhabitants were dislocated in time and place. And yet the priest demonstrates empathy, too; in the long excerpt quoted above, his more dubious assumptions combine with a genuine interest in the culture of the pueblo Indians. He certainly seems more sympathetic and knowledgeable than, for example, the high-ranking bureaucrats Tom petitions in Washington.

However, Father Duchene's conjectures about the peoples' fate again rely on a simplistic "good Indian"–"bad Indian" opposition:

They were probably wiped out, utterly exterminated, by some roving Indian tribe without culture or domestic virtues, some horde that fell upon them in their summer camp and destroyed them for their hides and clothing and weapons, or from mere love of slaughter. I feel sure that these brutal invaders never even learned of the existence of [the cliff city], honeycombed with habitations. If they had come here, they would have destroyed. They killed and went their way. (221)

Of course this scenario makes good novelistic sense. As David Harrell points out, Duchene's is one of several potentially plausible explanations, any of which could have been supported by scientific and historical evidence:

[B]ut the important point is that [Cather] chose this explanation for the disappearance of the cliff dwellers over others that were also advanced by the people she read or met: simple migration, which would have been too mundane; and a prolonged siege by enemies, which would have been too threatening to the sanctity of the mesa. Cather chose instead to sacrifice the cliff dwellers but to leave the mesa inviolate so that, when Tom Outland finds it, it remains . . . a holy place where ideals of all kinds— natural, physical, intellectual, and spiritual—can flourish and can inspire a receptive and harmonious soul. (114–115)

The problem with Duchene here is not that he must conjecture in accordance with Cather's artistic decisions but rather that he invents cartoon Indians virtuous or vicious to the extent that they cooperate with social evolutionist notions of progress. Also, the mesa does not seem particularly "holy" to the holy man—perhaps because in its inviolate state it awaits and soon experiences the violations of excavation and, a little later, commercial transactions. Unransacked, it awaits the romantically colored, construed, and justified ransacking set in motion by Roddy Blake and Tom Outland.

Duchene's concluding strokes participate in a recognizable variant of Frederick Jackson Turner's mischievous but influential frontier thesis:

> Wherever humanity has made that hardest of all starts and lifted itself out of mere brutality, is a sacred spot. Your people were cut off here without the influence of example or emulation, with no incentive but some natural yearning for order and security. They built themselves into this mesa and humanized it. (221)

Nothing about the cliff city invites this "lifted itself out of mere brutality" interpretation, with its clear assumption that any Native American ancestry reaches straight (and not very far) back to a state of "mere brutality." Instead of assuming complex, adaptable cultural processes, stories, and beliefs, the priest gives the distinct impression that while once these Indians were mere brutes, ungraced by (white, Christian, Euro-American) "example or emulation," the cliff city demonstrates that they evolved to roughly the condition of mammals with opposable thumbs, directed not by technological sophistication and cultural intelligence but by "some natural yearning" for a warm and cozy nest. Finally, the priest's racist proclivities come together with a revealing sexism when he speculates as to why the female mummy—Tom and Roddy name her "Mother Eve"—was screaming. Recall that the two men found that "there was a great wound in her side, the ribs stuck out through the dried flesh. Her mouth was open as if she were screaming, and her face, through all those years, had kept a look of terrible agony" (214). Duchene has a ready answer:

> "I seem to smell," he said slyly, "a personal tragedy. Perhaps when the tribe went down to the summer camp, our lady was sick and would not go. Perhaps her husband thought it worth while to return unannounced from the farms some night, and found her in improper company. The young man may have escaped. In primitive society the husband is allowed to punish an unfaithful wife with death." (223)

In this short and unpleasant speculation, the priest combines cheap domestic melodrama and a sort of men's night out on the mesa to produce a fictional narrative that efficiently blames the woman's agony on the woman. Beyond the facts that his "in primitive society" generalization is untrue as stated and that his fussy "in improper company" applies Victorian middle-class morality to ancient pueblo peoples, the whole invention of this adultery story looks altogether egregious. Is Cather exposing a (nonnative) cultural tendency whereby women who come to grief are then blamed for grieving? As usual with Cather, it is hard to say for sure yet unlikely that she would let a literary sketch double as a political or cultural critique. Still, though the image of "Mother Eve" is horrifying, the male response to her looks at least as ugly. "Smelling" this ambiguous "personal tragedy" (is it the cuckolded man's or the "unfaithful" wife's?), Duchene once again displays an unreflective disrespect for what is to him the rank odor of a dead woman and a dead culture.

"He didn't believe her death could throw any light on the destruction of her people" (223), mainly because he demonstrates an unwillingness and inability to imagine that it might. There is no place for "Mother Eve" in *The Professor's House;* when her twentieth-century dispossessors drop her over the side of the cliff and "lose" her, they in effect extravagantly reenact rather than question the disappearance of the Indian, more specifically the disappearance of the maternal Indian woman who is always already dead.[9]

Tom Outland tells his story some five years after the facts and spends more than three of those years steadfastly resisting the St. Peters, who just as persistently tempt him to stop brooding and start narrating, and yet the story itself when finally told evinces remarkably little tension between firsthand experiences and intervening reflections. Like Duchene, Outland displays an ease of presentation that sometimes suggests the limits or constraints that underlie his more highly and frequently touted virtues. Tom, in other words, behaves as though his formative past remains vividly, freshly present despite himself, as if he both does and does not reflect on that past. Not given to telling his auditors what things mean either to him or to them, Tom interrupts himself but sparingly even when returning to his deepest regrets, such as his terminal quarrel with Roddy Blake. The fullest statement of his feelings is this assemblage of four terse (and still quite Hemingwayesque) sentences: "But the older I grow, the more I understand what it was I did that night on the mesa. Anyone who requites faith and friendship as I did, will have to pay for it. I'm not very sanguine about good fortune for myself. I'll be called to account when I least expect it" (253). His vague fatalism informs the story through and through, in all of its laconic coolness about what happens to him, as for example when he chaperones the drunk Blake home after Blake has cleaned up in a poker game at Pardee, New Mexico:

> I struck a match and lit a candle. The bed took up half the room; on the dresser was a grip with his clean clothes in it, just as he'd brought it in from his run. I took out the clothes and began picking up the money; got the bills out of his hat, emptied his pockets, and collected the coins that lay in the hollow of the bed about his hips, and put it all into the grip. Then I blew out the light and sat down to listen. I trusted all the boys who were at the Ruby Light [saloon] that night, except Barney Shea. He might try to pull something off on a stranger, down in Mexican town. We had a quiet night, however, and a cold one. I found Blake's winter overcoat hanging on the wall and wrapped up in it. (182–183)

This night marks the beginning of their intimate friendship, but Tom doesn't quite say so; instead, all the familiar details, such as wrapping himself in the other man's winter coat, suggest in physical gestures all that Tom means to express about their soon-to-flourish emotional attachment. Unlike the explicit speculation about "Mother Eve's" adulterous heterosexual intimacies, the homoerotic inflections of Tom's relationship with Roddy remain implicit. In his best Hemingway manner, Tom works in short declarative sentences, in a journalistic plain style concerned with the seeming facts of the matter, the important things that happen and, when relevant, the things that importantly don't. Noticeably distinct from the book's other narrator, Tom relies primarily on nouns and verbs as he evokes the romantic possibilities of his experiences to the extent that he suppresses Romantic expostulation, reflection, and ornamentation. In fact, when (in his most sublime moments) the plain style fails him, Tom turns to expressions of his inability to express himself. And each time he says "I can't describe it," he calls attention to a narrative style unself-conscious except for the times it breaks down and is unable to perform with its usual smooth detachment. "Happiness," this voice asserts, "is something one can't explain. You must take my word for it. Troubles enough came afterward, but there was that summer, high and blue, a life in itself" (253). According to the code this terse philosophy sets down, personal inability to explain something translates into a recognizable and acceptable general condition, the power of one's word nonetheless remains an article of faith, and above all, no matter how bad one's troubles get, one holds on to the "high and blue" yet explicitly bounded past.

The Professor's House somewhat paradoxically stresses Tom's vital importance to Professor St. Peter and to the novel at the same time it flattens his voice and thus his character. Of course, Tom is dead throughout the book, and the flatness of his presence may be a polite way of reinforcing his stubbornly immutable absence, his ghostliness. But whatever the explanation, Tom, like the pueblo Indians, does not participate of his own accord in the life of the novel's narrative present. While St. Peter regrets the things left unsaid and undone by Tom's early death, and while Tom regrets pretty much the reverse when thinking of Roddy, the plain style of "Tom Outland's Story" leaves various significant things unremarked (or, as with the interpretation of "Mother Eve," overremarked). For instance, no one in the text makes any move whatsoever toward evaluating Father Duchene's conclusions, so that while they are not specifically celebrated, neither are they contested. Tom only explains why Duchene came up to the mesa and informs his listeners that he wrote the priest's conclusions down. These narrative spaces of uncertain provenance and spotty visibility are obviously complicated: are they more or less unmediated spaces that simply say what they mean and show, both directly and implicitly, who characters are? Or are they instead oblique reflections of Cather? Is the Indian problem Duchene's, or is it hers?

Even when phrased in terms more complex than these either/or options, the basic question remains unanswerable, though the critical consensus in favor of biographically informed readings points toward the author's mirrored implication in her narratives (see for example O'Brien, 403–420). In reaching a spiritual possession of the mesa after losing four thousand dollars' worth of Indian relics, Tom Outland ends up regretting the loss of his friendship with Roddy Blake more than the loss and commodification of pueblo pottery, clothing, tools, and other material remains, including a human body. In finding (in 1912, before the writing of *O Pioneers!*) an artistic inspiration in the Southwest after several frustrating years of derivative publications, Willa Cather ends up mourning not Tom Outland specifically but what Tom represents, standing as he does with one foot on top of an ancient indigenous Mesa Verde civilization and the other six feet under Flanders Field. The dislocation, as Cather understands it, is intolerable. In the Southwest of *The Professor's House,* a whole series of related, significant losses leads to a sort of complacency, stasis, or sublimation against that very modern and very crushing significance. Tom's final quarrel with Roddy figures this entrapment well; for all the painful hashing out of what the Indian relics mean to whom and who "owns" and deserves them, the argument is, as they both fully realize, pointless and fruitless. Both men's misreadings of the other have already done their work, the relics are already gone, and neither the material objects nor the abstract ideals are coming back.

Indeed, the novel's major key may very well be discussion after the fact. Tom's postmortem quarrel with Roddy over now-lost relics emanates outward to wider concentric circles: Tom recounts that quarrel with the knowledge that it loses him Roddy; St. Peter remembers "Tom Outland's Story" after the war that cost him Tom, and in the context of the impending loss of his old house, the deepening loss of his own youth, and the full expectation that he himself will be dead in a matter of months; Cather brackets the novel with two great cultural catastrophes, the extinction of the Mesa Verde pueblo and the Great War, and reflects on the consequences of both in relation to each other. Tom, Roddy, the mesa relics, the professor's house, the near past, the pueblo Indians, time itself—"Time, bearing away the youth who was struggling to snatch his palm" (260)—all are going or gone. And all throughout, chance, accidents, and misunderstandings quietly menace all of the book's narrators and authors as they struggle to come to terms with time's spaces and the inescapable after-the-fact quality of personal, historical, and cultural retrospection. Here circulates and broods the "moral melancholy" Michael Warner identifies as "the distinctive note of her mature style" (85). Of course the widest concentric circle in the book involves the vast, open spaces of deserts and centuries, but the various overseas voyages—the relics' exportation through Mexico to Germany, the numerous trips members of the St. Peter family make to Europe, Tom's final one-way voyage out across the Atlantic—evoke an international context no less active and influential for being positioned, more often than not, offstage or outside the canvas's frame.[10] As Joseph R. Urgo argues, "American culture, as examined through Cather's texts, is rooted in the vigilant maintenance of unsettled lives, impermanent connections, and continuous movements in space and time" (15). Perhaps especially in *The Professor's House,* it "is difficult . . . to be at home in a Catherian America" (16).

By way of a compact professorial flashback late in the novel, Cather attempts to chart the historical dimensions and dislocations of postwar America. Indians are, in this flashback, deeply removed and only returned to after a complicated series of travels; the passage takes what may very well be the most circuitous "Indian detour" in southwestern American literature. As the professor works his way through the years and the volumes of his *Spanish Adventurers in North America*, he travels back in time with Tom Outland to the Southwest. Beginning with "the copy of Fray Garces' [eighteenth-century] manuscript that the Professor had made from the original in Spain" (259), the two men retrace the priest's New World steps. "Tom could take a sentence from Garces' diary and find the exact spot at which the missionary crossed the Rio Colorado on a certain Sunday in 1775" (259); here, the relationship between text and place is perfectly secure. Then they go further back in time while also returning to Tom's much more recent past:

> It was on that trip that they went to Tom's Blue Mesa, climbed the ladder of spliced pine-trees to the Cliff City, and up to the Eagle's Nest. There they took Tom's diary from the stone cupboard where he had sealed it up years ago, before he set out for Washington on his fruitless errand. (259)

Now the pueblo is explicitly marked as "Tom's Blue Mesa," replete with physical and nominal signs that recall and reaffirm his habitation and possession. Moreover, Cather follows a textual trail from the copy of Garces's diary to the recovery and use of Tom's to the Book 3 broodings that in deeply self-reflective ways constitute the professor's most significant sense of himself as an actor in as well as an interpreter of history:

> The next summer Tom went with the Professor to Old Mexico. They had planned a third summer together, in Paris, but it never came off. Outland was delayed by the formalities of securing his patent, and then came August, 1914. . . .
> To this day St. Peter regretted that he had never got that vacation in Paris with Tom Outland. He had wanted to revisit certain spots with him . . . to stand with him before the monument to Delacroix and watch the sun gleam on the bronze figures—Time, bearing away the youth who was struggling to snatch his palm—or was it to lay a palm? Not that it mattered. It might have mattered to Tom, had not chance, in one great catastrophe, swept away all youth and all palms, and almost Time itself. (259–260)

In fact, they never do "arrive" at or return to the Pueblo Indians. This intricate, complex web of pasts and presents, returns and regrets, places and countries and uprootings, memories and monuments, includes the broad spatial and temporal canvas of the Southwest. No longer quite the same topography Euro-Americans perceived before, a place isolated and alienated from world and country and all but a few hardy (and more often than not "savage") people, the Southwest in Cather's American 1920s nonetheless represents, despite its great aesthetic power, a seemingly inescapable sense of overwhelming, Euro-American loss.

Though the cliff city nestled deep inside Blue Mesa serves as a model for the way the whole second book tucks the inset Southwest inside a "larger" form and story, it is ultimately much more and much less than a delicate artistic structure. Though the Great War oppositely remains at arm's length, "outset" and never directly treated, the Southwest of *The Professor's House* is subtly closed in on all novelistic sides by a narrative present quietly yet profoundly haunted and dislocated by that world war. Prewar international relations, including historiographical syntheses such as St. Peter's, return in both ironic and tragic guises to this postwar world of new magnitudes and new enormities. The Southwest and especially the pueblo Tom rediscovers seem at first blush a turn away from the modern world. But as it turns out even before hostilities open, the mesa is no mere refuge, no safe unspoiled haven from the twentieth century. Just as the pueblo is enclosed by the Blue Mesa facing the colonial expanses of the modern world on all sides, the whole novel encloses characters and things and at the same time touches and fearfully, frighteningly registers a very modernist preoccupation with the modern presences—and ghostly war-produced relics and absences—it can neither let in nor let go. As a result of this process, Tom Outland becomes the faint and fainter traces of more and less ephemeral narratives: his diary, his remembered oral tale, his place inside the more and less reliable memories of those who knew him. "You know," St. Peter's son-in-law Scott McGregor remarks to him, "Tom isn't very real to me any more. Sometimes I think he was just a—a glittering idea" (111). In this ephemeral manifestation, Tom resembles no one so much as Jay Gatsby. As Laura Winters has pointed out, Tom, like Jay Gatsby, may be "the prototypical American" (45); I would add that this prototype hinges on both characters'—and both narratives'—fraught negotiations with American history. The pueblo Indians' "one great catastrophe," the catastrophic devastation of twentieth-century global warfare, the silently screaming mummy, the transfer of relics from the home of the dead southwestern culture to Germany just a few years before the war: in the disconnections between cultures, Cather paradoxically and very subtly suggests profound and prototypical cultural dislocation. The silence of the pueblos, the misreadings those silences make possible, the commodification and exportation of indigenous materials—all of these acts and circumstances together mean something; all of these have profound consequences. All in all, Outland comes to seem a very modern place and a disturbingly modern condition.

9 Krazy Kat I

Contexts and Crossings

In *Krazy Kat* (1913–1944), George Herriman approaches, enters, and represents the Southwest in ways that suggest a moving beyond the raw ahistorical brutality of Frank Norris, the colonial self-promotions of Mary Austin, and the carefully controlled, racialized detachment of Willa Cather. Norris, Austin, and Cather are clearly very interested in the Southwest; Cather in particular links her visits there to her own development as a woman writer. But Herriman is much more multiculturally fluent than his more canonical EuroAmerican literary counterparts. He was not an American Indian, but his birth certificate lists him as "colored"—possibly Creole, possibly African American—and his mixed-blood straddling of ethnicities is crucial to an understanding of his work (McDonnell, O'Connell, and de Havenon, 30).[1] Even so, critics variously describe *Krazy Kat* as modernist, Victorian, Chaplinesque, surreal, or, conversely, "a self-contained aesthetic universe largely impervious to history" (Orvell, 131)—everything, it seems, but ethnically inflected. Some of Herriman's hybrid styles and arrangements, such as his injections of modernist techniques into comic-strip art, were noticed and praised as early as the 1920s; critics have been very interested in how he blurs the class boundaries between, for example, "high" and "low" art. But they have been significantly less interested in his blurrings of racial and gender boundaries. They tend to overlook the important interactions between *Krazy Kat* and Navajo culture, for example, through which Herriman unprogrammatically moves away from his contemporaries' colonialism toward a more postcolonial paradigm of cultural exchange.

Before investigating these particular interactions in detail, though, this chapter discusses various other crossings and contexts that inform the strip. For most of *Krazy Kat*'s thirty-one years, Herriman moved the same three main characters through the same basic narrative, daily and Sunday. Yet it is also true that his repetitions of this narrative—a love triangle involving a male police dog, a male mouse, and a deliberately ungendered "kat"—gave him almost unlimited room for improvisation. Moreover, the southwestern topographies of *Krazy Kat* work the same way; lithic and monumental, they are also exceptionally fluid and mobile, so much so that even the most recognizable rock formations nonetheless often vanish, appear, or change shapes suddenly from panel to panel. At other moments, these structures appear to be more "artificial" than "natural," more "imported" than "indigenous"; as their contours change, their identities seem to change as well. Further still, as the characters circulate around, across, and through this simultaneously stabilized and destabilized narrative space, Herriman presents his main character, Krazy Kat, as an androgynous figure: "that Kat can't be a he or a she. The Kat's spirit—a pixie—free to butt into anything. Don't you think so?" (McDonnell, O'Connell, and de Havenon, 54). He thus places other characters, and readers, in the interesting position of deciding whether, or how, to impose gender identity on a character so "free" and so capable of disrupting things. (Critical convention thus far has been to refer to Krazy Kat as female, "[f]or the sake of consistency," as Miles Orvell explains [132]. However, I will refer to the Kat as "he" to call attention to other consistencies and other possibilities, including the underemphasized homoerotic implications of the love triangle.) All in all, Herriman's southwestern dispositions publicize a multicultural, multispecies, multidirectional Southwest that is highly fluid and extremely ambiguous rather than colonially disciplined. He is willing not only to cross and recross a variety of geographical, racial, sexual, and gender boundaries but also to place these migratory movements into national circulation, diffusing and connecting this extraordinarily mobile Southwest to readers nationwide.

↙

Nearly fifty years after Herriman's death, cultural critic and art historian Adam Gopnik takes one of only a few long views of *Krazy Kat:* "Herriman has been for so long the single okay figure among comic-strip artists—the figure, like Chaplin or Duke Ellington in their realms, whose apparent atypicality made him acceptable—that comic-strip historians [c. 1990] are occasionally inclined to debunk him" (Varnedoe and Gopnik, 168). As E. E. Cummings more graphically puts it in a 1946 essay, "[R]ecelebrating Krazy would be like teaching penguins to fly." Of course, Cummings immediately adds, "Penguins (as a lot of people don't realize) do fly—not through the sea of the sky but through the sky of the sea—and my present ambition is merely . . . to show how their flying affects every non-penguin" (323). He also pays affectionate tribute to his predecessor Gilbert Seldes, whose pioneering 1924 book, *The Seven Lively Arts,* places *Krazy Kat* at the very heights of both popular culture and "high" modernism: "*Krazy Kat,* the daily comic strip of George Herriman is, to me, the most amusing and fantastic and satisfactory work of art produced in America today" (Seldes, *Seven Lively Arts,* 231).

Still, Seldes is then compelled to qualify, invert, or otherwise scramble his opening remark:

> It happens that in America irony and fantasy are practiced in the major
> arts by only one or two men, producing high-class trash; and Mr. Herri-

man, working in a despised medium, without an atom of pretentious-
ness, is day after day producing something essentially fine. It is the result
of a naive sensibility rather like that of the *douanier* Rousseau; it does
not lack intelligence, because it is a thought-out, a constructed piece of
work. In the second order of the world's art it is superbly first rate—and
a delight! (*Seven Lively Arts*, 231)

These qualifications, cautions, and playful reversals definitely recognize and
celebrate Herriman, but they also betray uncertainty about what to do with
him, where to put him, how to position and contextualize his impressive,
"constructed," yet assuredly "naive" work. Even Gopnik, who of these three
critics most demonstratively resists giving an easy response to this matter, returns to bounded genres and hierarchical measurements: "[I]n his own
small realm, Herriman played a crucial part in this century's emancipation of
the tradition of the sublime landscape from the decorum of high seriousness"
(Varnedoe and Gopnik, 168). To these critics, ultimately, *Krazy Kat* belongs
not in the Southwest (where it is so powerfully and imaginatively set), not in
the city (where it was first forged and where it returns, in syndication, bearing clear evidence of its urban origins), and not in the complicated crossings
and blendings that make up an increasingly multicultural twentieth-century
American mass culture. Instead, they put *Krazy Kat* in a "despised medium,"
a "small realm"—Robert Warshow writes, not disdainfully, of its "complete
disregard of the standards of respectable art" (quoted in Orvell, 131)—and
then forgive it this unrespectable "realm" or "medium." They keep it, finally
and for whatever critical motives, inside the spatially, temporally, and generi-
cally constricted panels and borders of disposable newspapers and comic-strip
history. They compare it to jazz, cubism, and Chaplin, but ultimately, they
suggest that the strip really belongs in the more limited, sentimentalized context of comic-strip history, grouped with "Old Cunning Stagers: Long-Lived
Stars of the Comic Strip's Second Two Decades, 1916–1936," for instance, or
"The Innocents: The First Generation of Comics."[2]

The problem with this categorical de-positioning of Herriman's work is
simply that *Krazy Kat* breaks free from and reinvents the categories as it
makes active, unpredictable contact with all sorts of cultural processes,
products, and experiences. Gopnik, to his credit, suggests a number of intriguing possibilities for recontextualizing the strip when he persuasively places
Herriman among an international set of modern painters—including one,
Joan Miró, who is rarely associated with *Krazy Kat*. Orvell similarly describes
the strip as cosmopolitan, arguing that it "adapts a surrealistic vocabulary to
the cubistic angular style and layout of the cartoon page" (132); Ronald Paulson in three pages links it variously to James Joyce, the Marx Brothers, Marcel
Duchamp, Dada, Robert Rauschenberg, Philip Guston, Pablo Picasso, Willem
de Kooning, the surrealists, Charlie Chaplin, and Buster Keaton (113–115).
But this internationalizing, combined with the retrograde positioning of the
strip in comic-book history, leads most critics to downplay its local, cross-

cultural, southwestern American contexts, particularly but not exclusively the Navajo contexts. This chapter seeks to reconstruct some of Herriman's local travels in the hope of restoring his work to its original places, not only the Southwest but also the fundamentally ephemeral and disposable medium of the newspaper. And, although beyond this chapter's scope, such a reading can also redirect discussions of how newspapers intersect with modernism, making and circulating news and, in cubist paintings and collages as well as in modernist films like *Citizen Kane* (1941), taking on further complex meanings as both metaphors for and ironic commentaries on the "new" as idea and image.

That modernist painters and collagists work with newspaper fragments is well known; that Herriman also reimagines newspapers as changing, unpredictable collages of verbal and visual images and narratives is less frequently discussed. In some fundamental ways, newspaper publishers themselves construct and market juxtapositions that they do not directly explain or explore. Theoretically, the production and reproduction of a daily newspaper resembles in some important ways the production and reproduction of modern art, particularly collages; both collages and newspapers tend both to suppress and to exploit the internal logic of their highly selective arrangements. In addition, readers can read newspapers selectively and creatively, at different speeds, in different contexts, and with different emphases from day to day. Alan Trachtenberg observes further that this reading experience provides "a private opening to a world identical to that of one's companion on a streetcar, a companion likely to remain as distant, remote, and strange as the day's 'news' comes to seem familiar, personal, and real" (*Incorporation*, 125). While each day's newspaper is "a replica of hundreds of thousands of others," its very familiarity, combined with its built-in disposability, estranges its readers: "the physical form itself of the familiar, the personal, the unique, made the represented experience seem unreal" (Trachtenberg, *Incorporation*, 125). Potentially, then, newspapers can be as defamiliarizing as collages or as Armory Show paintings—or more so, in that the papers appear to be deceptively familiar, deceptively material texts: "Assuming separation [of information and experience] in the very act of seeming to dissolve it, in their daily recurrence the newspapers expressed concretely this estrangement of a consciousness no longer capable of free intimacy with its own material life" (Trachtenberg, *Incorporation*, 125).[3]

The point is that *Krazy Kat* strips should not be read, critically or otherwise, at the same speed always, and they should not be extracted from their immediate contexts or from the cultural process Trachtenberg articulates. In other words, one way of reading *Krazy Kat* is to reposition it in and among the particular, collagelike contexts of particular daily and Sunday newspapers associated with particular cities, states, or regions. The strip is surrounded by other comic strips and by a whole range of news reports, features, public records, advertisements, photographs, and other print texts at once familiar, highly ephemeral, and estranging. At the same time, it comments on the material-yet-estranging nature of not only the medium but also the "reality" that it both represents and deconstructs. Reimagining *Krazy Kat* as an active part of these ever-changing yet recognizably ordered cultural collages-in-the-making sets up the possibility of describing and debating some consequences of its serious playfulness across and through these contextual spaces where the strip interacts with national, state, and local concerns. *Krazy Kat* is clearly all about the play of dematerialized topographies, familiar (though complex) characters, and very concretely material bricks. In fact, because of its kinetic geography and fluid architecture alone, the strip constantly recontextualizes itself, so that my work toward recontextualizing it really takes its cue from the very nature and design of this most improvisational yet most repetitive of comic strips. *Krazy Kat*, in other words, invents and reinvents textual metaphors for, among other things, its own medium.

Cummings's "not through the sea of the sky but through the sky of the sea"—crossings of habitats and habits of crossing, exemplified by his syntax and propelled by his metaphors—offers a useful conceptual paradigm for reading *Krazy Kat*. Rhetorically, the crisscross, or chiasmus, is a structural device that both reinforces antitheses and reveals surprising likenesses. Here, the vast differences between sky and sea lead directly to a recognition of similarities; these two amorphous sites can be imagined as each other. Because of this flexible interconnectedness, Cummings's conceptual shift about flightless waterfowl flying begins to come intuitively near to *Krazy Kat*. For one thing, the strip itself migrated from New York City to the Southwest by 1916 without leaving behind its urban genealogy. Herriman continually merges the skies and seas of Manhattan and Arizona, representing both places by way of an astonishing range of unlikely and generally unproblematic passageways, crossings, and exchanges in topographies that are themselves constantly in motion. The southwestern terrain is of course recognizable as a mixture of two actual adjoining and complementary places, Kayenta in northeastern Arizona and the Monument Valley area of northern Arizona and southern Utah.[4] But as Herriman urbanizes these places and circulates the Southwest nationally, he also reinvents them as surreal, abstract, jerry-built, figurative sites. At once kinetic, ephemeral, and monumental, *Krazy Kat* proposes a variety of daring transnational blurrings and transcultural crossings.

At the same time, though, Herriman carefully contains the stories he tells. They represent, in effect, thirty years' worth of jazz scatting on the same basic love triangle: Ignatz Mouse always invents new plots to bean Krazy with a brick; Krazy always desires the brick as a token of love; Offissa Pupp always sets out to foil the mouse and sentimentally romance the kat. But the characters' strategies and the artist's techniques never relax into unself-conscious predictability; the borders between sea and sky, cat and mouse, cat and dog, cat and kat, Coconino and Kokonino, repetition and improvisation, are typically fluid and indistinct. In the texts by Norris, Austin, and Cather, careful delineations of various borders make possible selective border crossings and (less often) critiques. In *Almanac of the Dead*, Leslie Marmon Silko looks toward a postborderlands pluralism most powerfully engineered by tribal peoples; in writing the novel, she participates in this reconstruction of the Americas as a transcultural, Indian-centered alliance. Herriman in some ways seems to tap into the energy with which Silko questions and dismantles boundaries; Paulson argues that Herriman "broke the series of closed boxes that traditionally constituted the comic strip" (113–114) and that the characters "break out of the boxes; the boxes themselves are jumbled, their lines dissolved, and characters float free in space; or the boxes become circles or irregular figures [see fig. 10]. In short, the diachronic structure of a comic strip narrative is fractured" (114).[5] Without directly critiquing the act of closing boxes or the maintaining of closed boxes, Herriman opens them and in the process dislodges various prevailing, seemingly compulsory, seemingly "closed" narratives of race, class, gender, and culture. He too resituates the borderlands, but, unlike Silko, he rarely offers explicit critiques of contemporary political and social matters. The range of his implicit cultural criticism is, however, quite broad.

One way to link the southwestern texts discussed in this book is to consider their willingness to represent the varied and often paradoxical difficulties of being grounded in particular "regional" places. Clearly, all of these narratives are often though not always grounded in some way, linked to particular American places and spaces that they construe as both southwestern and American. They acquire popular, literary, or even iconic status to the extent that they can be regarded, somewhat like Trachtenberg's newspaper, as simultaneously familiarizing and defamiliarizing. Granted, "grounded" and "regional" are not necessarily synonymous; indeed, as argued throughout this book, "regional" texts contravene "regionalism" in a variety of ideologically loaded ways, in part by making and disguising links between the region and the nation. For instance, Donna Haraway explains "Teddy Bear Patriarchy" by defamiliarizing the ways Theodore Roosevelt and his iconographers locate "[e]very aspect of the fulfillment of manhood" in topographical space, especially but not exclusively in "Nature" (28). Similarly, Roosevelt as icon continues to be situated in relation to particular geographies (museums and national parks, to give but two examples): "Roosevelt is the perfect *locus genii* for the [American Museum of Natural History's] task of regeneration of a miscellaneous, incoherent urban public threatened with genetic and social decadence, threatened with the prolific bodies of the new immigrants, threatened with the failure of manhood" (Haraway, 29). "Region" is an ideological strategy rather than an unadulterated "natural" space. As innocent, even "saintlike"[6] as Herriman often appears to be, his unmoorings of particular geographical spaces are particularly interesting as negotiations and mixings of southwestern and urban ground. Of course, he is not the first American artist to link city and country; much of western American literature and art has been made by transplanted easterners, and a good portion of it has been made in the East, with eastern cultural centers and markets in mind. Hollywood Westerns trace their origins back to New Jersey; the Frederic Remington Museum is in Ogdensburg, New York. Norris wrote a draft of *McTeague* while at Harvard; Cather wrote *The Professor's House* in Manhattan and at Grand Manan, New Brunswick, Canada. Cummings's sea/sky paradigm begins to map such cultural exchanges but not in geographically, demographically, or ideologically specific ways.

Patricia Nelson Limerick helps further, especially by providing a metaphor that depends less than Cummings's on the clean symmetry of penguin logic. In a 1992 essay, she argues that

> the cultural study of verbal activity . . . can remind western historians that we are ourselves fundamentally interpreters, standing at an intersection where many groups—racial, ethnic, religious, national—have met and will meet. At that crossing our mission is to find order, pattern, and meaning in a swirl of perplexing events and perspectives. ("Making the Most of Words," 183–184)

Limerick's paradigm invites all sorts of specific approaches to and readings of the intersections she so confidently figures. It allows for comings and goings and mixtures without overdetermining or polarizing them. She seeks patterns without expecting or demanding absolute precision or ideological paralysis: order, in her sense, does not superimpose itself on, and thereby erase, perplexity. All in all, she argues for an opening up of western cultural history by, paradoxically, generalizing and even normalizing it without discarding the specifics that distinguish western topographies (including of course textual, imaginative topographies). But she envisions interpretation as an act of standing still rather than a more flexible and even migratory process or disposition; her western historian acts as a sort of eyewitness but is not really part of the process she or he interprets.

Herriman's particular mixtures of verbal and visual (hyper)activity, of urban and southwestern geographies, suggest an alternative way of reading western cultural history—as a loose collection of intersections, more a means than an end, more circulatory than marginal, more migratory than boxed in. He proposes that the Southwest is implicated in much that is not explicitly "southwestern." In *Krazy Kat*, urban artistic vocabularies (and nonindigenous animal species) migrate to Monument Valley, intersect with already migratory southwestern Indian cultures, and set in motion a process by which "urbanized" southwestern cultures and communities return, in arresting comic form, to national popular culture, in newspaper syndication. Even though the strip was not overwhelmingly popular,[7] it was highly accessible, and it regularly made these crossings and recrossings visible. Daily and Sunday, it represented the migration of urban dialects, styles, and sensibilities to the desert as it celebrated a variety of multicultural intersections. It suggested as well that these mixings and mergings of the Southwest, the American city, the newspaper (as medium and metaphor), and modernism were good things; in *Krazy Kat*, personal and cultural transformations are occasions for optimism. In other words, Herriman typically does not use his comic strip as a venue for critiquing American culture; only occasionally does he comment directly on problems faced by the Navajo or caused by inflexible constructions of gender, for example. This temperamental mildness may seem overly deferential, and Herriman's art may consequently appear to be almost blandly celebratory despite its pyrotechnical verbal and visual performances. However, one basic reason why his love triangle remains in circulation for so long is that he refuses his characters an entirely happy ending; the three main characters are often at odds with each other, and the brick signifies pain and alienation as well as love. Still, Herriman does move, with *Krazy Kat*, toward a modern, nationally distributed comic art that is multiple by design and covertly subversive.

↙

As discussed earlier in this book, the American Southwest in late-nineteenth-century America was becoming more visible and available to increasing numbers of Americans, both as a physical space and as figurative currency. Urban American slums and southwestern deserts were developed into journalistic, literary, and by extension aesthetically charged terrains at about the same time, the early 1890s, in popular writings like Jacob Riis's *How the Other Half Lives* (1890), Stephen Crane's *Maggie: A Girl of the Streets* (1893), Henry B. Fuller's Chicago novel, *The Cliff-Dwellers* (1893), and, a bit later, Norris's *McTeague* (1899), John Van Dyke's *The Desert* (1901), Jack London's *The People of the Abyss* (1903), and Upton Sinclair's *The Jungle* (1906). To varying extents, these are all heroic adventure narratives in which the male narrator/writer positions himself as a reformer who risks something of himself to expose dangers and injustices or to reveal new spectacles to readers less experienced than he is.

Additionally, these texts all appear in the cultural context of Frederick Jackson Turner's frontier thesis (see Etulain, 31–42, 47–50). In defining the actual western frontier as closed, Turner paradoxically opens up possibilities (and perhaps needs and desires) for reimagining the metaphor of the frontier in relation to various sites, regions, psychologies, and cultures. Earlier, this book described some of the ways in which outlaws are rehabilitated and incorporated into national mythologies that contravene Turner's monumental and restrictive myth. Like these "outlaw" texts, Austin's early work also reflects her active, polemical thinking about the nature and cultural status of frontiers. *The Land of Little Rain* (1903), rooted in the California desert but first published (through *Atlantic Monthly*) in Boston and perhaps influenced by Boston-area regionalists like Sarah Orne Jewett,[8] clearly criticizes Turner-esque assumptions and formulations about heroic male westward expansion. Far from ossifying into a closed frontier, Austin's western deserts, home to strong, creative women artists, go by their Indian-derived name, the "Land of Lost Borders." And in the gap between "closed" and "lost" lies the argument between Turner and Austin.[9]

The city and the desert both come to be understood as spectacles calling forth ambivalent responses as something suspiciously like aesthetic pleasure complicates the more deeply entrenched fear, loathing, and suspicion of such seeming desolations. Riis crosses a frontier line that is at least to some extent a romantic construction every time he travels, camera in hand, into the slums; his readers vicariously cross this line, too, and in so doing participate, however uncertainly, in a process of re-forming and reimagining American cultural geographies (see Kaplan, *Social Construction*, 45–46).[10] Like Turner's colonial re-formers of the western frontier, Riis constantly crosses the imaginary and aesthetically teasing social line between poverty and wealth, "culture" and "desert," "civilized" and "uncivilized," "immigrant" and "native," "ethnic" and "nonethnic." As reformers attempt to transform social distresses into disciplined, disciplinary, and artful narratives and as surveillance strategies begin visibly to undergo the cultural processes of being packaged textually, readers encounter complex and sometimes uncomfortable blurrings of ethnography, criminology, sociology, reformist politics, and aesthetics. The photographs, as closed boxes, dramatically expose urban poverty but, at pretty much the same time, work as guided tours that permit safe unreciprocated entry into spaces whose details—faces, furniture, clothing, alleys, cellars—make close textual study possible and even desirable. Such texts are designed to reassure as well as to instigate change; reformers simultaneously maintain and challenge selected cultural "frontiers" and boundaries.

The first recontextualization of *Krazy Kat*, then, positions it as a slightly younger relative of these larger cultural processes of revealing "unknown" American spaces to an uninitiated readership and encouraging contact between urban and southwestern spaces. At the same time, though, Herriman's impetus is to open or dissolve the ideological boxes that usually remain closed in the texts of Riis, Turner, and (to a lesser extent) Norris and Austin. Such impulses often work in concert with ideas of travel and migration, and indeed Herriman's life was characterized by migration. He was born in New Orleans in 1880, but from about age six on, he mainly lived in either New York or Los Angeles, with side trips to Arizona (he might have relocated there permanently but for one crucial problem: the absence of a Monument Valley post office). He lived in Los Angeles for the better part of the 1890s, but in 1900, at age twenty, he stole a train ride from L.A. to New York and found work as a barker and billboard painter at a Coney Island sideshow. (For biographical information on Herriman, see McDonnell, O'Connell, and de Havenon.) From 1900 to 1905, he stayed in New York pretty much continuously, publishing first "one-shot" and then "continuing character" comics for the Pulitzer newspapers. In the ten years or so before easing into *Krazy Kat*, Herriman worked energetically, producing a variety of comic strips such as *Professor Otto and His Auto* (1902), *Acrobatic Archie* (1902–1903), *Lariat Pete* (1903), *Major Ozone's Fresh Air Crusade* (1904 and 1906), *Grandma's Girl—Likewise Bud Smith* (1905–1906), *Mr. Proones the Plunger* (1907), *Baron Mooch* (1909), *Gooseberry Sprigg* (1909), and *The Dingbat Family* (1910–1916). He

moved back to Los Angeles in mid-1905, then was summoned back to New York in 1910 by one of the editors of William Randolph Hearst's *New York Evening Journal.* And then, on July 26, 1910, everything (including this argument) came together in one historic creasing of a feline cranium (Figure 1). At the bottom of each panel of *The Dingbat Family,* Herriman's urban apartment comic strip, a cat-and-mouse game transpires with a comic reversal: the mouse chases, and beans, the cat. According to Herriman, this cat-and-mouse play was a sort of extra comic-within-a-comic, created (he said) "to fill up the waste space," the blank white space near the border of the composition (McDonnell, O'Connell, and de Havenon, 52). Beyond the loose associations set in motion by his metaphor, no southwestern wasteland appears here. The "waste space"—the margin—is urban and (de)valued.

As Gopnik writes of *The Dingbat Family,* the apartment is the most beautiful thing about the strip: it is "a spare world of white walls, geometric moldings, bare hanging bulbs, and gridded windows—the desert of the lower-middle-class apartment" (Varnedoe and Gopnik, 168–169). Though perhaps colored by hindsight, Gopnik's perception nicely illuminates the continuities between New York and Coconino County, city and desert; so too does Herriman's drawing of Offissa Pupp remarking that certain rock formations in Monument Valley "look like a lotta Woolworth Buildings looking for rooms—and not finding any" (Figure 2). If the Dingbats' New York apartment can appear to be a desert, the desert's volcanic rock formations can likewise be read in light of a New York skyscraper well known in the early twentieth century as a cultural centerpiece, "the cathedral of commerce." [11]

Gopnik writes that "sometime around 1910, Herriman visited the Monument Valley of Arizona—the sublime western landscape of natural skyscrapers and endless horizons. . . . For Herriman, it was like Turner discovering Venice" (Gopnik, 22). Moreover, drawing from conversations with Saul Steinberg, Gopnik suggests that American art deco elements can be located in *Krazy Kat:*

Figure 1. *The Dingbat Family*, 26 July 1910. Ignatz Mouse beans Krazy Kat for the first time. Reprinted with special permission of King Features Syndicate.

the terraced and set-back needles of Monument Valley were a formal current that nourished the romantic American skyscraper: block up the windows of the RCA building and plonk it into the middle of Arizona, and it wouldn't look a bit out of place. . . . [Herriman's drawings,] with their constant ambiguity about what in his metamorphosing backgrounds is natural and what man-made, perhaps seem so evocative to us because they seem to mediate so perfectly between Rockefeller Center and Monument Valley. (Gopnik, 22)

Herriman's contemporaries noted the resemblance as well. In a 1923 article, "Arizona: The Land of the Joyous Adventure," Austin describes Arizona "as a land of many-storied cities, true prototype of the modern American skyscraper" (37), while Cather's friend Elizabeth Shepley Sergeant mobilizes the connection differently, remarking on "New Mexico communities . . . [that] are dominated by spectral fears from which those who rub elbows under the shadow of skyscrapers are liberated" (254). In a thoroughly obscure 1913 text, *Through Our Unknown Southwest*, Agnes C. Laut writes, "'It was not until the nomadic robbers forced the pueblos that the Southwestern people adopted the crowded form of existence,' says Archaeology. Sounds like an explanation of our modern skyscrapers and the real estate robbers of modern life, doesn't it?" (vi). Even Carl Jung enters into this discourse. Remembering his trip to Taos Pueblo, New Mexico, in 1924–1925, Jung writes that "on its opposite bank stood a second pueblo of reddish adobe houses, built one atop the other toward the center of the settlement, thus strangely anticipating the perspective of an American metropolis with its skyscrapers in the center" (40). Like Wile E. Coyote, who in the more recent southwestern cartoon *Road Runner* frantically ships in items from the outside world as represented by the Acme Company, *Krazy Kat* often imports such signs of a world "outside" Coconino County: technologies, commodities, political and cultural issues, literary conceits and allusions, and so forth. Unlike the indigenous Wile E., who fails to catch the roadrunner in part because he depends on these imported,

Figure 2. Original drawing of Krazy Kat, Offissa Pupp, Ignatz Mouse, and friends, c. 1925. Reprinted with special permission of King Features Syndicate.

human-made products rather than on his inherited talents as a predator, the characters in *Krazy Kat* settle comfortably into a desert community that intersects often and well with the urban world "outside."

The three main characters and the three corners of the comic love triangle in the desert—the "crack-brained" Kat, the fiendishly vagrant Ignatz Mouse, and the staunch but sentimental police dog Offissa B. (Bull) Pupp—all hail from urban places. Writes Gopnik, "With his Keystone Cop's helmet and double-breasted jacket, Offissa Pupp is clearly drawn not as a western sheriff but as a Gotham cop on the beat, transplanted into an alien milieu of the West in a reversal of the sitcom cliché" (Gopnik, 23–24). Though "reversal" is not quite right—it implies movement in one direction only rather than the more complicated exchanges at work in newspaper production and syndication as well as in southwestern cultural crossings—a similar transplantation of city to Southwest (as well as various countertransformations) manifests itself in Ignatz and Krazy. Both, after all, can be traced back to the Dingbats' urban floorboards. And though their move to the Southwest happens gradually and easily, without any abrupt, dramatic uprooting, their city speech and mannerisms do not correspondingly fade away out of sight. Most obvious of all is Krazy's language, or "lenguage." Ignatz Mouse in another strip calls it "plain language in a higher plane"—a fanciful mixture of Dickensian comic bluster, Lower East Side Yiddish/German accents, and various other voices and languages, including perhaps a touch of Irish in a canine airplane pilot's "Gimme back me poipa" (Figure 7). Patrick McDonnell, Karen O'Connell, and Georgia Riley de Havenon describe this language as

> an outrageous alphabet soup of Coconino patois, Spanish, French, Brooklyn Yiddish, onomatopoetic juxtapositions—and almost anything else that came to Herriman's mind. The lilting voices of the inhabitants of the capricious Kat world were perhaps nascent in a boyhood spent in the Creole quarter of New Orleans. (63)

Franklin Rosemont offers that this language sounds "something like a synthesis of Emily Brontë and Groucho Marx" (124). These intersections of citified language and modernized (but not overdeveloped) desert make for a fluid and fluent urbanization, a diverse mix characteristic of New York City and also very much like the Southwest.

For example, in a 1918 daily without desert trappings (Figure 3), Krazy asks "Why is 'lenguage,' 'Ignatz'?"—not a garden-variety comic-strip query— and conducts an investigation into the subject. With the postures and gestures of a highly theatrical prosecuting attorney, Krazy closes in on a conclusion more like a punch line than a logical deduction. At the same time, his topic invites a closer look at *his* language. Here, the noticeable characteristics of his speech include a sort of Germanic-Yiddish transformation of all short "a" vowels to short "e" vowels, a hardening of "th" ("other" becomes "udda"), and a suppressing of all definite articles. Further, his examples of "foreign language" speakers may, beyond the comic wallop of the words themselves, seem a bit odd: why, after all, "a Finn, or a Leplender, or a Oshkosher"? Lapland overlaps Finland; Oshkosh, Wisconsin, would not necessarily be "foreign" (or kosher) to an Americanized mouse. Krazy's examples don't support his contention as strongly as they might have; however, his overall performance, particularly his own dialect speech, both exemplifies and undercuts his conclusion that language facilitates misunderstandings. As a result, Krazy—and Herriman—suggest the possibility of moving beyond the binary (here, clarity and confusion as "good" and "bad," respectively) and toward a more ambiguous sense of language in complex motion.

In a 1935 daily strip (Figure 4) set in the desert Southwest, Krazy's lenguage gyrates and freelances as it did when he lived and worked in the big city; slang, fractured grammar, dialect speech, and a sort of dynamic improvisation converge. The processes of migrating into Krazyspeak call to mind other migrations in the strip (the characters' move from New York and the Dingbats' apartment to a Southwest populated by talking animals of various

species, for example) as well as a broader conception of loosely regulated, unending, inventive processes of cultural migration. In the July 22, 1935, strip, for example, Krazy sings about comings and goings. The song itself unmoors its narrative "facts"; thanks mostly to his verbs, it is difficult to tell just when he is going and coming, let alone where he is headed and where he has been. But much more important than paraphrasing the song is getting a loose feel for the movements it describes, movements that involve the city ("For I leff town a wikk iggo") by name and also by sound. The song's rhythm is urban, clipped, popular, jazz-based, and at the same time bluesy:

> Press my pents
> An' shine my shoes.
> Gimme twenny cents
> To pay my dews—
> For I'm goin' far a-waay—
> —Tidday—

Its jazz rhythm counterpoints and in a way illustrates Ignatz's travels, or, more precisely, his failed and not very well planned sneak attack: Krazy's "I'm goin' far a-waay—Tidday" might very well call to mind the emotional effects

Figure 3. *Krazy Kat*, 6 January 1918.
Reprinted with special permission of
King Features Syndicate.

of the brick he always longs for, but Ignatz somewhat inexplicably crawls right toward Offissa Pupp, whose police baton delivers a quiet rim shot after (or during) Krazy's third verse and refrain.

His language, as in the 1918 daily, does away with the short "a" vowel in favor of short "e," and other transpositions as well point playfully toward a variety of East Coast city accents:

twenny for twenty

tidday for today

brood for brewed

pot pooree for potpourri

timorra for tomorrow

yetz tidday for yesterday (or, less likely, yes, today)

dokk for dark

poily for pearly

Toots day for Tuesday

Figure 4. *Krazy Kat*, 22 July 1935.
Reprinted with special permission of
King Features Syndicate.

All these examples point toward a dialect speech that takes shortcuts, eliding certain consonants ("t," "r") rather than painstakingly articulating to the letter. The geolinguistic intersection between Brooklynese and the Southwest denigrates neither while helping to make a subtler point, a point conveyed by the refrains of each verse:

> For I'm goin' far a-waay—
> —Tidday—
> W'en I get comin' beck
> —Timorra—
> An' I may not go until
> —Yetz tidday
> For I leff town a wikk iggo
> —On Toots day.

Each refrain comments accurately on the nature of Herriman's medium. In broader terms, the popular song, like the popular (yet "despised") newspaper, is an extremely temporal, highly impermanent form. And the comings and goings encapsulated in Krazy's lenguage encapsulate in turn the departures and daily arrivals of these migratory forms.

To be sure, such playful speculations are not restricted to Krazy's language habits; in a daily printed on January 24, 1939, Ignatz Mouse incarcerates himself in Offissa Pupp's jail, claiming that he is "expiating a sin" that he will commit tomorrow. Much of the language is again quite self-conscious of Coconino County's multiple locations: Arizona and Hearst newspapers. Moreover, this self-consciousness very often appears in Herriman's visual images. Most obviously, the desert spaces constantly change shapes; but in a relatively early daily such as September 21, 1921 (Figure 5), the whole look of each panel changes in amazingly inventive ways, even as this changefulness is counterpointed by the two characters' casual disregard of it. As evoked by the dialogue of these dailies but also by the shifting, restless compositional structures, time as well as space work in strange ways; by positioning Krazy and Ignatz inside spectacular physical spaces, abstract squares and ovals, and even on a sheet of paper tacked to the "wall" of a panel, Herriman constructs collages as well as mirages. Blatantly artificial and ephemeral, these visual

Figure 5. *Krazy Kat,* 21 September 1921. Reprinted with special permission of King Features Syndicate.

images set in motion a sort of punctuated equilibrium; they "up settle" as they both fracture reality, but they also accumulate into a coherent strategy, a way of reconstituting that which it dislodges.

As Seldes asserts, "There must be ephemera. Let us see to it that they are good" (*Seven Lively Arts,* 348). The crossings of city and desert depend on a highly kinetic ephemerality or (there are many ways to phrase this) an openness to postcolonial processes in which unlike peoples and things come together: modern ephemera (especially those associated with technology) and a monumental "natural" Southwest; shifting miragelike perceptions and concrete material bricks; a mouse throwing bricks at a cat who loves being creased because he loves he who creases. The kat generously interprets each missile as a token of affection, and his response only infuriates the mouse whose not-so-loving obsession is to bean the kat again and again. But these misreadings generate rather than frustrate contact between them. Further, Herriman frequently throws quotation marks around particular words and names, enclosing them grammatically but at the same time opening signification up in surprising ways. The quotation marks work in the service of ephemerality, too. They comment archly on the nature of comic strip "reality," perhaps, and they devilishly dislodge signifiers that might otherwise be regarded as fixed and obvious—yet, again, these localized disruptions accumulate and ultimately cohere into a more or less familiar strategy. Each gap between signifiers and each nudge/wink of quotation marks enacts in miniature the visual and verbal lenguage games and explorations of *Krazy Kat;* as Krazy asks, "Why is lenguage?"

Often, too, Herriman represents such gaps structurally in his compositions; the February 5, 1922, Sunday page (Figure 6) can be and of course is read left to right, horizontally and panel by panel. But it can also be read top to bottom, right down the middle, through the liminal zone where Krazy and Ignatz keep passing each other without ever quite meeting. This zone works in at least two ways as a visual metaphor for their relationship: first, blank white spaces and sparse deserts represent the absence of contact between them; these appear to be abstract spaces except for the explosive passage of locomotives between Kaibito and Coconino. Technology connects "urban" places by cutting through whiteness and desert, importing industrial and rec-

Figure 6. *Krazy Kat*, 5 February 1922. Reprinted with special permission of King Features Syndicate.

reational transportation systems that paradoxically make the terrain legible in the act of overrunning it while also failing to bring about the connections Krazy and Ignatz desire. And second, of course, their railroad travels and missed connections figure the kat-mouse relationship in general, predicated as it is on misunderstandings and misreadings of each other's gestures, speech, and motives. At the same time, all this riding on trains across the desert leads finally to visual and verbal punning—"I'll not miss him again" and "I'll miss him no more, y'bet"—that adds intriguing layers to the kat-mouse relationship. Their lines, for one thing, resemble each other tellingly. And, investing so much energy in the other, both Ignatz and Krazy pun toward not only a lost traveler's paradoxical recognition (I can find my way only if I stop traveling) but also toward a lover's desire not to miss or be missed by his beloved. Meanwhile, these passings and crossings cast metaphorical light on the homoerotic geography of the relationship between a kat and a mouse who both miss their connection and remake it again and again. Finally, to return the strip to its original, newspaper context, the "news" Krazy and Ignatz and Herriman make—for all its desire and ability to imply, to suggest, to imagine, to improvise—sublimely stays its course.

And it drops from the sky. Krazy, alone in the shape-shifting desert, remarks, "Well, here I are, all alone with nobody around but myself. S'turbil" (Figure 7). Immediately thereafter, what should enter but a low-flying airplane, dropping a newspaper to the ground—which of course enables Krazy in this comic strip to discover Krazy in a comic strip. Metaphysical discussions ensue. In the process, Krazy's startled innocence about his comic-strip existence quickly modulates into a winning fascination with the plot of the strip he is reading; rather than puzzling out the mechanics of the paper's sudden appearance, Krazy adapts by rethinking his own identity. He blurs the already hazy differences between life as he knows it and life as it is textually constructed. What Krazy reads begins to happen all around him, so that he narrates both strips; but as he gets more and more involved in the newspaper strip, he ironically grows oblivious to the action "around" him right then and there. This metaplot intensifies to the point where, in the lower left-hand corner, Krazy moves from narrator to critic and Herriman then suppresses both the newspaper rendition and the pooch's live-action "werra roughish and werra uncootish lengwidge." Krazy's reading thus overlaps ours. At the same time, however, readers can notice things that he may or may not notice. The strip all in all plays out a sort of paradigm in which something—here, modern technology represented by planes and newspapers—paradoxically enters Coconino from outside the strip's borders while at the same time underscoring that Coconino is already "outside" itself, in part because of *its* positioning in a mass-produced newspaper that is itself an example of modern technologies. This convergence point between the Southwest and technology is purposefully too slippery to go very far in the direction of permanent settlement. It emphasizes the somewhat random nature of newspaper distribution, and it savors the accidental, the found object, the non sequitur. In other words, the

Figure 7. *Krazy Kat*, 16 April 1922. Reprinted with special permission of King Features Syndicate.

Figure 8. *Krazy Kat,* 11 June 1939. Reprinted with special permission of King Features Syndicate.

airplane introduces modern(ist) sophistication without imposing colonial designs. Herriman's narrative does not really try to disguise, justify, or foreshadow this accidental postcolonialism. However, looking at the narrative from its conclusion back to its abrupt beginning, and rereading the whole thing in light of *Krazy Kat*'s larger life as a newspaper comic, it is possible to see how the self-reflexivity in the strip dissolves as each panel itself represents in the moving terrain and enacts in the narrative the very nature of its disposable medium: the newspaper comes, at times very suddenly, and can be very interesting, even gripping. But the newspaper also goes.

At other times, Herriman goes without words in favor of a sort of silent-film pantomime. And even without verbal language, he invents a visual idiom sophisticated in its crossings and mixings of "art" and "illusion." Here (Figure 8), the strip plays with notions of representation, again by way of the comic within a comic. Amid the ever-fluctuating southwestern setting, Ignatz sketches a rectangular box in the air, a box that turns out to be an artist's sketch pad or canvas—or an animator's cel, as the figures drawn by Ignatz begin almost immediately to move on their own—or as much "on their own" as the figures drawn by Herriman. All this movement seems a bit supernatural, especially given that the canvas, like the jail, floats in the air (or stands up by itself) throughout, easel-less. Maybe they are just drawing on the air, after all, and inviting readers to make the interesting perceptual leap of seeing and understanding these two-dimensional line drawings on air *as* a canvas, a jail, a what-have-you. All this of course raises questions about how to read the other boxes. In the lower bar, at the very bottom, such questions reach further still, as they are translated into verbal language: "But he's a 'ott krittik,' ain't he?" "Yes, but he's also a 'woodpecker.'" "Ah-h." As the shifting topographies and idioms indicate, Herriman loves to set in motion multiple, intersecting meanings that are not so much articulated—"Ah-h"—as enacted.

That's one angle. But the strip also unfolds as an extraordinarily ingenious Ignatz Mouse plan to distract Offissa Pupp so that Ignatz can bean Krazy's noodle. Ignatz's obsession is prefigured in the drawings, and the drawings work as accomplices. But just as Herriman gets his readers to the verge of thinking that the illusory brick-beaning on canvas is different from the "actual" brick incident, he pulls up. Again, the strip evanesces not into resolutions, not into disciplined questions and answers, but into open speculations and musings. "Why is lenguage?" indeed. Krazy's response, "Language is, that we may *mis*-unda-stend each udda," is, ironically, precisely right—it beautifully sums up Krazy and Ignatz's relationship—but Krazy doesn't know how right he is. And that is the suspended comic point—or, more accurately, the comic gap or question—Herriman explores over and over again, in detailed and inventive delight. The comic strip within a comic strip, like the play within a play, is another way of crossing the sea of the sky and the sky of the sea and a way of considering, questioning, complicating, and playing with the act and art of convergence.

10 Krazy Kat II

Navajo Aesthetics

In moving, with *Krazy Kat*, toward an unprogrammatic postcolonial paradigm of cultural exchange, George Herriman never loses sight of the local and personal, the interactions between particular people and particular places. Patrick McDonnell, Karen O'Connell, and Georgia Riley de Havenon rightly insist, "There can be no true understanding of George Herriman, and only a limited understanding of *Krazy Kat*, without some knowledge of the Navajo country, which includes [among other places] the settlement of Kayenta as well as Monument Valley and straddles Arizona and Utah" (69). As this quotation implies, it is difficult to understand this place without also considering the Navajo people, migrants to the Southwest who were able to "alter their culture . . . to place themselves within their new homeland" (Iverson, 108). In broad terms, the Navajo found ways of bringing their stories with them when they migrated from the Northwest and ways of relocating these stories conceptually and aesthetically to southwestern places. Clearly, these cultural processes of adaptation and continuation resemble Herriman's repetitive yet highly adaptive work. However, this book is less interested in causality—who influenced whom—than in a more random and disorderly Southwest in which "postcolonial" refers at once to both local and migratory conditions. Both *Krazy Kat* and "Navajo aesthetics," then, are grounded in particular southwestern places, and both circulate through and across these places. At times they resemble each other in more specific ways as well.

Hertha Dawn Wong explains, "Defining a Native American identity is an especially treacherous endeavor, since such diverse native cultures and nations cannot be collapsed into one undifferentiated category" (13). Working against "romanticized notions of communal identity, even within a specific tribe," she urges caution and restraint in generalizing about tribal identity (13). As Herriman seems to have recognized, a circumspect specificity is a sign of respect for all concerned, which is not to say that generalizations about any and all tribes are in some absolute way impossible but simply to suggest, along with Wong, that "[f]or all the tribal and individual distinctions . . . it is possible to make *a few* generalizations about the concepts of self, life, and language shared by many of the pre-Columbian indigenous peoples of what is now the United States" (13, emphasis added). While some general-izations about the five hundred years since Columbus's arrival in America are also possible, I try to make them as rarely as possible, preferring instead to work against transforming particular early-twentieth-century northeastern Arizona Navajo into a uniform, generic "Navajo" (or, broader still, "Indian").

The places Herriman most frequently visited and incorporated into *Krazy Kat,* Kayenta and Monument Valley, make up a relatively small portion of the Navajo reservation. These topographies, however, have entered into na-tional iconography in large part because of director John Ford, who made all or part of nine Western films there.[1] McDonnell, O'Connell, and de Havenon write that

> Monument Valley is an elevated desert, a land of hogans, mesas, and buttes, dogs herding sheep, wild horses grazing, and tumbleweed blow-ing across the land. Majestic orange-colored corrugated rock formations stand in awesome stillness, casting purple shadows across the vast ex-panse. Only the whirling wind whistling through the monuments dis-rupts the quiet and hallowed serenity. One feels as if one were on sa-cred ground where time stands still. Like *Krazy Kat,* this valley exists in its own "world" and is a geographic counterpart of Herriman's peaceful spirit. (69)

Though slightly overwrought—the alliteration is one warning sign—this passage gives a useful general idea of what Monument Valley evokes and rep-resents. These authors regard the wind as disruptive, for example, and inter-ject a romantic lyricism, yet they perceive that the place works as a spiritually invested, temporally nonlinear, self-sufficient ecosystem whose monumen-tality is not necessarily defined and certified by spectators from an "outside" world.[2] Asa Bazhonoodah, an eighty-three-year-old Navajo woman arguing against a coal company's open-pit mining on Black Mesa, says,

> A long time ago the earth was placed here for us, the people, the Navajo, it gives us corn and we consider her our mother.
> When Mother Earth needs rain we give pollen and use the prayers that was given us when we came from the earth. That brings rain. Black Mesa area is used to ask for rain. And afterward (after the mining) we don't know what it will be like. We make prayers for all blessings for Mother Earth, asking that we may use her legs, her body and her spirit to make ourselves more powerful and durable. After this the pollen is thrown into the water.
> Air is one of the Holy Elements, it is important in prayer. Wooded areas are being cut down. Now the air is becoming bad; not working. The herbs that are taken from Mother Earth and given to a woman during childbirth no longer grow in the cut area. The land looks burned. . . .
> When we were first put on Earth, the herbs and medicine were also put here for us to use. These have become part of our prayers to Mother Earth. We should realize it for if we forget these things we will vanish as the people. That is why I don't like the coal mine. (398–399)

Speaking at a Washington, D.C., hearing in 1971, Asa Bazhonoodah seeks to explain and teach a complex and deeply rooted way of seeing to an audience largely unfamiliar with the ways of the Diné, the People. There is much here, perhaps most prominently the conviction that the land and the people take care of each other, circulate through each other in ways that keep both "more powerful and durable." The Navajo depend on the vitality of the land and the reciprocal processes through which each sustains each. When Asa Bazhonoodah speaks of the "herbs that are taken from Mother Earth and given to a woman during childbirth," she exemplifies these reciprocal, cyclical exchanges: nourishing Indian mothers, Mother Earth ensures her own nourishment. Taking care of the earth, the Navajo are taken care of by the earth. Entering as a catastrophically disruptive third party, the mining interest breaks down this relationship between land and people, scarring the earth, hurting the people, and contaminating—breaking—essential natural and spiritual processes. The air is "not working"; the connections between place and people are being destroyed, and as a result the people, like the earth, may vanish. Not only does Asa Bazhonoodah set out to explain all this to Washington; she also sets out to explain it *in* Washington, where she must try to articulate a sense of place to an audience significantly less familiar than she is with Black Mesa. In a telling analogy, she introduces what strikes her as a white concern of comparable import and power: "Black Mesa is to the Navajo like money is to the whites. Our Mother gives birth to the animals, plants, and these could be traded for money. Black Mesa is my billfold" (399).

Of course, Euro-American colonization in the Southwest had been underway for a long time before this Navajo woman gave her testimony. When Herriman arrived in Kayenta sometime around 1910, the Navajo had already spent almost fifty years on reservation land. Following their military subjugation by Kit Carson (1863), they were removed—temporarily, as it turned out—and forced on a Long Walk comparable in harshness to the Trail of Tears, the forced migration of Cherokees, Creeks, Choctaws, Chickasaws, Seminoles, and others from their southeastern homelands to Oklahoma Indian Territory. Exiled to the barren Bosque Redondo Reservation on the Pecos River (1864–1868), the Navajo finally returned in 1868 to the homeland so crucial to their very existence and survival as the Diné (see Utley, *Indian Frontier*, 82–86). For centuries prior to this forced march and changeover to reservation life, the Navajo were in contact with Spanish conquistadors, missionaries, capitalists, and other colonists as well as with many other southwestern native tribes, including Pueblos, Apaches, and Utes (see, for example, Richard White, 12–13, 21). Still, though particular Navajo responded and continue to respond in various ways to these various cultural intersections and conflicts, Asa Bazhonoodah is not alone among the Navajo in her perceptions of a tribal common ground that persists and, in the face of struggle, remains firm. It is probably safe to generalize, with Wong, that "[t]his [spiritual] awareness of interdependence [of self and cosmos] results in a deep respect for everything in the natural world as well as a profound personal responsibility for helping to maintain balance" (14). As Peggy V. Beck, Anna Lee Walters, and Nia Francisco write,

> Everything, though having its own individuality and special place, is dependent on and shares in the growth and work of everything else. This means, for example, that if you take the life of an animal you have to let that animal know why you are doing so and that you take full responsibility for your act. Why? One reason is because it is a way of showing that you understand the balances that exist in all natural systems. . . . Another reason . . . is because human beings and animals have a relationship to one another . . . [and] our survival depend[s] on maintaining the relationships between animals, plants, rivers, feeding grounds, etc. (12)

This grounded, interactive sense of sacred relationships and exchanges, glimpsed in various American Indian stories and writings from various parts of the Americas, begins to give a sense of what Herriman may have been permitted to enter into, to some unknown extent, in Arizona.

As the authors of *The Comic Art of George Herriman* demonstrate in an excellent though necessarily summary overview, Herriman loved Monument Valley and respected and admired the Navajo: "Those mesas and sunsets out in that ole pais pintado . . . a taste of that stuff sinks you—deep too—" he wrote in a 1938 letter to a close friend (McDonnell, O'Connell, and de Havenon, 71, 88). In another context he said of the Southwest,

> That's the country I love and that's the way I see it. I can't understand why no other artists ever use it. All those Indian names mean something to me and they "fit" somehow whether or not the readers understand their meaning. I don't think Krazy's readers care anything about that part of the strip. But it's very important to me and I like it nearly as well as the characters themselves. (McDonnell, O'Connell, and de Havenon, 68–69)

Proclaiming himself unaware of other artists working with the Southwest, Herriman points up most of all his characteristic modesty; he is unassuming about taste making and unassuming about his own "artistic" or "literary" status. Herriman characteristically stays out of the spotlight. He is also most likely writing before Ford descended upon Monument Valley to film *Stagecoach* (1939). In any event, Herriman interestingly regards the Southwest as out of the public eye, even as he himself circulates images of it seven days a week, year after year, in the Hearst newspapers. More to the point, he assumes that his national readership is not interested in Indian names and "that [Indian-focused] part of the strip"; in effect, he publicizes personal, even private, meanings while both distributing them to and distancing them from his readers. His position as he sees it may be vaguely romantic about Indians, but it is also decisively not colonial.

Herriman seems to have enjoyed a strong, mutually respectful relationship with the Navajo. McDonnell, O'Connell, and de Havenon write that

Herriman never lost his affinity with the ways of the Navajo people. . . .
He always wore a silver Navajo bracelet and owned many books about
American Indians. On trips down to Navajo country he would bring a
huge five- or ten-gallon jar of hard candy for the Indian children. In appreciation of Herriman's kindness and his concern for them, the Navajos
sent him a handsome handmade book of photographs of Monument Valley, taken by photographer Josef Muench. The women loomed him a rug
in black, white, and gray with his name woven across it: GEO. HERRIMAN.
He treasured these gifts and displayed them prominently. (76)

In keeping with the technological nature of some of these gifts, Herriman
introduced sound movies to Kayenta—a gift two different southwestern acquaintances of his recall, though only in tantalizingly sketchy detail:

> He was very generous. He sent a movie projector to the T.B. sanitarium
> in Kayenta, as a gift. Then he arranged for films to be sent every Friday.
> Those were the first "talkies" in Kayenta. (Betty Zane Rodgers, adopted
> daughter of Kayenta traders the Wetherills, in McDonnell, O'Connell,
> and de Havenon, 72).

> [W]e met George Herriman in Kayenta, he always stayed with Mr. John
> [Wetherill], and was very interested in the Navajo people, and wanted
> them to know some of the things we did out in the world, so sent in the
> first movies they had ever seen. Once a week at the old sanitarium we
> could all gather and see Tom Mix or some kind of movie. Great fun, the
> Navajos always laughed at the sad scenes! (Mike Goulding, who, with her
> husband, Harry, set up a Monument Valley trading post and later brought
> Ford there, in McDonnell, O'Connell, and de Havenon, 72–73)

From these remembrances, a few tentative conclusions are possible: first
of all, they watched Westerns ("Tom Mix"). Mix himself was possibly part
Cherokee and, according to film historian Kevin Brownlow, was a highly dramatic storyteller: "He told haphazard tales of adventure so wild that his career eclipsed for sheer action and breathless pace the first few chapters of the
Bible" (300–301). He got his start in silent movie Westerns in 1909, often
shooting on location at southwestern sites such as the Grand Canyon, and
made his last film, a serial, in 1935. If Navajos and Euro-Americans sat down
together to watch cowboy-and-Indian pictures, what did they say about them?
The movies seem to have served as cultural mediators, helping to create (or
reinforce) a sort of cross-cultural comic intersection at which Navajo audiences laugh at all the sad bits, reversing the expectations of Euro-American
narratives and of the people who make and distribute them. In any event, the
links to *Krazy Kat* are irresistible: moving, kinetic, cinematographic pictures
in their own right, Herriman's strips also generate comedy by engineering a
major reversal of a conventional Euro-American narrative. Rather than the
expected cat-chases-mouse story, Herriman's mouse chases his kat, and the
brick, creasing the kat's cranium, means both love and war.

Herriman frequently joins Monument Valley images with Navajo designs, motifs, philosophies, and humor. In the furnishings of characters' houses—rugs, pottery, lamp shades, curtains, pillows, blankets, and so on—in the exterior topographies of this border country, as well as in the compositional borders, the crevices between panels, and the title panels (Figure 9), he unpresumptuously brings modern (here, collaged and cinematographic) styles, newspaper production technologies, and Navajo design elements into contact. In two Sunday pages from September 1922, for example, Navajo images appear on pottery and on a mesa (Figure 10) as well as in petroglyphic style (Figure 11, top left); the pottery is of course handcrafted, but the mesa's zigzag posits a much more startling fusion. In fact, much of the imagery in Figure 10 cannot be taken literally. What, for example, are the things on either side of Ignatz Mouse in the sixth "scene," immediately to the right of the circle? On the riverbank to his left rests something that looks like a potted Italian loaf spearing a tire while the tire defies conventional gravity, an image odd enough that it may distract attention from the anthropomorphic thing looming over the river to Ignatz's right, perhaps a hill or a desert mirage transformation of the seemingly more natural structures behind the figures inside the circle—but the river thing has arms, an eye, perhaps a trunk. The point is that this world remains in motion. Structures behind figures change from panel to panel, even where the characters themselves have not changed position. The potted bush at the far left of the final box/panel might best be taken as something possibly natural, possibly handcrafted, definitely handcrafted, *and* bearing a Navajo imprint that itself changes any seemingly stabilizing reading of the image as it moves toward a sort of zone where identities and perceptions can be and often are fluid.

However, these ephemera-in-process carry and convey deeper aesthetic and philosophical meanings, meanings fundamentally Navajo. According to anthropologist Gary Witherspoon, the Navajo have "over three hundred thousand (356,200 by my calculation) distinct conjugations of the verb 'to go'" (21), and this number of "to go" conjugations (instead of "to be," for example), coupled with "the astonishing degree to which the Navajo language is dominated by verbs" (48), "seems to indicate a cosmos composed of processes and

Figure 9. *Krazy Kat,* 17 August 1920.
Reprinted with special permission of King
Features Syndicate.

events, as opposed to a cosmos composed of facts and things" (49). Witherspoon writes that "the world is in motion" and that "the essence of life and being is movement" (48). In his autobiography, Navajo Blessingway singer Frank Mitchell points out that "[t]here were only two styles of hogan in the beginning . . . [but] as time went on they changed the styles and made them in all different ways" (171). And, Mitchell continues,

> Nowadays we have songs about that. The first song says: "It's being talked about. . . ." those are the words of the first song: "It's being talked about, it's being discussed." Then later songs say: "It's being set in position. . . ." and so on. There is a song for each action as the house is being built. (171)

Mitchell's and Witherspoon's discussions of a world in motion also make sense in relation to *Krazy Kat,* particularly in that Navajo traditionals also see this world as balanced between processes of change and processes of repetition. Early in his discussion of Navajo songs, Witherspoon observes that "Repetition is a motif found all through Navajo life and culture. It is associated with the concepts of renewal, regeneration, rejuvenation, revolution, and restoration" (155–156). Along the way, repetition is accompanied by a sort of countermelodic variation; just as Mitchell, in talking about hogan-building songs, repeats the sentence "It's being talked about" and varies it ("it's being discussed"), just as Herriman improvises to "adorn" and "enliven" (Witherspoon, 156) a fundamentally repetitive plot triangulation, so do Navajo songs create and rehearse a play of repetition and what musicologist David McAllester calls "the subtle and constant variations . . . such modes of variation as interruption, alternation, return, pairing, progression, transection, and ambiguity. These may be seen as contrapuntal to the theme of repetition" (quoted in Witherspoon, 156). Still, as Mitchell emphasizes, it is crucial to sing sacred songs properly: "The words in that [Shootingway] song have a meaning; they are very sacred and should not be sung just for fun" (153). A man Mitchell knows errs greatly when he sings this song without "using the regular words in the song; instead he was just making up some words" (153). There is an important distinction between respectful variations in proper contexts and foolish improvisations undertaken in improper contexts.

Figure 10. *Krazy Kat,* 3 September 1922. Reprinted with special permission of King Features Syndicate.

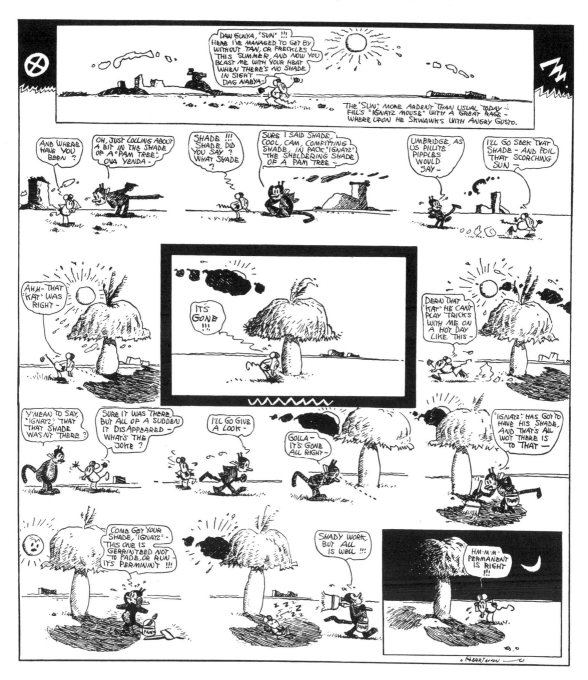

Figure 11. *Krazy Kat,* 24 September 1922. Reprinted with special permission of King
Features Syndicate.

In the January 25, 1942, Sunday cartoon (Figure 12), Herriman engages in a deceptively tedious self-reflexivity; here, what seems to be an exposure of the strip's utterly repetitive, absolutely familiar plot actually improvises further variations on the old theme. Again, the characters demonstrate full awareness of their comic-strip existence—except that Krazy himself upon closer examination behaves very uncharacteristically. Unusually silent in the presence of both Ignatz Mouse and Offissa Pupp, he in fact does not even seem to be listening to them, a circumstance hinted at by his abstracted and possibly distracted expression and then completely borne out in panels three and four, when he falls asleep just as his beloved brick "magically" appears. He seems tired of it all, and indeed upon creasing his cranium, the brick produces no heart, no joyful celebration, no song. Are the characters just rehearsing? Certainly the language throughout suggests artificiality, whether theatricality or simply trite imagery: "picture," "plot," "Like a bud—the plot . . . flowers," "climax," "finale," "overture." This sounds like the plot stripped bare, its energy sapped and its improvisational magic reduced to mere mechanical contrivance. The horizontal bar at the bottom of the strip furthers the notion that Ignatz, like Pupp, only works here, acting a familiar part. And yet, this lower bar—which usually houses some sort of commentary on the action above it—presents a startling reversal: a brick hurtles toward an unsuspecting Ignatz, and the brick thrower stands offstage, his/her identity a mystery. Is the brick thrown by Krazy? by Pupp? by Herriman? by an unsatisfied customer, a member of the audience? It is impossible to know for sure, and all in all, the strip's ambiguity, progression, pairing (of Pupp and Mouse from the first panel on, another variation on usual Coconino behavior), alternation, and interruption—to borrow some of McAllester's words—contrapuntally adorn and upset what looks at first blush like an exercise in sheer repetition. The changes are not merely foolish.

In Kayenta, Herriman by one account attended Navajo ceremonies, and while specific information or detailed stories about what he thought and what the Navajo thought of him remain largely unavailable, it is clear from the strips themselves that he adapted elements of Navajo philosophy as well as designs. He knew, for example, Navajo prayers such as this one:

> With beauty before me, I walk
> With beauty behind me, I walk
> With beauty above me, I walk
> With beauty below me, I walk
> From the East beauty has been restored
> From the South beauty has been restored
> From the West beauty has been restored
> From the North beauty has been restored
> From the zenith in the sky beauty has been restored
> From the nadir of the earth beauty has been restored
> From all around me beauty has been restored.

(Witherspoon, 153–154)

Figure 12. *Krazy Kat*, 25 January 1942. Reprinted with special permission of King Features Syndicate.

Here, formal, structural repetitions both contain and generate significant variations as the prayer describes cardinal points coming together as circles toward a unified expression and incarnation of beauty. As Elsie Lee, a Navajo quoted in *The Sacred*, says, "These Beauty Way songs that is what you are yearning for. . . . The Beauty Way songs are priority to all . . . merits above all" (Beck, Walters, and Francisco, 269).

Compare Offissa Pupp's soliloquy:

Officer Pupp:
Today my world walks in beauty.
Beneath me a good earth—
A gracious glebe, lies in beauty—
Shifting sands dust its cheeks in powdered beauty—
And now I will turn my eye to the empyrean—
where stars' gleam moon's beam—
and sun's sheen abides in beauty . . .
So—I'll nap in beauty.

The Brick (off in the distance): ZIP—

Ignatz Mouse: Today—my world walks in beauty.

Officer Pupp: HIS world—Yaaaa

(McDonnell, O'Connell, and de Havenon, 74)

Delivered in Pupp's finest "poetic" diction, this soliloquy demonstrates Herriman's familiarity with the Navajo prayer as well as his respectful refusal to appropriate it. Most of all, Pupp's language combined with his dramatic situation is funny: his phrasing keeps threatening to sink into bathos, especially when he gets embroiled in possessives, and Ignatz efficiently irks the police dog by winging the brick but also by taking up the words "Today—my world walks in beauty." While the pooch's version comes close enough to be identifiable as both a repetition of particular elements and another variation on the song as a whole, Herriman clearly and carefully presents the soliloquy as a comic performance, not (for example) as an untoward attempt to practice Navajo medicine or religion. He gently adds further variations, loosening the prayer's formal repetitions; Pupp drifts back to the central concept, "in beauty," as his speech drifts toward its punch line and the nap that awaits him. The Navajo version of the song begins each line "With beauty" and then "From the," while the epistrophe ("I walk" and "has been restored") reinforces closure and continuity, deliberate processes of self- and world restoration. Witherspoon remarks, "If a Navajo is to be truly happy and healthy, beauty must dominate his thought and speech, and harmony must permeate his environment" (191). Mitchell offers, "As for the prayers, you say, 'Beauty shall be in front of me, beauty shall be in the back, beauty shall be below me, above me, all around me.' On top of that you say about yourself, 'I am everlasting, I may have an everlasting life. I may live on, and lead an everlasting life with beauty.' You end your prayers that way" (219). Herriman does nothing to menace that sense of beauty, even as he dislodges it by applying it to Pupp.

Witherspoon concludes *Language and Art in the Navajo Universe* by describing a "Navajo aesthetic style" that creates and sustains "dynamic symmetry" (198). In other words, "The total impact of Navajo works of art is a unity of diversity, a synthesis of differences, a harmony of divergence, and a confluence of contrast" (200). Combining with this aesthetic style is a "Navajo intellectual style" rich with "dynamic synthesis" (198): "In their thinking and in their daily behavior Navajos are constantly and creatively integrating and synthesizing. The outward trappings of their whole culture seem to be made of creative syntheses of diverse customs from divergent cultures" (200–201). So, too, "Ectospasms" (Figure 13), where astonishing improvisations of plot and transpositions of language lead "william and nilliam" to—of course—the brick. Visually as well as verbally, this strip takes amazing flights *and* returns the characters and plot to solid ground. "Dynamic symmetry" brings two apparently separate plots together as it links two different sonic and visual images, the balloon's POP and the brick's POW, in ectospasmic glory.

Krazy Kat, finally, resembles or at least comprehends the Navajo art of sandpainting; in both, dynamic symmetry characterizes the work from its making to its evanescent public form and its assured replacement by another painting or the next day's *Krazy Kat*. Thus, each particular work repeats certain important narrative and thematic elements while in the same breath articulating a complex balancing of transience and memory. Tom Ration, a Navajo silversmith who "specializes in the Male Beauty Way Chant (*Hozhoné Biká'ji Hatáál*) which connects to the Mountain Way Chant (*DziX K'ihji Ba'áádi*)," has said,

> In all the ceremonies which have sand paintings, not one has the same sand painting. The figures, the lines, colors, sizes, they all differ. We who have this wonderful knowledge have long memorized all these in our minds and we know exactly what to put into the sand painting because the picture is right in our heads. We instruct our assistants just how to make the figures, colors, and sizes, as it comes into our mind how it is supposed to be made. (Beck, Walters, and Francisco, 29)

The dynamic qualities of this process come clearer on a brief look at the work of Jackson Pollock. Born in Cody, Wyoming, Pollock traveled a great deal in the Southwest; he said of his southwestern Indian influences, "On the floor I am at ease. I feel nearer, more a part of the painting, since this way I can walk around it, work from the four sides and literally be 'in' the painting. This is akin to the method of the Indian sand painters of the West" (quoted in Witherspoon, 175–176). As W. Jackson Rushing explains in *Native American Art and the New York Avant-Garde*, both sandpainting and drip painting

Figure 13. *Krazy Kat,* 11 June 1922. Reprinted with special permission of King Features Syndicate.

work ritually, from memory, toward bringing about acts of transformation and a transformative art (186–187).

These descriptions and positionings of a Navajo aesthetic that is deeply rooted and sacred as well as fundamentally dynamic and transient in practice give further clues to Herriman's Navajo influences and artistic habits. In a strip printed on October 28, 1928, Krazy makes a sandpainting of Ignatz while saying, "Well if he can't be here in person, he can be here in pitcher—I'll draw him in the sand" (McDonnell, O'Connell, and de Havenon, 74). As Pupp says in his soliloquy grounded in a Navajo prayer, "Shifting sands dust [the earth's] cheeks in powdered beauty." Writes Witherspoon, "To the Navajo the artistic or aesthetic value of the sandpainting is found in its creation, not in its preservation. Its ritual value is in its symbolic or representational power and in its use as a vehicle of conception" (152). And after each sandpainting serves its ceremonial purpose, it is destroyed. Although his art is in an important sense secular, whereas Navajo sandpainting is sacred, Herriman, in every strip set in Navajo country and then placed in a daily newspaper, also participates in cultural processes both repetitive and improvisational, both stable and ephemeral.

In conclusion, the interactions among Herriman, Navajo people, and Navajo places resemble the interactions among Herriman, urban spaces, and the Southwest. The strip is distinctively and powerfully "southwestern" not only because of its physical setting but also because Herriman is so well aware of the region's migratory mixtures of indigenous and nonindigenous cultures, forms, and styles. This exceptionally open-ended, fluent, multidirectional understanding of southwestern peoples and places can be read as an implicitly political construction as well as, more explicitly, an aesthetic one, a postcolonial paradigm all the more striking in that it emerges in the contexts of a prevailing early-twentieth-century American colonialism that generally positions both the Southwest and American Indians very differently. When Herriman enters and reenters Navajo country, he regards both the place and the people as active, vital parts of it all; even the Navajo border motifs in particular strips work integratively rather than as marginalizing forces. More importantly, he resists regarding himself as the colonial imposer or arbiter of meaning. (He would probably resist much of what this book ascribes to him for precisely that reason.) The place, finally, sinks Herriman deep yet turns him loose artistically, as his work repeatedly and paradoxically dissolves toward a powerful comprehension of ephemerality. Both verbally and visually, ephemera as metaphor and medium transfix him. Though biographical information remains (aptly) sketchy and fleeting, the authors of *The Comic Art of George Herriman* report that Herriman wanted his life to come to a natural end in the Southwest; Gilbert Seldes recalled him speaking of "lying down on a cactus leaf until he was shrivelled up and blown away by the wind"

(quoted in McDonnell, O'Connell, and de Havenon, 88). He died in his sleep in April 1944, leaving on his Hollywood work table "a week's worth of unfinished *Krazy Kats*" (McDonnell, O'Connell, and de Havenon, 88); his ashes were scattered, as he wished, over Monument Valley.

In larger terms, this analysis moves toward a recontextualization of the Southwest and also of the American nation at large. The impermeable boundaries and more permeable border cultures I describe show the Southwest to be not merely a regionalist outback but rather a shifting collection of deeply connected yet discrete, settled yet powerfully unsettling, local and regional yet multinational and multidirectional constructions (McDonnell, O'Connell, and de Havenon, 28). Without doubt, the Southwest can be arresting, beautiful, captivating, and aesthetically charged in its own right, both physically and metaphysically, both topographically and figuratively. As the discussions of texts by Geronimo and Leslie Marmon Silko have suggested, the region can be and is recharged again and again by indigenous peoples (and less frequently by Euro-American artists) who find ways of setting its enormously mobile elements in textual motion. Navajos and many other southwestern peoples still face crushing poverty, disease, racism, and indifference, as well as less lethal but nonetheless irritating appropriations and romanticizations. Herriman, along with a few others, comes to represent encouragement. He models in *Krazy Kat* a generally successful, promising, migratory circulation of animate characters, modern artistic styles, indigenous peoples, and a new pictorial medium (newspaper comics) to *and* from and through *and* across the Southwest. His images themselves, both verbal and visual, are mostly migrants, and he turns, in a modest and respectful manner, toward American Indian cultural currency as well. He is willing, in other words, to inhabit multiple and potentially conflicting cultural positions: "colored" and "white," "regional" and "national," "Euro-American" and "Navajo." His stylistic habit of "quoting" all these and much more is itself a postcolonial move.

In constructing a deceptively difficult, deceptively different kind of modernist text, he builds a bridge that is not transatlantic to London and Paris and is quite different from what is more often recognized as "conventional," "traditional" Euro-American high modernism. As Houston A. Baker says of an earlier generation of critics, "[T]here seems to be an identifiable pleasure in listing features of art and writing that begin to predominate . . . on or about December 1910" (3). Regarding the Euro-American modernists themselves, Baker's sterling mock bewilderment shape-shifts into something much edgier:

> And it was only a rare one among them who did not have some formula— some "ism"—for checking a precipitous toppling of man and his towers. Futurism, imagism, impressionism, vorticism, expressionism, cubism— all offered explicit programs for the arts *and* the salvation of humanity. Each in its turn yielded to other formulations of the role of the writer and the task of the artist. (Baker, 5)

Krazy Kat encounters various modern "isms" but admits them into a constantly circulating multicultural environment, thereby transforming them, relaxing their explicit programs into implicit subtleties, and describing an altogether different sort of pleasure. Herriman may be one of Baker's rare exceptions, or, more likely, such rarity is but a matter of context. For, just as Baker recontextualizes Charlie Chaplin, Duke Ellington, Booker T. Washington, and Ma Rainey as, literally, household words, so too does this book recontextualize *Krazy Kat*. Herriman does not reject Baker's "isms," but neither does he practice them religiously or programmatically; he is not naive, but he is certainly unassuming about his own considerable sophistication as a modern American artist. As a result, he makes remarkably gentle, remarkably subversive American art.

Like the intersections located and described in *Krazy Kat*, the connections between modernism and what follows it are fluid and often indistinct. "Postmodernism," for example, is not a frontier as much as it is a sort of permeable wall through which much passes, in many directions. Herriman himself saw *Krazy Kat* as something like gentle debris forged in "waste space," set in a southwestern "wasteland," printed in a medium "disposable" by design; he once wrote that "K.K. hasn't so many followers—he's not big enough to stand out in the crowd—so he just bums around along the Baseboards."[3] Maybe it is time to recontextualize "baseness" and reassess this American comic "wasteland," listening (especially) to its urban bop Navajo rhythms as they move not only through the sea of the sky but also through the sky of the sea. Maybe it is time as well to rethink the virtues of the fleeting as well as the paralyses of the colonial, which is to suggest softening but not abandoning potentially untoward metaphors of baseboards, waste, the disposable.

This discussion has suggested something of Herriman's open faith and artistic confidence in the recurrent pleasures of being ephemeral, as well as his happily unpresumptuous relationships with Navajo people and culture. While ceremonies and adaptations, repetitions and improvisations are necessarily cooperative, necessarily cross-cultural processes in the American Southwest, it remains clear that many southwestering people, including several of the writers discussed here, have abused and undercut these processes even in the act of contributing something to a larger, longer view of the Southwest. Herriman, in contrast to these writers, gently straddles worlds and respectfully crosses boundaries in ways that make meaningful and noncolonizing engagements between cultures possible. But to what end? As post–World War II Euro-American cultures turn increasingly to the Southwest as an alien site, and as contemporary American Indian novelists increasingly depict the Southwest as a place where monsters actively interfere with native lives, it is advisable to hold any optimism in check. In an earlier version of this chapter, I concluded it as follows:

> In the open spaces of the American Southwest, where the meetings of
> earth and sky and peoples and texts trick the sense of time and challenge

the fixities of cultures, such keys turn into the audible and visible tones of a new and ancient world. Maybe, as Krazy himself puts it, "just imegine having your ectospasm running around william and nilliam among the unlimitliss etha—golla, it's imbillivibil."

Now I can only urge cautious attention to the Southwest as a crucial national and multinational site that continues to change as it continues to be entered, crossed, recrossed, bounded, overlooked, and resituated by various peoples with various motives in various contexts. Migration, finally and not finally, makes waste of both colonial and postcolonial conditions.

Conclusion

Cross-Purposes and Purposeful Crossings

Beginning with the alien wreckage of a mythologized UFO crash at Roswell, New Mexico, this book has worked through and across a variety of textual passages that reflect cultural migrations and their consequences. As James Clifford suggests, "the worldly, historical routes which both constrain and empower movements across borders and between cultures" (6) interact in complex ways with personal, cultural, and other roots. "[W]hat is at stake," Clifford argues, "is a comparative cultural studies approach to specific histories, tactics, everyday practices of dwelling *and* traveling: traveling-in-dwelling, dwelling-in-traveling" (36). What is at stake, clearly, is the stability of "our" notions of "home," whether "home" refers to people, to built structures, or to tribe, neighborhood, village, city, ethnicity, gender, sexuality, religion, culture, nation, or world, as these notions themselves shift, merge, conflict, and dissolve. The entry of the "otherworldly" alien into Roswell speaks quite directly to these very worldly, translocal, and transcultural matters. Paradoxically, the exceptional yet domesticated "alien" from space is mobilized in ways that crowd out wide varieties of "alien"-"native" encounters in, around, and across contested "home" places. There is no place for American Indians in the Roswell stories; in the most decontextualized versions of these stories, there is no such thing as "alien"-"native" history before the summer of 1947.

This book has tried to rectify such omissions. But Roswell, intriguing as it is, makes for fairly easy game in a relatively narrow field; further, the issues raised by Roswell circulate, in a variety of forms and trajectories, through many other southwestern texts, places, and contexts. And so this volume is not merely a counterhistory of Roswell but rather argues for a multiplicity of American Southwests, through and across which American Indian and Euro-American cultures have been migrating, most often against each other, for a very long time. That the textual passages illuminate the physical migrations is not particularly surprising; that "traveling-in-dwelling, dwelling-in-traveling" is so rampant in multicultural southwestern American literature and yet so unarticulated (in the Roswell narratives as well as in many literary-critical studies of the West, the Southwest, American Indian literature, and more) revitalizes my respect for the texts, writers, and places I return to and arrive at throughout this study. *Almanac of the Dead*, typically, provides the best example. Given the directions of my readings and reflections, readers might expect me to disagree with Joy Harjo when she claims that "*Almanac of the Dead* change[s] the shape and concept of the American novel. It will never be the same" ("World Is Round," 207). But in fact it has become abundantly clear that if there is one paradigmatic text, one text that more than any other exemplifies and yet continually surprises the ideas ventured here, it is *Almanac of the Dead* in all its revolutionary, even chaotic, power. This emerging yet deeply rooted power involves a wide variety of previously unsuspected, unbroached migratory possibilities. Harjo brilliantly observes, for example, "It wouldn't surprise me if Silko disappeared into the pages of one of her novels" ("World Is Round," 210). In some ultimate, doubtless tactical act of both traveling and homing in, Leslie Marmon Silko and her storytelling might very well cross physical and textual borders to the extent that they merge into each other, probably generating new stories in the process. She would disappear, that is, but her stories would not.

This is more than idle speculation. *Almanac of the Dead* surprises even Silko in its ways of actively displacing and deauthorizing its own author; she has spoken of the novel as an entity unto itself, a 763-page text that once stretched as far as 1,793 pages (Perry, 328). She speaks wonderingly of her own obsessive writing of the book—or, perhaps more accurately, the book's obsessive writing of her—and jokes about "these dear little people that love *Ceremony*, what's going to happen to them when they get sucked into the maelstrom of *Almanac!*" (Perry, 331). The implicit suggestion here is that *Almanac of the Dead* goes places that *Ceremony* (and *Storyteller*) simply do not go, and it goes there as a hungry, dangerous, even monstrous text, a "maelstrom" that seems to have an undisciplined agency of its own. In other words, it is able and transgressively willing to cycle, to turn and return, even to risk the creation of monsters—or the transmutation of itself, and perhaps its author, into monsters. "It is as if I am compelled to violate the scope of any outline or plan," Silko writes; "it is as if the writing does not want me to know what is about to happen" (*Yellow Woman*, 135). In other words, she links these violations to the book's sometimes monstrous autonomy: the book makes her transgress, makes her move in unexpected directions. *Almanac of the Dead* is, like each of the Mayan Almanac codices, a fragmentary, migratory text that purposefully redefines, strategically takes control of, and tricksterishly disrupts the ways of the "alien"-"native" Southwest, including the designs and movements of its own author or authors.

Like Mary Shelley's *Frankenstein* (1818), then, *Almanac of the Dead* at times appears to be a monstrous text that consumes its own author and generates itself, a text that describes and enacts, among other things, the monstrosities of consumption (see Halberstam, particularly Chapter 2). As Silko points out, "I also had the feeling that it was *Almanac* trying to keep hold on me because it really didn't want to end. Simon and Schuster made the *Alma-*

nac end. I, the one who was in the day-to-day world, made it end. But the *Almanac* didn't want to end" (Perry, 338). Silko offers this remark as a sympathetic gesture to her quite possibly unsettled and overwhelmed readers, and she also suggests that she has transgressed out of necessity. She knows full well the dangerousness and inefficacy of supplying this grisly, funny, perverse, polemical material to her readers, and she supplies it anyway. Silko explains, "I asked myself, 'Do I really have to write about all this incredible twisted sexual torture? Do I have to write about America's fascination with blood and violent death?' But I knew I had to because nobody really wants to talk about it" (Perry, 327). In a sense, the very prevalence—indeed, the repeatability—of the horrific risks clashing with the improvisational repeatability of storytelling grounded in oral traditions. But the horrific, in all its recurring transgressive power, also directly contributes to the urgency of the revolutionary countermovements Silko describes and advocates.[1]

In part because it comes to seem such a restlessly, unpredictably, and even monstrously paradigmatic text, *Almanac of the Dead* should be reread. As readers go through the narrative again (and again), they enter at least partially into the kinds of migratory processes that the characters and the text evince. The point of rereading is not to wrest control of the stories away from the text. Rather, these processes of reading and rereading help make visible the many ways in which characters go through things again (and again); stories recur, indigenous peoples return to their lands, obsessed characters repeat and intensify their obsessions, international and other borders are crossed and recrossed. These routes and roots seem necessarily to include characters and scenes so horrifying that, as in the work of William S. Burroughs, they induce perverse pleasure even—especially—when they most explicitly refuse to go away. Certainly it is clear that these excesses and monstrosities both obstruct and instigate indigenous peoples who strategically organize massive southwestern migrations as a crucial part of their work toward retaking the Americas.[2] Indeed, exposure to the horrors—reading and rereading, telling and retelling—urges a complex sense of complicity that may be more productive, politically and culturally, than detachment from them.

Perhaps these speculations help to explain why Silko tells Donna Perry, "I liked all my characters quite a bit. . . . A lot of the characters developed . . . and they saved their own lives" (329)—even the spoiled Alegría and the sadistic snuff-video peddler, Beaufrey. Sharon Holland takes a similar point and moves it in a different direction:

> *Almanac* centers itself both within and without various communities, as technocrats and corrupt officials meander through a succession of gross actions and the "people" who wish to "take back the land" also experience and wander through a maze of grotesque circumstances, couplings and terrains, so that the categories of "self" and "other," "inside" and "outside," become blurred in the telling of this story. . . . [W]ithin the terrain of *Almanac* is both the story of witchery and slavery and of revolution and freedom. (342–343)

These blurrings of identity provide Silko with one way of ensuring that in *Almanac of the Dead* much remains unresolved, or, perhaps more accurately, much continues to shift and grow in unsettling and exciting ways. It is also, of course, a self-consciously prophetic text, not (in this sense) an argument to be accepted or refuted so much as a self-proclaimed inevitability that both reveals and creates a sort of intuitive, energetic realm of possibility predicated on migrations across time as well as space. In this way, Silko both constructs and qualifies alliances or collaborations between herself, her readers, and a narrative that controls her even as she invents it. Rereading, then, not only resembles the migratory practices Silko advocates but also provides a way of magnifying the paradoxical heart of *Almanac of the Dead*, the center that moves as well as the movements that venture to fix and the moments that threaten to horrify and terrorize.

Links between the monstrous and the migratory appear, in various intensities, not only in *Almanac of the Dead* but in a wide range of contemporary southwestern American Indian fiction. In other words, reading and rereading *Almanac of the Dead* reveals and generates migratory monsters as well as "monstrous" migrations—personal and cultural identities under duress and in motion—and so, too, does reading across a range of contemporary Indian narratives grounded in the Southwest. Of course, a complex manifestation of witchery appears in Silko's own *Ceremony* (1977), as does a contravening power that circulates through some—not all—people, things, and stories, enabling them to shift, grow, and survive.[3] Ron Querry's *The Death of Bernadette Lefthand* (1993) involves Navajo witches who double as murderers and travelers. Anna Lee Walters's *Ghost Singer* (1988) cautiously discusses the ghosts of depatriated Indians who haunt the Smithsonian Institution (the place they have been removed to, by force); these ghosts appear to a variety of museum visitors, Indian and non-Indian, but move most aggressively against white museum employees who "specialize" in Indians. Responding to this very serious problem, a variety of Indian characters move closer to each other and travel to Washington as a sort of intertribal delegation. In Louis Owens's *Bone Game* (1994), psychopathic Euro-American serial killers and a painted, mixed-blood Gambler figure hauntingly roam the forests around Santa Cruz, California, and a displaced mixed-blood literature professor gradually resituates himself in relation to his family and his sense of home. He is able to do this in part because his relations travel from Mississippi to Santa Cruz to help him confront and control a dangerous array of personal and cultural demons. And in A. A. Carr's *Eye Killers* (1995), migratory vampires, invading New Mexico as both mythic and spectacularly physical aliens, come into complex contact with Navajo monsters—skinwalkers—as well as Navajo and non-Navajo elders, teenagers, and schoolteachers.

Even this short list of contemporary American Indian novels suggests an interesting conjunction among migration, monstrosity, and the American Southwest. Of course, as this book's introductory reading of Roswell conspiracy narratives demonstrates, alien presences are not at all exceptional in the Southwest; what is perhaps most odd about the Roswell aliens is that they are considered to be something new rather than a continuation of long-standing, even familiar southwestern encounters between "natives" and "aliens." In this sense, too, the role of the Southwest as atomic testing and development site should not be overlooked (although nuclear issues are beyond the scope of this book; see Caputi). But the vampires and witches that populate these recent Indian novels represent more than merely surrogate conquistadors, missionaries, U.S. soldiers, Indian agents, corporate tools, and nuclear physicists, to name no more. These monsters often signify most powerfully when they are in the process of being resituated, most often by full- or mixed-blood Indian characters. That is, Indians find ways of seeing and naming the monster; in doing so, they often move physically as well as metaphysically toward its shifting, frightening, dis-positioning domain. But the dangers and other complications of these often transgressive, often transcultural encounters between monsters and Indians loom large; the problems monsters cause or reflect threaten to subvert or explode Indian cultures, and these problems rarely go away permanently.

Most if not all of these narratives hinge on Indian recognition of the monsters both around and inside Indian communities. The "elderlies" (Carr's term) in *Eye Killers* recognize the vampires, at least partially, by positioning them in relation to Navajo and Keresan stories, eventually linking them to their loosely equivalent "Indian" counterparts, skinwalkers.[4] Similarly, in *Bone Game* various Choctaw characters, along with a cross-dressing Navajo anthropologist, work out an understanding of who the Gambler is and why he appears where and when he does. To do so, they rely on their knowledge of California Indian history but also recognize him as a sort of metaphysical migrant who appears, for instance, in the dreams and visions of Onatima Blue Wood even before she herself travels from her home place, Mississippi, to Santa Cruz, the current, haunted home place of her adopted grandson, Cole McCurtain. Onatima, Cole, their relations, and their Navajo friend, Alex Yazzie, must also untangle the story of the Gambler from the story of the serial killers, must learn to detach these stories despite their seeming connections. In each of the novels named above, Indian characters—many of them elders—develop responses to mysterious, monstrous, "alien" figures by patiently turning to flexible, selectively adaptable tribal stories and precepts that enable them to move closer to the monsters and to turn these dispositioning forces back on themselves.

In this way, both Carr and Owens are clearly indebted to Silko. In *Ceremony*, the witchery envelops Tayo's best friends (among others), and as the mixed-blood healer and philosopher Betonie explains, Tayo must learn to see the witches—and himself—in relation to, rather than in opposition to, Laguna Pueblo Indian culture. Owens acknowledges this debt explicitly, both in his language ("witches" and "their evil will turn against itself," 154) and in his act of naming a minor but dangerous witch after one of the most troubling witches in *Ceremony*, Emo. Carr, too, acknowledges *Ceremony* in a variety of ways, from the Betonie-like clutter of the Pachecos' living room (156) to the understanding that the evil is bigger than just white people (272) and that ceremonies must change to respond to changing situations and contexts (279). Owens familiarizes monsters by repositioning them both as victims of Luther Cole's Choctaw piss-hex and as recurring figures in an American Indian literary genealogy.[5] Carr similarly situates the monstrous in strong relation to the familiar. Taking responsibility for the monsters, wherever and however they surface, these contemporary southwestern Indian characters, stories, and writers turn and return to something like the flexible, migratory paradigm discussed throughout this book. Unlike the domestications of Roswell aliens, though, the reorientations of monsters in American Indian fiction also involve productive, if frightening and potentially unsettling, reorientations of Indians.

Because these contemporary Indian reinventions and repositionings of monsters work in such complicated ways as teachings, it is important to examine briefly some of the pedagogical applications of these texts, particularly in light of storytelling as a form of cross-cultural currency and survival. Greg Sarris has written persuasively about classroom uses and practices of storytelling, arguing for "the potential for storytelling to empower and engage culturally diverse students while providing, in turn, a context for strong sense critical thinking for all of us, students and teachers alike, such that the nature of our shared reality and our relationship to it is made more visible and less intimidating" (168). What Sarris urges here is remarkably similar to what the contemporary American Indian novelists discussed here do, however cautiously, with both their monsters and their readers. That is, the relationships Indian characters work out between themselves and monsters resemble the relationships Indian novelists work out between themselves and their readers. This is not to collapse the many distinctions among readers, vampires, and witches or to overlook Jana Sequoya-Magdaleno's cautionary point that

> many scholarly interpreters of Native American fiction seem to assume that the writer, however explicitly bicultural, however modern—as evidenced by appropriation of the novel form itself—is nevertheless transparent at some preconscious level, that is, really *is* the narrative position taken up for the sake of participating in the discursive conditions of the genre. (93–94)

But in constructing a "more visible and less intimidating" sense of "the nature of our shared reality and our relationship to it," characters, storytellers, readers, writers, students, and teachers alike participate in a form of migration—a process of resituating that urges respect for both the roots and the routes of everyone concerned. But storytellers often have to dis-position—however frightening, transgressive, or dangerous the stories may be—before they can reposition. And the Indian characters and writers in question must reorient themselves not only by changing the ceremonies and stories but also by anticipating and taking on the cultural consequences of these changes.

In *Eye Killers*, for example, a young Euro-American girl named Elizabeth

Mary Washburn, originally from Boone County, Kentucky, migrates west from Independence, Missouri, in 1849. En route, her family is attacked by monsters, and Elizabeth is bitten by the vampire, Falke. However, she does not transform entirely; she operates as both human and vampire, both nineteenth- and twentieth-century girl and woman, both abductor and abductee. She is both a mixed-blood character and a blood-mixing character. Eventually, this relentlessly liminal character finds herself in a willing, mutually respectful, even loving relationship with Navajo elder Michael Roanhorse, who is in the process of rescuing his granddaughter, Melissa, from these same vampires. Meanwhile, Carr admits a non-Indian character, high-school English teacher Diana Logan, fully into ceremony; she learns and is entrusted with sacred Navajo knowledge, in part because she tells a story that a Navajo medicine woman recognizes. This is not to say that Carr defers Navajo culture to Irish-American culture or to migratory vampires but rather to point out that Logan is guided and admitted into a carefully demarcated sacred space and taught a small portion of sacred knowledge. She acquires status as a sort of honorary and honored Navajo woman warrior, but the Indian elderlies allow her the opportunity to go to that space and help her to heal her own psychic wounds in the process. Similarly, Michael and Elizabeth move toward a partial but powerful "shared reality" that they can constitute only after telling each other their stories, dis-positioning themselves in order to reposition themselves. Michael and Elizabeth even reveal their scrupulously guarded real names to each other. Are these examples of transcultural adaptation gone too far? Or are they brilliant and daring pedagogical gestures, ways of instigating productive dispositions of routes and roots in non-Indians and Indians alike?

Carr represents Navajo culture as a sort of permeable, unwritten anthology, an adaptable collection of stories, ceremonies, and other forms of remembered knowledge. At the same time, by taking on the Euro-American vampire narrative, he interweaves another type of oral narrative and actively invites the puns, like "oral narrative," that come so easily here. This punning facility is to be expected, according to Judith Halberstam, who suggests—in a study of Gothic monsters—that "[p]unning creates or enacts a form of cultural remembering" (180). She is thinking about the intertextuality of vampire narratives, the ways they, like many American Indian stories, remember their textual ancestors. As a Navajo/vampire story, for example, *Eye Killers* is very much aware of Bram Stoker's *Dracula* (and various film adaptations of Stoker's novel) as well as of *Ceremony*. In Carr's narrative, though, the alpha vampire Falke's own story is blurry, badly preserved, and full of holes. And Falke's stories—like the one about the reincarnation of his nine-centuries-old true love, Christiane, as a contemporary woman—are tired and predictable, except that now the woman is a Navajo teenager, Melissa Roanhorse. It is as though Falke, for all his power, is controlled not so much by a blood inheritance as by a textual genealogy; clearly he is driven by this highly conventional "vampire narrative," which, although locally adaptable, adheres to a variety of generic contrivances. And precisely at these textual moments when the vampire narrative seems most familiar, Carr dis-positions his readers, not only by entangling the vampire stories with the Navajo stories but also by exposing complicities between readers and vampires. Many readers, Indian and non-Indian alike, will likely be more familiar with vampires than with Changing Woman, just as Silko's readership will probably be more familiar with atomic warfare than with Thought Woman. The trick in teaching *Eye Killers*, then, is to decenter vampire mythology while giving a sense of all the various ways in which vampires, Navajos, storytellers, and readers migrate toward each other and interact with each other in transgressive, unsettling, disengaging, and reengaging ways.

Clearly, Carr in *Eye Killers* regards the routes and roots of human (and nonhuman) relationships as pedagogical in nature. The vampires have to learn how to be vampires; they read books and mentor each other. Likewise, the Navajo have to learn how to be Navajo; Coyote, Changing Woman, the elderlies, and the stories themselves are all explicitly represented as teachers. These acts of teaching and learning acknowledge permeable boundaries and redefine cultural boundaries, as when the elders embrace Diana and transform her from high-school English teacher into student and quasi-Navajo. When Michael Roanhorse and the hyperliminal Elizabeth tell each other stories, they teach each other and even fall in love as they redefine cross-purposes as purposeful crossings. Clearly, Carr teaches not only the importance of stories but also the important relationships and transitions between stories. Everyone in the book has vampires (losses, ghosts, regrets, hauntings); everyone in the book has stories. The difference between Falke and Elizabeth is that she, like Michael, can tell and adapt her stories transculturally. Unlike Falke, Elizabeth and Michael come to understand that "adaptation" is not simply a convenient, abstract notion but rather a physical and metaphysical act of dis-positioning and repositioning. They recognize the tremendous problems and possibilities of migratory adaptability, this physical and metaphysical process that places both their roots and their routes at stake as it demands their full powers of intelligence, memory, imagination, and endurance.

"Navajo witches are human," one of the Navajo-Keresan elderlies, William Pacheco, tells Diana:

> Skinwalkers are evil humans. They eat stew and fried bread just like you and me. The Holy Ones are not human. They don't understand us people too well; or maybe too much. Coyote is one of our greatest teachers, yet I don't consider him to be human. But his stories are about people. He knows about us and teaches us the good and bad of our ways. I think these vampires that have stolen Melissa are to be respected, as we respect the Holy Ones and Coyote; even though we fear the vampires and hate them. (A.A. Carr 273)

As is more than evident by now, *Eye Killers* is not a simple story about identity. It avoids various kinds of simplifications: good versus evil, vampires versus Navajos, mortal humans versus immortal monsters. As William Pacheco explains, even fear and hate need not crowd out respect. Across 344 pages, Carr demonstrates how exceptionally difficult it is to learn what William teaches—and how exceptionally important it is. William's learning crosses temporal and spatial boundaries, and it works comparatively as it stretches to integrate vampires and much more—the white woman, for example, who finds herself grouped with both skinwalkers and Indian elders as humans who "eat stew and fried bread." Like Silko in *Almanac of the Dead*, Carr in *Eye Killers* risks much in dis-positioning both the "monsters" and the "humans." Both Carr and Silko insist on seeing the "monsters" or "aliens" in relation to the "humans," and both regard complicity as a form of responsibility.

It is crucial, finally, to see how these two novels—and many others, some of which this book discusses—use both monsters and migrations to reflect, critique, and reconstruct notions of the Americas. American Indians have been migratory for a long time, since well before the advent of European colonists; in other words, the southwestern dispositions discussed here can themselves be redefined, resituated as, first and foremost, American Indian dispositions. But for better or for worse, migrations rarely happen without countermigrations; cross-purposes and purposeful crossings motivate and complicate each other. And as William Pacheco understands, migrations and monsters are neither easily separable nor easily joined. Rather, both construct their own particular kinds of dispositions, and both challenge students and teachers not only to shift paradigms but to combine them and to keep traveling.

Clifford argues that "traveling-in-dwelling, dwelling-in-traveling" is an everyday global phenomenon. While the American Southwest does not reach quite that far quite that frequently, the most compelling southwestern and southwestering texts, read together, raise a rich variety of difficult questions about the nature and position of personal and cultural identity, questions that make clear the need for a critical resituating of the Southwest. American Indian novels such as *Almanac of the Dead* and *Eye Killers*, for example, represent and enact complex, sometimes monstrous migrations that implicate characters, readers, and writers in the places they move from, through, and toward. Though there is, finally, no magic formula for moving "students and teachers alike" toward and into Sarris's "shared reality," southwestern American Indian and Euro-American texts provide particularly incisive and interesting ways of loosening a variety of graven images and assumptions about regions, cultures, nations, and literary canons. As we map the cross-purposes, the routes and roots that implicate us in a multiplicity of American Southwests, we begin to articulate the southwestern dispositions that, in so many ways, make purposeful crossings and repositionings possible.

Notes

Introduction

1. Readers interested in navigating through the vast literature on the Roswell UFO crash might start with Berlitz and Moore, *Roswell Incident*, then turn to Randle and Schmitt, *Truth about the UFO Crash*. The latter text supersedes the former but does so in a highly self-conscious, sometimes defensive way, indicating tensions and disagreements among the Roswell "researchers." See also Benson Saler, Charles A. Ziegler, and Charles B. Moore, *UFO Crash at Roswell: The Genesis of a Modern Myth*. Washington, D.C.: Smithsonian Institution Press, 1997.

2. The U.S. Air Force released "The Roswell Report, Case Closed" in late June 1997. Associated Press wire stories about this report appeared in newspapers dated 24 June 1997.

3. Of course, both Robert Bloch's and Alfred Hitchcock's Bates Motels are deadly places, but they are different deadly places. Bloch's novel *Psycho* begins in Texas. Mary Crane, fleeing with money stolen from her workplace, drives through Oklahoma City and Tulsa, then heads north; in the novel, the Bates Motel appears to be in Kansas. However, in the movie, released in 1960, Hitchcock switches settings: probably to call further attention to the bird imagery, the movie begins in Phoenix. Marion Crane's flight takes her through Arizona toward California, and the Bates Motel is somewhere in this southwestern area.

Chapter 1

1. Clifford, *Routes*, 13, theorizes and enacts some of these and other questions of travel while also posing different, though related, questions: "Is it possible to locate oneself historically, to tell a coherent global story, when historical reality is understood to be an unfinished series of encounters? What attitudes of tact, receptivity, and self-irony are conducive to nonreductive understandings? What are the conditions for serious translation between different routes in an interconnected but not homogeneous modernity? Can we recognize viable alternatives to 'traveling West,' old and new paths?" See also MacCannell, *Tourist*.

2. I am indebted to James Clifford for this very suggestive and useful formulation, a variation of which I introduce in the first paragraph of this chapter. See Clifford, *Routes*, especially 24–25.

3. On Euro-American images and stereotypes of American Indians, see the

standard studies by Berkhofer, *White Man's Indian,* and Roy Harvey Pearce, *Savagism and Civilization.* For Indian critiques of European and Euro-American immigration to the Americas, Silko's *Almanac,* Deloria's *God Is Red,* and Allen's *Sacred Hoop* are three of the many excellent places to start. Flynn, "Christopher Columbus," recasts Columbus's "discovery" of the Americas as a Coyote story, "Christopher Coyote and the Seeds of the Sun." Revard, "Report," nicely turns the tables on all things colonial, Silko's "Tribal Prophecies" (in *Yellow Woman,* 146–148) speaks concisely to some of the salient issues also raised in *Almanac,* and, more generally, many American Indian autobiographies weigh in on this issue, sometimes by discussing Indian prophecies of European arrivals.

4. As my use of quotation marks only begins to articulate, "prehistory" is an enormously problematic term, one that I do not in any way endorse. Like related terms—"pre-Columbian," "preliterate," "precontact"—"prehistory" implies that there was no history, no contact, no literacy in the Americas before the advent of Europeans. In a slightly different way, "pre-Columbian" makes a similar gesture, suggesting that things—and cultures—really don't get underway in the Americas until Columbus arrives. For further discussion of these matters, see Krupat, *Native American Autobiography,* 19–21.

5. Readers interested in Paul Martin's work should begin by consulting Martin and Wright, eds., *Pleistocene Extinctions,* and Martin and Klein, eds., *Quaternary Extinctions.*

6. On Beringia, a thorough recent text is West, ed., *American Beginnings.* However, West does not, in his introduction to this large book, acknowledge American Indian opposition to the western construct of Beringia.

7. Greg Sarris criticizes Allen, not specifically for her work on Silko but for what he sees as her tendency to overgeneralize, in *Keeping Slug Woman Alive,* 124–130. Sarris argues that Allen "replicates in practice what she sets out to criticize" (126).

Chapter 2

1. Both Geronimo and Betzinez write extensively about hostilities between Apaches and Mexicans. In *Geronimo's Story of His Life,* Geronimo gives an entire section (Chapters 6–12) to these battles and their consequences. Betzinez is less interested in elaborating on Apache-Mexican relations, but he does begin *I Fought with Geronimo* by discussing them, and his attitude toward the Mexicans is clear and very similar to Geronimo's (see 1–9, 14–17, 93–96).

2. Limerick reads the desert as "aesthetic spectacle" in *Desert Passages,* especially 6–7, 91–94. Readers interested in Billy the Kid's academic career should begin with Tatum, *Inventing Billy the Kid.* Written for the centennial of Billy the Kid's death, this text studies both the formation of an iconic American outlaw and the various transformations this icon has undergone. Tatum both updates and usefully supplements Steckmesser's chapters on Billy the Kid in *Western Hero.* Utley, *Billy the Kid,* is a solid, more straightforwardly biographical work. Finally, see Tuska, *Billy the Kid,* which includes inconsistently persuasive critiques of rival scholars.

3. In *Billy the Kid,* 231–236, Tuska rightly notes Tatum's Turneresque assumptions, but readers should note in turn Tuska's disciplinary biases and blind spots.

Chapter 3

1. Of course, as Henry Adams's *Education* demonstrates, western autobiography can be and has been written in the third person. For a fascinating and powerful African-American autobiographical text written under a pseudonym and given a third-person title, see Jacobs, *Incidents*.

2. To his credit, Krupat, *For Those Who Come After*, explicitly acknowledges the places in his argument where evidence is scanty or altogether nonexistent. He parenthetically points out that "there does not seem to be an original manuscript [of *Geronimo's Story of His Life*] extant" (61–62), and he remarks, "It is not possible effectively to disprove" (70) the view that Geronimo sees things the way Barrett says he does—or that Geronimo has an argument and that that argument at least occasionally competes with Barrett's marks on and in the text. As will be clear from my argument, I generally sympathize with Greg Sarris's reading of Krupat's reading of Geronimo.

3. For an interesting gloss on these observations, see the chapter titled "At War with the U.S. Government" in Silko, *Almanac*, 128–132. In the complex structural geography of this novel, the chapter in question is the seventh of nine chapters in Book 5 ("The Border") of Part 1 ("The United States of America"). The chapter ends with the death of Lecha and Zeta's Yaqui grandmother, Yoeme, and contains Yoeme's sophisticated commentary on "the photographs that are labeled 'Geronimo'" (129) as well as suggestive links between these photographs and the interconnected, crucial problems of losing and preserving pages of the Almanac. For further discussion of Yoeme's remarks and of the "Geronimo" photographs, see Chapter 4 of this book.

4. Correctives to this view can be found, of course, in Geronimo, *Geronimo's Story of His Life*, and Betzinez, *I Fought with Geronimo*, as well as in historical and critical texts such as Debo's *Geronimo*.

5. While Betzinez appears to be extraordinarily and often uncritically good-natured almost by disposition, Geronimo exercises a more skeptical, cautious, critical view; thus, Geronimo's enjoyment of the Louisiana Purchase Exposition at St. Louis in 1904 is much harder earned and much more qualified than Betzinez's enjoyment of the prisoner-of-war train.

6. Nye's remarks here may seem to contradict a point I make earlier in this chapter, as well as in n. 4, above. Betzinez, like Geronimo, did not completely set aside bows and arrows; indeed, Debo, *Geronimo*, 18, points out that boys "practiced much with the bow and arrow" in the early part of the nineteenth century. But adult Apache warriors often used guns in the late nineteenth century.

Chapter 4

1. Of course, one of the most influential texts on the evanescence and mystery of photography is Barthes, *Camera Lucida*. For a more specifically focused discussion of the "magical power that seems to emanate from the photographic image," see Lee Clark Mitchell, "Photograph and the American Indian," xiv–xv.

2. In an interview published in Perry, *Backtalk*, Silko says that "I needed to rest after *Almanac*. . . . I also had the feeling that it was *Almanac* trying to keep hold on me because it didn't really want to end. Simon and Schuster made the *Almanac* end. I, the one who was in the day-to-day world, made it end. But the

Almanac didn't want to end. . . . *Almanac* has dominated me for so long" (338–339). Again, Silko refuses conventional disciplinary boundaries as she insists that *Almanac,* like *the* almanac, has temporal and spatial life and migratory power beyond the frames and covers of a single text or writer.

3. I am grateful to Shelley Reid for this insight.

4. In the interview published in Perry, *Backtalk,* Silko agrees to call Sterling "a moral center or a connection for the reader" (Perry's words), 330.

5. In *Navajo and Photography,* xi, Faris declares, "My purpose is also . . . polemical—to counter the hegemonic discourses currently commanding analysis of photography of Navajo and to suggest alternatives."

6. See the captivity narratives by Mary Rowlandson, Sarah Wakefield, and a host of other white women who, of course, have different experiences of captivity, which they then narrate in a variety of ways. A good, useful study of these and other writers and issues is Castiglia, *Bound and Determined.*

Chapter 5

1. The concept of "leisure" is highly elastic, and information on early-twentieth-century leisure can be located in a wide variety of sources. It would make sense to begin with Veblen, *Theory.* Recent studies include Banta, *Taylored Lives,* and Bill Brown, *Material Unconscious.*

2. This discussion of O'Keeffe's "centering on the margins" and "marginal center" bears in mind her conscious decision to construct a distant yet active link between her northern New Mexico home and the Manhattan gallery of her husband, Alfred Stieglitz. Critical work on O'Keeffe's negotiations (or lack thereof) with southwestern American Indians remains scanty; however, Momaday visited with O'Keeffe and wrote a poem about their meeting, "Forms of the Earth at Abiquiu," which is published in *Gourd Dancer,* 60.

3. These romantic narratives and solutions are so accessible that they may not need to be elucidated in great detail here. I will content myself with recommending revisionist historiographies such as Limerick's *Legacy of Conquest* and decisive critiques of dominant American culture such as Deloria's *God Is Red*—books, in other words, that give a sense of the romantic narratives, discuss the romancers' motives, and offer important correctives. Readers interested in the romantic narratives themselves might begin by consulting Berkhofer, *White Man's Indian,* and Roy Harvey Pearce, *Savagism and Civilization.*

4. In 1890, Bandelier published *The Delight Makers.* Readers interested in Cushing's writings might begin with Green, ed., *Cushing at Zuni.* Crane's accounts of his journalistic travels in the region can be found in Katz, ed., *Stephen Crane.*

5. Doyle's *A Study in Scarlet* (1887), in *Complete Sherlock Holmes* (3–88), moves rather abruptly between London and the American desert. Weigle and White's *Lore* abundantly illustrates the range of late nineteenth- and twentieth-century texts that take the desert as their subject or setting and charts the increasing popularity of these texts.

6. One useful source on corporate involvement with natural spectacles is Hyde, *American Vision.* Readers might also consult Weigle and Babcock, eds., *Great Southwest,* and Kathleen L. Howard, *Inventing the Southwest.*

Chapter 6

1. David W. Teague's *The Southwest in American Literature and Art: The Rise of a Desert Aesthetic* was published while *American Indian Literature and the Southwest* was in the process of publication.

2. Pizer, *Novels,* especially 56–63, discusses the influence of Lombroso and Nordau on Norris.

3. Similarly, as Chase notes in *American Novel,* 191, "One reason for the abstractness that makes so notable a part of the book is that McTeague himself is semilegendary; we should have to change our feeling about him if his name were Joe McTeague, say, instead of apparently just plain McTeague." Given the astonishing abstraction and vacancy swirling in and sometimes around McTeague, any specific details indicating his tastes and preferences become genuinely fascinating as curiosities; for example, he "would have a son, whose name would be Daniel, who would go to High School, and perhaps turn out to be a prosperous plumber or house painter" (Norris, *McTeague,* 191–192). The play of vast personage and small but telling detail in turn recalls Samuel Johnson's theories of biography and their application in, among other texts, Boswell's *Life of Johnson.* Boswell remarks, "I remain firm and confident in my opinion, that minute particulars are frequently characteristick, and always amusing, when they relate to a distinguished man" (25). Though Boswell and Johnson are of course not beset by McTeague's strain of baffled abstraction, the idea that small details reveal great (or huge or enormously limited) people pertains to both the dentist and the lexicographer—as does the nearly sublime impact of the "minute particular" when seen in relation to the vast and often more abstract potentiality.

4. See Cullick, "Configurations," and Dean, "Domestic Horizons." Both Cullick and Dean describe how seeming disjunctions in the narrative structure of *McTeague* in fact maintain thematic and structural continuities. As I suggest I argue that these disjunctive continuities magnify emptiness or nothingness.

5. Dillingham, *Frank Norris,* is especially good on Norris's years as an art student in Paris and elsewhere; see especially Chapter 1, "The Would-Be Painter."

Chapter 7

1. The question of why Americans travel is of course a large one. Good places to begin formulating a response include Clifford, *Routes,* MacCannell, *Tourist,* and Caesar, *Forgiving the Boundaries.*

2. Though Abbey gets quite a few things wrong and evidently only reread the first three or so pages of Austin's book before writing his introduction to it, he nonetheless makes an excellent foil for her, especially when it comes to gendered language: "Our nature writers are such a sober, solemn, misty-eyed lot. . . . But, what the hell, after a few pages the tolerant reader ceases to be troubled by Austin's poetical, elliptical, sometimes periphrastical phraseology. If it seems too fussy, even prissy at first, you are soon absorbed by the accuracy of her observational powers and learn to overlook, then ignore, and finally forget the pretty archaisms, the invertebrate verbs" (introduction, xi–xii).

3. Ammons, *Conflicting Stories,* 94, continues: "Coming out of Austin's understanding of Indian art, in combination with nineteenth-century western sketch tradition, the book, more than anything else, resembles a collection of

Seyavi's bowls. Each individual narrative unit represents a variation on the same form. As is true of the earth, the source of both Austin's and Seyavi's art, there exists both endless subtle difference and profound sameness, repetition. We can move the units, arrange the bowls in any order, and the result varies yet remains the same. . . . All of the pieces tell us that we are part of the earth; our patterns are its; its harmony ours."

4. Ruoff, "Three Nineteenth-Century American Indian Autobiographers," 261, states unequivocally that Winnemucca's *Life among the Piutes* is the first Native American autobiography written by a woman. Georgi-Findlay, "Frontiers," 222, however, says only that Winnemucca's is "one of the first autobiographical narratives written by a Native American woman." I should add here that *Life among the Piutes* is usually published under Winnemucca's married name, Hopkins; however, I have elected to follow critical convention and refer to her as "Winnemucca" throughout.

5. Ruoff begins to suggest links between Winnemucca and Jacobs in "Three Nineteenth-Century American Indian Autobiographers," 251–269.

6. Here I disagree with Sands's assertion that "[t]he text is not a polyphony; only the single voice of Winnemucca actually narrates dramatic events and characters" ("Indian Women's Personal Narrative," 278). Not only is the distinction between "single" and, say, "tribal" voice quite unclear—in Winnemucca's autobiography as well as in a variety of other nineteenth- and twentieth-century American Indian autobiographies—but the very structure of *Life among the Piutes*, especially the apparatus, suggests something much more like a multivocal collage than a single voice speaking soliloquies.

Chapter 8

1. Reynolds, *Willa Cather*, 123, for example, writes of *One of Ours*, "The unevenness of the text, the technical failures and clashing discourses, testify to Cather's difficulties in gauging the true 'national significance' of the war."

2. Cordell, *Prehistory*, 58, 102–104, explains that the "Mesa Verde" Indians were Anasazi who abandoned the cliff city around 1300. Cordell points out that urban communities such as this one develop (among other identities) a collective identity as residents of a city; I am arguing that for Cather, this collective identity is superseded by a different collective identity—the Indians as dead and vanished. Of course, as Cordell is well aware, doing ethnographies of "missing persons" is very difficult. See Cordell, *Prehistory*, 21, 118–119, for some discussion of these problems.

3. See for example Michaels, *Our America*, 7, 8, in which Michaels reads Cather's representation of Louis Marcellus as a racial "other"; there is, writes Michaels, a "sense that what is outside the family is also outside the race."

4. Similarly, Stout, "Willa Cather," 50, argues, "Even if Tom had succeeded in his goal of getting government officials to remove the relics to a museum, of course, the result would have been the despoiling of the beautiful remains of a past life—a less crass and less objectionable despoiling, to be sure, but the destruction of the site as it had been."

5. Ammons, *Conflicting Stories*, 101–102, has written forcefully about modernist appropriation: "In the history of modernism the appropriation by white

artists of the cultural perspectives of people of color has almost always been racist and exploitative. . . . Modernism is rooted in repeated raids by the twentieth-century west, for its own psychic and artistic purposes, on cultures it has defined as less 'civilized' or more 'primitive.' . . . Indeed, it may be that any attempt by a white person in the twentieth century to participate intellectually in the cultures of nonwhite peoples is by definition corrupt, given the pervasively discriminatory construction of race, class, culture, and nationality in the modern world."

6. The best of these few arguments critical of Duchene is Schwind, "This Is a Frame-Up."

7. Duchene may very well also be influenced by functionalism, the view (upheld, for example, by Frank Lloyd Wright) that form follows function. In this context, Duchene's remarks about "convenience" may be intended to praise and enhance the aesthetics and artistry of the cliff city. Additionally, functionalism was closely associated with primitivism and constructions of nature and "the natural." I am indebted to my colleague Linda Leavell for calling my attention to this important context.

8. Wheeler, *"Modernist" Women Writers,* consistently refers to both the Southwest and the cliff cities as "nature," making strikingly little mention of any human inhabitance or architectural design. Among the "many complications" of "Tom Outland's Story" that she perceives are "the relation of author to reader, creation to interpretation, and the problem of the nature of language and communication" (34)—not, for example, Cather's assumptions about dead Indians. Wheeler writes that, in Cather's work, "*brute* experience is raised to a high, imaginative quality" (38, emphasis added), and Wheeler romanticizes the cliff city even more than Cather herself does, describing it as "magical," "incredible," "extraordinary," and "fascinating" (39). When, after eleven pages of unrelieved ethnocentrism, Wheeler finally mentions that Indian objects were found in the ruins, she calls these items "furnishings" (42). Fourteen pages into her sixteen-page disquisition, she mentions the Indians themselves, only to write them off and write them out of her reading as she pursues her interpretation of the city as Precious Aesthetic Object. Wheeler writes, "Excavation is valuable in itself" (45) and remarks, amazingly, that "nature is our nature as humans" (46). In a single endnote, she grudgingly allows, "Cather's Outland story anticipates much of the criticisms engendered recently by the five hundredth anniversary of Columbus's discovery of America, the implication being that it was a disaster for the indigenous peoples" (194). Beyond the difficulties of taking Cather seriously as a prophet of anti-Columbus discourse and an avatar of native resistance to the quincentenary, I need only observe that Wheeler's endnote does not, in its marginality and in its halfheartedness, adequately acknowledge, let alone address, major issues of race and cultural appropriation in "Tom Outland's Story."

9. My reading steers clear of the Christian overtones of the name "Mother Eve," in part because I take them to be obvious and clearly implicated in the arguments I make about race and gender relations. However, as Linda Leavell has pointed out to me, it could be argued that Duchene distinctly backs away from the Judeo-Christian premise that Eve's temptation is responsible for the fall of humankind. In these contexts, Michaels's arguments in *Our America* about American nativism and collective identity are particularly suggestive. The maternal figure of Eve seems, in "Tom Outland's Story," to be subject to limitless appro-

priation; conversely, Indianizing Eve also, in a potentially subversive way, links the book of Genesis to the ruination of Mesa Verde.

10. For a different approach to this matter, see Moseley, "Concentric Texts."

Chapter 9

1. I would like to acknowledge Susan Brill for her insightful and extremely helpful responses to my readings of *Krazy Kat*.

2. "Old Cunning Stagers" hails from Blackbeard and Williams, ed., *Smithsonian Collection*. "The Innocents" is Berger's phrase, used in his *Comic-Stripped American*.

3. Although I have excerpted several of Trachtenberg's remarks (see *Incorporation*, 122–129) here, his full discussion is well worth consulting.

4. Coconino County overlaps with the Navajo and Hopi Indian reservations, but the Kayenta and Monument Valley areas are farther east, in Navajo and Apache Counties. Herriman took a bit of artistic license in stretching the boundaries of Coconino County.

5. *Calvin and Hobbes* cartoonist Bill Watterson has written that, along with *Peanuts* and *Pogo*, *Krazy Kat* was "tremendously inspirational" to his work (*Calvin and Hobbes Tenth Anniversary Book*, 14). Watterson argues, "The prevailing Sunday format was invented to standardize comic strip layouts so as to give newspapers the utmost flexibility in printing them" (14). Herriman's experiments with the layouts of both his Sunday and daily strips constitute a breaking away from standardization, even though *Krazy Kat* ultimately remained subject to a system of production and distribution that, as Watterson is well aware, readily frustrates experimentation. Still, from relatively early on in the print career of *Calvin and Hobbes*, Watterson was actively "trying to escape the tyranny of panels" (36) and seeing Herriman as a crucial precursor.

6. Cartoonist Harry Hershfield, speaking at Herriman's funeral service, said, "If ever there was a saint on earth, it was George Herriman" (McDonnell, O'Connell, and de Havenon, *Krazy Kat*, 88).

7. *Krazy Kat* was syndicated through Hearst newspapers. McDonnell, O'Connell, and de Havenon, *Krazy Kat*, 65, report that "William Randolph Hearst, among other things a fervent patron of the comic strip and possibly the sole reason *Krazy Kat* continued through its later, less popular years, was a great fan of George Herriman's." The strip peaked in popularity in the 1920s, when Seldes's articles "Golla, Golla" and "The Krazy Kat That Walks by Himself" (in *Seven Lively Arts*) appeared, when the John Alden Carpenter/Adolph Bolm jazz-pantomime ballet *Krazy Kat* was first performed (New York, 1922), and when Herriman was inducted into the *Vanity Fair* Hall of Fame (April 1923). But from the late 1930s until Herriman's death in 1944, "[i]n spite of the renewed vigor of the strip, it was appearing in fewer and fewer papers. By 1944 *Krazy Kat* could be found in only thirty-five papers, not a large number compared with a strip like *Blondie*, which ran in over a thousand" (McDonnell, O'Connell, and de Havenon, *Krazy Kat*, 82).

8. Pryse, xv–xvii, develops possible connections between Jewett and Austin in her very useful introduction to her recent edition of Austin's *The Land of Little Rain* and *Lost Borders*. And for suggestive comparisons as well as contrasts between Jewett and Austin, see Ammons, *Conflicting Stories*, Chapter 6.

9. For American Indian perspectives on westward expansion, two good start-

ing points are Nabokov, ed., *Native American Testimony*, and Utley, *Indian Frontier*. See also Calvin Martin, ed., *American Indian*, and the many nineteenth- and twentieth-century Indian autobiographies, novels, and poems that speak to westward expansion.

10. My argument about Riis and the urban frontier is also indebted more generally to Kaplan's work.

11. The Woolworth Building was commonly called the cathedral of commerce. See for example Douglas, *Terrible Honesty*, 566.

Chapter 10

1. Although John Ford often seems to have discovered Monument Valley for Hollywood, in fact he was not the first director to make movies there; one pre-Ford picture of note is *The Vanishing American*, filmed there in 1926. Ford's association with Monument Valley began famously with *Stagecoach* (1939); all told, he made all or part of nine movies there (Bogdanovich, *John Ford*, 10). Bogdanovich also records Monument Valley trader Harry Goulding celebrating Ford's relationship with the Navajos, claiming that to them, "Mr Ford's holy, sorta. . . . [He] came here to make *Stagecoach*, and gave a score of jobs to the Navajos and a lotta lives was saved" (14–15). If accurate, Goulding provides a fascinating link between two of his acquaintances, Ford and Herriman. Finally, Andrew Sarris observes in *John Ford*, 83, "Anyone who has followed Ford's career with any consistency since *Stagecoach* must respond to the landscape of Monument Valley as to the New York skyline; that is, as to a fixed landmark of our visual imagination."

2. The term "investment" is Momaday's (Coltelli, *Winged Words*, 91): "The American Indian has a very long experience of the North American continent, say, going back thousands of years, maybe thirty thousand. So I think of that as being a very great investment, a kind of spiritual investment in the landscape, and because he has that experience he is able to think of himself in a particular way, think of himself in relation to the land, and he is able to define for himself a sense of place, belonging, and to me that is very important."

3. Etulain, *Re-Imagining the Modern American West*, discusses "The West as Postregion." However, Etulain's reluctance to read ideologically, related to his resoundingly canonical reading of the West, leads me to wonder what exactly he is re-imagining and what exactly is "post" about his "postregion." (Despite a back-cover blurb boasting that Etulain "stresses important works of ethnic writers, including Leslie Marmon Silko, Rudolfo Anaya, and Amy Tan," he actually gives only three and a half sentences to Silko and restricts his remarks to her most canonical novel, *Ceremony*. Tan and Anaya fare only slightly better.) Like almost all historians and literary critics who take up the West and Southwest, Etulain does not mention *Krazy Kat*. I have set out, in Chapters 9 and 10, to map some of the places Herriman allows readers to go, and I have indicated some of the important differences between relatively traditional, relatively immobile readings such as Etulain's and the mobile, migratory readings Herriman actively encourages.

Conclusion

1. For example, Halberstam, *Skin Shows*, 21, 13, argues that "Gothic novels are technologies that produce the monster as a remarkably mobile, permeable,

and infinitely interpretable body" that is nonetheless also subject to obsessive repetitions of the same interpretations, motivated by both fear and desire. These seemingly infinite repetitions often implicate the monstrous with "class and race, sexual and national relations."

2. Silko does not essentialize this indigenous project, however. In a 1985 interview printed in Coltelli, *Winged Words*, 153, she refers to "the old thing, which is very simpleminded in a way, that it's 'our land,'" and she distinguishes between the actions of the character who upholds "the old thing" and her own work in *Almanac*.

3. These hauntings are of course not restricted to the American Indian Southwest. As Reid, "Still Haunting," has pointed out, Louise Erdrich's June Kashpaw haunts her way through *Love Medicine* (both versions, 1984 and 1993), *The Bingo Palace* (1994), and even *Tales of Burning Love* (1996) as an absent presence and a powerful survivor.

4. See, for example, the conversation between Michael Roanhorse and Emily Sandoval in Chapter 32 of A. A. Carr's *Eye Killers*, 153, where Emily reminds Michael, "You have kept your sheepcamp at the edge of the Keresan reservation, to watch for enemies or bad things. The Keresan are happy about that. A long time ago, the old Navajos, passing through on their sad walk, left your great-grandmother with the Keresans. Your father understood the Keresan language. After he died, when your mother died too, the Keresans took care of you and raised you to be strong. You are family with them, *ba'ba'ah*. Like me. You and William and myself are Navajo, but we are Keresan, also."

5. In Chapter 30 of Owens's *Bone Game*, 125–130, Luther Cole inflicts a Choctaw piss-hex on the witches. The name "Emo" appears on p. 126. And this scene takes place outside of Gallup, New Mexico, as Luther Cole and Hoey McCurtain travel from Mississippi to Santa Cruz. Much of *Bone Game* takes place in California, but the book's various southwestern locations and dispositions are also important.

Works Cited

Abbey, Edward. *Desert Solitaire: A Season in the Wilderness.* New York: Touchstone, 1968.
———. Introduction to *Land of Little Rain,* by Mary Austin. New York: Penguin, 1988.
Adams, Ansel, with Mary Street Alinder. *Ansel Adams, an Autobiography.* Boston: Little, Brown, and Company, 1985.
Adams, Henry. *The Education of Henry Adams.* Boston: Houghton Mifflin, 1961.
Alexie, Sherman. *The Lone Ranger and Tonto Fistfight in Heaven.* New York: Atlantic Monthly Press, 1993.
Allen, Paula Gunn. "The Autobiography of a Confluence." In *I Tell You Now,* ed. Swann and Krupat, 143–154.
———. Interviews. In Perry, *Backtalk,* 1–18, and Coltelli, *Winged Words,* 11–39.
———. *The Sacred Hoop: Recovering the Feminine in American Indian Traditions.* Boston: Beacon, 1986.
———. "Special Problems in Teaching Leslie Marmon Silko's *Ceremony.*" *American Indian Quarterly* 14 (1990): 379–386.
Ammons, Elizabeth. *Conflicting Stories: American Women Writers at the Turn into the Twentieth Century.* New York: Oxford University Press, 1992.
———. "Gender and Fiction." In *Columbia History of the American Novel,* ed. Emory Elliott, 267–284. New York: Columbia University Press, 1991.
Anderson, Eric Gary. "Manifest Dentistry, or Teaching Oral Narrative in *McTeague* and Old Man Coyote." In *Tricksterism in Turn-of-the-Century American Literature: A Multicultural Perspective,* ed. Elizabeth Ammons and Annette White-Parks, 61–78. Hanover, N.H.: University Press of New England, 1994.
Anderson, John Q., Edwin W. Gaston Jr., and James W. Lee, eds. *Southwestern American Literature: A Bibliography.* Chicago: Swallow Press, 1980.
Anzaldúa, Gloria. *Borderlands/La Frontera: The New Mestiza.* San Francisco: Aunt Lute Books, 1987.
Asa Bazhonoodah. "Dark Sky over Black Mesa" (editor's title). In *Native American Testimony,* ed. Nabokov, 397–400.
Austin, Mary. *The American Rhythm: Studies and Re-expressions of Amerindian Songs* (1923). Boston and New York: Houghton Mifflin, 1930.
———. "Arizona: The Land of the Joyous Adventure" (1923). In *These United States: Portraits of America from the 1920s,* ed. Daniel H. Borus, 37–44. Ithaca: Cornell University Press, 1992.

———. *The Land of Little Rain* (1903). Reprinted in *Stories from the Country of Lost Borders*, ed. Marjorie Pryse. New Brunswick, N.J.: Rutgers University Press, 1987.

———. *Lost Borders* (1909). Reprinted in *Stories from the Country of Lost Borders*, ed. Marjorie Pryse. New Brunswick, N.J.: Rutgers University Press, 1987.

Baker, Houston A. *Modernism and the Harlem Renaissance.* Chicago: University of Chicago Press, 1987.

Bandelier, Adolf F. *The Delight Makers: A Novel of Prehistoric Pueblo Indians* (1890). New York: Harvest/Harcourt, 1971.

Banta, Martha. *Taylored Lives: Narrative Productions in the Age of Taylor, Veblen, and Ford.* Chicago: University of Chicago Press, 1993.

Barnes, Kim. "A Leslie Marmon Silko Interview." In *Leslie Marmon Silko*, ed. Graulich, 47–65.

Barrett, S. M. *Geronimo's Story of His Life.* New York: Duffield and Company, 1906.

Barthes, Roland. *Camera Lucida: Reflections on Photography.* Trans. Richard Howard. New York: Hill and Wang, 1981.

Beck, Peggy V., Anna Lee Walters, and Nia Francisco. *The Sacred: Ways of Knowledge, Sources of Life.* Tsaile, Ariz.: Navajo Community College Press, 1992.

Berger, Arthur Asa. *The Comic-Stripped American.* New York: Walker and Company, 1973.

Berkhofer, Robert. *The White Man's Indian: Images of the American Indian from Columbus to the Present.* New York: Vintage, 1978.

Berlitz, Charles, and William L. Moore. *The Roswell Incident.* New York: Grosset and Dunlap, 1980.

Betzinez, Jason, with Wilbur Sturtevant Nye. *I Fought with Geronimo.* Harrisburg, Pa.: Stackpole, 1959.

Blackbeard, Bill, and Martin Williams, eds. *The Smithsonian Collection of Newspaper Comics.* Washington, D.C.: Smithsonian Institution Press and Harry N. Abrams, 1977.

Bloch, Robert. *Psycho.* 1959. New York: Award, 1975.

Bogdanovich, Peter. *John Ford.* Berkeley: University of California Press, 1978.

Boone, Elizabeth Hill. "Aztec Pictorial Histories: Records without Words." In *Writing without Words*, ed. Boone and Mignolo, 50–76.

Boone, Elizabeth Hill, and Walter D. Mignolo, eds. *Writing without Words: Alternative Literacies in Mesoamerica and the Andes.* Durham, N.C.: Duke University Press, 1994.

Boswell, James. *Life of Johnson.* Ed. R. W. Chapman. Oxford: Oxford University Press, 1980.

Brown, Bill. *The Material Unconscious: American Amusement, Stephen Crane, and the Economics of Play.* Cambridge: Harvard University Press, 1996.

Brown, E. K. *Willa Cather: A Critical Biography.* 1953. Lincoln: University of Nebraska Press, 1987.

Brownlow, Kevin. *The War, the West, and the Wilderness.* New York: Alfred A. Knopf, 1979.

Brumble, H. David, III. *American Indian Autobiography.* Berkeley: University of California Press, 1988.

Bryant, Marsha, ed. *Photo-Textualities: Reading Photographs and Literature.* Newark: University of Delaware Press, 1996.

Burns, Walter Noble, *The Saga of Billy the Kid.* Garden City, N.Y.: Doubleday, Page & Co., 1926.

Caesar, Terry. *Forgiving the Boundaries: Home as Abroad in American Travel Writing.* Athens: University of Georgia Press, 1994.

Cain, William E. "Presence and Power in *McTeague.*" In *American Realism: New Essays,* ed. Eric J. Sundquist, 199–214. Baltimore: Johns Hopkins University Press, 1982.

Calderón, Hector, and José David Saldívar, eds. *Criticism in the Borderlands: Studies in Chicano Literature, Culture, and Ideology.* Durham, N.C.: Duke University Press, 1991.

Calloway, Colin. *New Worlds for All: Indians, Europeans, and the Remaking of Early America.* Baltimore: Johns Hopkins University Press, 1997.

Canfield, Gae Whitney. *Sarah Winnemucca of the Northern Paiutes.* Norman: University of Oklahoma Press, 1983.

Caputi, Jane. "The Heart of Knowledge: Nuclear Themes in Native American Thought and Literature." *American Indian Culture and Research Journal* 16 (1992): 1–27.

Carr, A. A. *Eye Killers.* Norman: University of Oklahoma Press, 1995.

Carr, Helen. *Inventing the American Primitive: Politics, Gender, and the Representation of Native American Literary Traditions, 1789–1936.* New York: New York University Press, 1996.

Castiglia, Christopher. *Bound and Determined: Captivity, Culture-Crossing, and White Womanhood from Mary Rowlandson to Patty Hearst.* Chicago: University of Chicago Press, 1996.

Castro, Michael. *Interpreting the Indian: Twentieth-Century Poets and the Native American.* Albuquerque: University of New Mexico Press, 1983.

Cather, Willa. *The Professor's House.* 1925. New York: Vintage, 1973.

Cawelti, John. *Adventure, Mystery, and Romance: Formula Stories as Art and Popular Culture.* Chicago: University of Chicago Press, 1976.

Chase, Richard. *The American Novel and Its Tradition.* Baltimore: Johns Hopkins University Press, 1957.

Clifford, James. *Routes: Travel and Translation in the Late Twentieth Century.* Cambridge: Harvard University Press, 1997.

Coltelli, Laura. *Winged Words: American Indian Writers Speak.* Lincoln: University of Nebraska Press, 1990.

Cordell, Linda S. *Prehistory of the Southwest.* Orlando, Fla.: Academic Press, 1984.

Cowart, Jack, Juan Hamilton, and Sarah Greenough. *Georgia O'Keeffe: Art and Letters.* Exhibition catalog. Washington, D.C.: National Gallery of Art; Boston: New York Graphic Society Books, 1987.

Crane, Stephen. *Maggie, a Girl of the Streets* (1893). New York, Norton, 1979.

Cronon, William, George Miles, and Jay Gitlin, eds. *Under an Open Sky: Rethinking America's Western Past.* New York: Norton, 1992.

Cullick, Jonathan S. "Configurations of Events in the Narrative Structure of *McTeague.*" *American Literary Realism* 27 (1995): 37–47.

Cummings, E. E. *A Miscellany Revised.* Ed. George J. Firmage. New York: October House, 1965.

Dasenbrock, Reed Way. "Southwest of What?: Southwestern Literature as a Form of Frontier Literature." In *Desert, Garden, Margin, Range: Literature on the American Frontier,* ed. Eric Heyne, 123–132. New York: Twayne, 1992.

Dean, Thomas K. "Domestic Horizons: Gender, Genre, Narrative Structure, and the Anti-Western of Frank Norris." *American Literary Realism* 27 (1995): 48–53.

Debo, Angie. *Geronimo: The Man, His Time, His Place.* Norman: University of Oklahoma Press, 1976.

Deloria, Vine, Jr. "Afterword." In *America in 1492,* ed. Josephy, 429–443.

———. *God Is Red: A Native View of Religion.* 1972. Golden, Colo.: Fulcrum, 1994.

Dillingham, William B. *Frank Norris: Instinct and Art.* Lincoln: University of Nebraska Press, 1969.

Dilworth, Leah. *Imagining Indians in the Southwest: Persistent Visions of a Primitive Past.* Washington, D.C.: Smithsonian Institution Press, 1996.

Doughty, Francis W. *Old King Brady and Billy the Kid; or, the Great Detective's Chase.* New York Detective Library, No. 411. (New York: Frank Tousey, 1890).

Douglas, Ann. *Terrible Honesty: Mongrel Manhattan in the 1920s.* New York: Noonday, 1995.

Doyle, Arthur Conan. *The Complete Sherlock Holmes.* Garden City, N.Y.: Garden City Publishing Company, 1938.

Dreiser, Theodore. *Sister Carrie.* 1900. 2d ed. Ed. Donald Pizer. New York: Norton, 1991.

Drinnon, Richard. *Facing West: The Metaphysics of Indian-Hating and Empire-Building.* 1980. New York: Schocken, 1990.

Durham, Jimmie. "Geronimo!" In *Partial Recall,* ed. Lippard, 54–58.

Etulain, Richard W. *Re-Imagining the Modern American West: A Century of Fiction, History, and Art.* Tucson: University of Arizona Press, 1996.

Evers, Larry, ed. *The South Corner of Time: Hopi Navajo Papago Yaqui Tribal Literature.* Tucson: University of Arizona Press, 1980.

Faris, James C. *Navajo and Photography: A Critical History of the Representation of an American People.* Albuquerque: University of New Mexico Press, 1996.

Fergusson, Erna. *Our Southwest.* New York: Alfred A. Knopf, 1940.

Flynn, Johnny. "Christopher Columbus and the Problem of History." *American Indian Culture and Research Journal* 17 (1993): 11–16.

Foote, Kenneth E. *Shadowed Ground: America's Landscapes of Violence and Tragedy.* Austin: University of Texas Press, 1997.

Fuller, Henry B. *The Cliff Dwellers.* New York: Harper & Brothers, 1893.

Garrett, Pat F. *The Authentic Life of Billy the Kid. 1882.* (Norman: University of Oklahoma Press, 1954).

Georgia O'Keeffe: Exhibition of Oils and Pastels. Exh. brochure, "An American Place." New York: Metropolitan Museum of Art, 1988.

Georgia O'Keeffe: Art and Letters. Jack Cowart, Juan Hamilton, and Sarah Greenough. Exhibition catalog. Washington, D.C.: National Gallery of Art; Boston: Graphic Society Books, 1987.

Georgi-Findlay, Brigitte. "The Frontiers of Native American Women's Writing: Sarah Winnemucca's *Life among the Piutes.*" In *New Voices in Native American Literary Criticism,* ed. Arnold Krupat, 222–252. Washington, D.C.: Smithsonian Institution Press, 1993.

Geronimo, with S. M. Barrett. *Geronimo's Story of His Life.* New York: Duffield and Company, 1906.

Gopnik, Adam. "The Genius of George Herriman." Review of *Krazy Kat: The Comic Art of George Herriman,* by Patrick McDonnell, Karen O'Connell, and Georgia Riley de Havenon. *New York Review of Books,* 18 December 1986, 19–28.

Graulich, Melody, ed. *Leslie Marmon Silko, "Yellow Woman."* New Brunswick, N.J.: Rutgers University Press, 1993.

Green, Jesse, ed. *Cushing at Zuni: The Correspondence and Journals of Frank Hamilton Cushing, 1879–1884.* Albuquerque: University of New Mexico Press, 1990.

Halberstam, Judith. *Skin Shows: Gothic Horror and the Technology of Monsters.* Durham, N.C.: Duke University Press, 1995.

Haraway, Donna. *Primate Visions: Gender, Race, and Nature in the World of Modern Science.* New York: Routledge, 1989.

Harjo, Joy. "Ordinary Spirit." In *I Tell You Now,* ed. Swann and Krupat, 265–270.
———. "The World Is Round: Some Notes on Leslie Silko's *Almanac of the Dead." Blue Mesa Review* 4 (1992): 207–210.

Harrell, David. *From Mesa Verde to "The Professor's House."* Albuquerque: University of New Mexico Press, 1992.

Hart, Albert Bushnell, and Herbert Ronald Ferleger, eds. *Theodore Roosevelt Cyclopedia.* New York: Roosevelt Memorial Association, 1941.

Herriman, George. *Krazy Kat: The Comic Art of George Herriman.* Ed. and comp. Patrick McDonnell, Karen O'Connell, and Georgia Riley de Havenon. New York: Harry N. Abrams, 1986.

Hofstadter, Richard. *The American Political Tradition and the Men Who Made It.* New York: Vintage, 1973.

Holland, Sharon. "'If You Know I Have a History, You Will Respect Me': A Perspective on Afro–Native American Literature." *Callaloo* 17 (1994): 334–350.

Hollon, W. Eugene. *The Southwest: Old and New.* New York: Alfred A. Knopf, 1961.

Hough, Emerson. "Billy the Kid, the True Story of a Western 'Bad Man.'" *Everybody's Magazine,* 5 (September 1901): 302–310.
———. *The Story of the Outlaw.* (New York: D. Appleton, 1897).

Howard, June. *Form and History in American Literary Naturalism.* Chapel Hill: University of North Carolina Press, 1985.
———. "Unraveling Regions, Unsettling Periods: Sarah Orne Jewett and American Literary History." *American Literature* 68 (1996): 365–384.

Howard, Kathleen L. *Inventing the Southwest: The Fred Harvey Company and Native American Art.* Flagstaff, Ariz.: Northland, 1996.

Hyde, Anne Farrar. *An American Vision: Far Western Landscape and National Culture, 1880–1920.* New York: New York University Press, 1990.

Iverson, Peter. "Taking Care of the Earth and Sky." In *America in 1492,* ed. Josephy, 85–117.

Jacobs, Harriet. *Incidents in the Life of a Slave Girl Written by Herself.* Ed. Jean Fagan Yellin. Cambridge: Harvard University Press, 1987.

Jennings, Francis. "American Frontiers." In *America in 1492,* ed. Josephy, 339–367.

Josephy, Alvin M., Jr., ed. *America in 1492: The World of the Indian Peoples before the Arrival of Columbus.* New York: Vintage, 1991.

Jung, Carl. "The Pueblo Indians." In *The Spell of New Mexico,* ed. Tony Hillerman, 37–43. Albuquerque: University of New Mexico Press, 1976.

Kane, Sean. *Wisdom of the Mythtellers.* Peterborough, Ont.: Broadview Press, 1994.

Kaplan, Amy. "'Left Alone with America': The Absence of Empire in the Study of American Culture." In *Cultures of United States Imperialism,* ed. Amy Kaplan and Donald E. Pease, 3–21. Durham, N.C.: Duke University Press, 1993.

———. *The Social Construction of American Realism.* Chicago: University of Chicago Press, 1988.

Katz, Joseph, ed. *Stephen Crane in the West and Mexico.* Kent, Ohio: Kent State University Press, 1970.

Kaywaykla, James, and Eve Ball. *In the Days of Victorio: Recollections of a Warm Springs Apache.* Tucson: University of Arizona Press, 1970.

Krupat, Arnold. *For Those Who Come After: A Study of Native American Autobiography.* Berkeley: University of California Press, 1985.

———, ed. *Native American Autobiography: An Anthology.* Madison: University of Wisconsin Press, 1994.

———. *The Turn to the Native: Studies in Criticism and Culture.* Lincoln: University of Nebraska Press, 1996.

Langlois, Karen S. "Marketing the American Indian: Mary Austin and the Business of Writing." In *A Living of Words: American Women in Print Culture,* ed. Susan Albertine, 151–168. Knoxville: University of Tennessee Press, 1995.

Laut, Agnes C. *Through Our Unknown Southwest.* 1913. New York: Robert M. McBride and Company, 1921.

Lee, Hermione. *Willa Cather: Double Lives.* New York: Pantheon, 1989.

Leibsohn, Dana. "Primers for Memory: Cartographic Histories and Nahua Identity." In *Writing without Words,* ed. Boone and Mignolo, 161–187.

Lejeune, Phillippe. "The Autobiographical Pact." In *On Autobiography,* 3–33. Minneapolis: University of Minnesota Press, 1989.

Limerick, Patricia Nelson. *Desert Passages: Encounters with the American Deserts.* Albuquerque: University of New Mexico Press, 1985.

———. *The Legacy of Conquest: The Unbroken Past of the American West.* New York: Norton, 1987.

———. "Making the Most of Words: Verbal Activity and Western America." In *Under an Open Sky,* ed. Cronon, Miles, and Gitlin, 167–184.

———. "Second Views and Second Thoughts: Mark Klett and the Re-exploration of the American West." In *Revealing Territory: Photographs of the Southwest,* by Mark Klett. Essays by Patricia Nelson Limerick and Thomas W. Southall. Albuquerque: University of New Mexico Press, 1992.

Lippard, Lucy, ed. *Partial Recall.* New York: New Press, 1992.

London, Jack. *The People of the Abyss.* 1903. New York: Archer House, 1963.

Lyman, Christopher M. *The Vanishing Race and Other Illusions: Photographs of Indians by Edward S. Curtis.* New York: Pantheon, 1982.

MacCannell, Dean. *The Tourist: A New Theory of the Leisure Class.* New York: Schocken, 1976.

Martin, Calvin, ed. *The American Indian and the Problem of History.* New York: Oxford University Press, 1987.

———. *In the Spirit of the Earth: Rethinking History and Time.* Baltimore: Johns Hopkins University Press, 1992.

Martin, Paul S., and Richard G. Klein, eds. *Quaternary Extinctions: A Prehistoric Revolution.* Tucson: University of Arizona Press, 1984.

Martin, Paul S., and H. E. Wright Jr., eds. *Pleistocene Extinctions: The Search for a Cause.* New Haven: Yale University Press, 1967.

McDonnell, Patrick, Karen O'Connell, and Georgia Riley de Havenon, ed. and comp. *Krazy Kat: The Comic Art of George Herriman.* New York: Harry N. Abrams, 1986.

Messinger, Lisa Mintz. *Georgia O'Keeffe.* New York: Metropolitan Museum of Art, 1988.

Michaels, Walter Benn. *The Gold Standard and the Logic of Naturalism: American Literature at the Turn of the Century.* Berkeley: University of California Press, 1987.

———. *Our America: Nativism, Modernism, and Pluralism.* Durham, N.C.: Duke University Press, 1995.

Mitchell, Frank. *Navajo Blessingway Singer: The Autobiography of Frank Mitchell, 1881–1967.* Ed. Charlotte J. Frisbie and David P. McAllester. Tucson: University of Arizona Press, 1978.

Mitchell, Lee Clark. *Determined Fictions: American Literary Naturalism.* New York: Columbia University Press, 1989.

———. "The Photograph and the American Indian." In *The Photograph and the American Indian,* by Alfred L. Bush and Lee Clark Mitchell, xi–xxvi. Princeton: Princeton University Press, 1994.

Momaday, N. Scott. "The Becoming of the Native: Man in America before Columbus." In *America in 1492,* ed. Josephy, 13–19.

———. *The Gourd Dancer.* New York: Harper and Row, 1976.

———. Interviews. In Woodard, *Ancestral Voices,* and in Coltelli, *Winged Words,* 89–100.

———. *The Way to Rainy Mountain.* Albuquerque: University of New Mexico Press, 1969.

Moseley, Anne. "Concentric Texts in *The Professor's House.*" *Western American Literature* 31 (1996): 35–47.

Murray, David. *Forked Tongues: Speech, Writing, and Representation in North American Indian Texts.* Bloomington: University of Indiana Press, 1991.

Nabokov, Peter, ed. *Native American Testimony: A Chronicle of Indian-White Relations from Prophecy to the Present, 1492–1992.* New York: Penguin, 1991.

Nelson, Robert M. *Place and Vision: The Function of Landscape in Native American Fiction.* New York: Peter Lang, 1993.

Norris, Frank. *McTeague: A Story of San Francisco.* 1899. Ed. Kevin Starr. New York: Penguin, 1985.

Norwood, Vera, and Janice Monk, eds. *The Desert Is No Lady: Southwestern Landscapes in Women's Writing and Art.* New Haven: Yale University Press, 1987.

O'Brien, Sharon. *Willa Cather: The Emerging Voice.* New York: Fawcett Columbine, 1987.

O'Keeffe, Georgia. "About Myself." In Messinger, *Georgia O'Keeffe.*

Orvell, Miles. *After the Machine: Visual Arts and the Erasing of Cultural Boundaries.* Jackson: University Press of Mississippi, 1995.

Owens, Louis. *Bone Game.* Norman: University of Oklahoma Press, 1994.

Paulson, Ronald. *Figure and Abstraction in Contemporary Painting.* New Brunswick, N.J.: Rutgers University Press, 1990.

Pearce, Roy Harvey. *Savagism and Civilization: A Study of the Indian and the American Mind.* Berkeley: University of California Press, 1988.

Pearce, T. M. *Mary Hunter Austin.* New Haven, Conn.: College and University Press, 1965.

Pérez-Torres, Rafael. *Movements in Chicano Poetry: Against Myths, against Margins.* New York: Cambridge University Press, 1995.

Perrigo, Lynne I. *The American Southwest: Its Peoples and Cultures.* New York: Holt, Rinehart, and Winston, 1971.

Perry, Donna. *Backtalk: Women Writers Speak Out.* New Brunswick, N.J.: Rutgers University Press, 1993.

Pizer, Donald. *The Novels of Frank Norris.* Bloomington: University of Indiana Press, 1966.

Pollitzer, Anita. *A Woman on Paper: Georgia O'Keeffe.* New York: Touchstone, 1988.

Pryse, Marjorie. Introduction. In *Stories from the Country of Lost Borders,* by Mary Austin, ed. Marjorie Pryse, vii–xxxviii. New Brunswick, N.J.: Rutgers University Press, 1987.

Querry, Ronald B. *The Death of Bernadette Lefthand: A Novel.* Santa Fe, N.M.,: Red Crane Books, 1993.

Randle, Kevin, and Donald R. Schmitt. *The Truth about the UFO Crash at Roswell.* New York: Avon Books, 1994.

Reid, E. Shelley. "Still Haunting After All These Years: The Returns of June Morrissey Kashpaw Mauser." Paper presented at the annual meeting of the Southwest/Texas Popular Culture Association/American Culture Association, San Antonio, 29 March 1997.

Revard, Carter. "History, Myth, and Identity among Osages and Other Peoples." *Denver Quarterly* 14 (1980): 84–97. Reprinted in Revard, *Family Matters, Tribal Affairs.* Tucson: University of Arizona Press, 1998.

———. "Report to the Nation: Claiming Europe." *American Indian Quarterly* 6 (1982): 305–318. Reprinted in Revard, *Family Matters, Tribal Affairs.* Tucson: University of Arizona Press, 1998.

Reynolds, Guy. *Willa Cather in Context: Progress, Race, Empire.* New York: St. Martin's, 1996.

Riis, Jacob. *How the Other Half Lives: Studies among the Tenements of New York.* 1890. New York: Dover, 1971.

Robinson, Roxana. *Georgia O'Keeffe: A Life.* New York: Harper and Row, 1989.

Roosevelt, Theodore. "Across the Navajo Desert." In *The Works of Theodore Roosevelt,* national ed., 3:204–224. New York: Scribner's, 1926.

Rose, Wendy. *Bone Dance: New and Selected Poems, 1965–1993.* Tucson: University of Arizona Press, 1994.

———. Interview. In *Winged Words,* by Coltelli, 121–133.

———. "Neon Scars." In *I Tell You Now,* ed. Swann and Krupat, 253–261.

———. *What the Mohawk Made the Hopi Say.* New York: Strawberry Press, 1993.

———. *What Happened When the Mohawk Hit New York.* New York: Strawberry Press, 1982.

Rosemont, Franklin. "Surrealism in the Comics I: Krazy Kat (George Herriman)." In *Popular Culture in America,* ed. Paul Buhle, 119–127. Minneapolis: University of Minnesota Press, 1987.

Rosowski, Susan J. *The Voyage Perilous: Willa Cather's Romanticism.* Lincoln: University of Nebraska Press, 1986.

Rudnick, Lois. "Re-Naming the Land: Anglo Expatriate Women in the Southwest." In *The Desert Is No Lady,* ed. Norwood and Monk, 10–26.

Ruoff, A. LaVonne Brown. "Ritual and Renewal: Keres Traditions in Leslie Silko's 'Yellow Woman'." In *Leslie Marmon Silko,* ed. Graulich, 69–81.

———. "Three Nineteenth-Century American Indian Autobiographers." In *Redefining American Literary History,* ed. A. LaVonne Brown Ruoff and Jerry W. Ward Jr., 251–269. New York: Modern Language Association, 1990.

Rushing, W. Jackson. *Native American Art and the New York Avant-Garde: A History of Cultural Primitivism.* Austin: University of Texas Press, 1995.

St. Clair, Janet. "Death of Love/Love of Death: Leslie Marmon Silko's *Almanac of the Dead.*" *MELUS* 21 (1996): 141–156.

———."Uneasy Ethnocentrism: Recent Works of Allen, Silko, and Hogan." *Studies in American Indian Literatures* 6 (1994): 83–98.

Sands, Kathleen Mullen. "Indian Women's Personal Narrative: Voices Past and Present." In *American Women's Autobiography: Fea(s)ts of Memory,* ed. Margo Culley, 268–294. Madison: University of Wisconsin Press, 1992.

Sarris, Andrew. *The John Ford Movie Mystery.* Bloomington: Indiana University Press, 1975.

Sarris, Greg. *Keeping Slug Woman Alive: A Holistic Approach to American Indian Texts.* Berkeley: University of California Press, 1993.

Schwind, Jean. "This Is a Frame-Up: Mother Eve in *The Professor's House.*" *Cather Studies* 2 (1993): 72–91.

Seldes, Gilbert. "Golla, Golla, the Comic Strip's Art." *Vanity Fair,* May 1922.

———. *The Seven Lively Arts.* New York: Harper and Brothers, 1924.

Seltzer, Mark. *Bodies and Machines.* New York: Routledge, 1992.

Sequoya-Magdaleno, Jana. "Telling the *Différance:* Representations of Identity in the Discourse of Indianness." In *The Ethnic Canon: Histories, Institutions, and Interventions,* ed. David Palumbo-Liu, 88–116. Minneapolis: University of Minnesota Press, 1995.

Sergeant, Elizabeth Shepley. "New Mexico: A Relic of Ancient America." 1923. In *These United States: Portraits of America from the 1920s,* ed. Daniel H. Borus, 249–255. Ithaca: Cornell University Press, 1992.

Shelley, Mary Wollstonecraft. *Frankenstein, or the Modern Prometheus.* 1818. University of California Press, 1984.

Silko, Leslie Marmon. *Almanac of the Dead.* New York: Simon and Schuster, 1991.

———. *Ceremony.* New York: Penguin, 1977.

———. "A Geronimo Story." In *The Man to Send Rain Clouds: Contemporary Stories by American Indians,* ed. Kenneth Rosen. (New York: Viking Press, 1974), pp. 3–8.

———. Interview. In *Backtalk,* ed. Perry, 313–340.

———. Interview. In *Leslie Marmon Silko,* ed. Graulich, 47–65.

———. Interview. In *Winged Words,* by Coltelli, 134–153.

———. *Storyteller.* New York: Arcade, 1981.

———. *Yellow Woman and a Beauty of the Spirit: Essays on Native American Life Today.* New York: Simon and Schuster, 1996.

Sinclair, Upton. *The Jungle.* 1906. New York: New American Library, 1990.

Smith, Patricia Clark, with Paula Gunn Allen. "Earthly Relations, Carnal Knowledge: Southwestern American Indian Women Writers and Landscape." In *Leslie Marmon Silko,* ed. Graulich, 115–150.

Steckmesser, Kent Ladd. *The Western Hero in History and Legend.* Norman: University of Oklahoma Press, 1965.

Stout, Janis P. "Willa Cather and Mary Austin: Intersections and Influence." *Southwestern American Literature* 21 (1996): 39–59.

Sundquist, Eric J. Introduction to forum, "American Literary History: The Next Century." *American Literature* 67 (1995): 793–794.

Swann, Brian, and Arnold Krupat, eds. *I Tell You Now: Autobiographical Essays by Native American Writers.* Lincoln: University of Nebraska Press, 1987.

———, eds. *Recovering the Word: Essays on Native American Literature.* Berkeley: University of California Press, 1987.

Tagg, John. *The Burden of Representation: Essays on Photographies and Histories.* 1988. Minneapolis: University of Minnesota Press, 1995.

Tatum, Stephen. *Inventing Billy the Kid: Visions of the Outlaw in America, 1881–1981.* Albuquerque: University of New Mexico Press, 1982.

Teague, David W. *The Southwest in American Literature and Art: The Rise of a Desert Aesthetic.* Tucson: University of Arizona Press, 1997.

Trachtenberg, Alan. *The Incorporation of America: Culture and Society in the Gilded Age.* New York: Hill and Wang, 1982.

———. *Reading American Photographs: Images as History, Mathew Brady to Walker Evans.* New York: Hill and Wang, 1989.

Turner, Frederick Jackson. *The Frontier in American History.* New York: Henry Holt and Company, 1920.

Tuska, Jon. *Billy the Kid: His Life and Legend.* Westport, Conn.: Greenwood Press, 1994.

Urgo, Joseph R. *Willa Cather and the Myth of American Migration.* Urbana: University of Illinois Press, 1995.

Utley, Robert M. *Billy the Kid: A Short and Violent Life.* Lincoln: University of Nebraska Press, 1989.

———. *The Indian Frontier of the American West, 1846–1890.* Albuquerque: University of New Mexico Press, 1984.

Van Dyke, John. *The Desert: Further Studies in Natural Appearances.* New York: Scribner's, 1901.

Varnedoe, Kirk, and Adam Gopnik. *High and Low: Modern Art and Popular Culture.* New York: Museum of Modern Art, 1990.

Veblen, Thorstein. *The Theory of the Leisure Class: An Economic Study of Institutions.* New York: Macmillan, 1899.

Walters, Anna Lee. *Ghost Singer.* Albuquerque: University of New Mexico Press, 1988.

Warner, Michael. "Weird Science." Review of *The Life of Mary Baker G. Eddy and the History of Christian Science,* by Willa Cather and Georgine Milmine. *Village Voice,* 17 August 1993, 85.

Warrior, Robert Allen. *Tribal Secrets: Recovering American Indian Intellectual Traditions.* Minneapolis: University of Minnesota Press, 1995.

Watterson, Bill. *The Calvin and Hobbes Tenth Anniversary Book.* Kansas City, Mo.: Andrews and McMeel, 1995.

Weber, David J. *The Spanish Frontier in North America.* New Haven: Yale University Press, 1992.

Weigle, Marta, and Barbara Babcock, eds. *The Great Southwest of the Fred Harvey Company and the Santa Fe Railway.* Phoenix: Heard Museum, 1996.

Weigle, Marta, and Peter White. *The Lore of New Mexico.* Albuquerque: University of New Mexico Press, 1988.

Welch, James. *Fools Crow.* New York: Penguin, 1986.

West, Frederick Wadleigh, ed. *American Beginnings: The Prehistory and Palaeoecology of Beringia.* Chicago: University of Chicago Press, 1996.

Wheeler, Kathleen. *"Modernist" Women Writers and Narrative Art.* New York: New York University Press, 1994.

White, G. Edward. *The Eastern Establishment and the Western Experience: The West of Frederic Remington, Theodore Roosevelt, and Owen Wister.* New Haven: Yale University Press, 1968.

White, Richard. *"It's Your Misfortune and None of My Own": A New History of the American West.* Norman: University of Oklahoma Press, 1991.

Wiget, Andrew. *Native American Literature.* Boston: Twayne, 1985.

Winnemucca, Sarah. *Life among the Piutes: Their Wrongs and Claims.* 1883. Reno: University of Nevada Press, 1994.

Winters, Laura. *Willa Cather: Landscape and Exile.* Selinsgrove, Pa.: Susquehanna University Press, 1993.

Witherspoon, Gary. *Language and Art in the Navajo Universe.* Ann Arbor: University of Michigan Press, 1977.

Wong, Hertha Dawn. *Sending My Heart Back across the Years: Tradition and Innovation in Native American Autobiography.* New York: Oxford University Press, 1992.

Woodard, Charles L. *Ancestral Voices: Conversations with N. Scott Momaday.* Lincoln: University of Nebraska Press, 1989.

Wyatt, David. *The Fall into Eden: Landscape and Imagination in California.* New York: Cambridge University Press, 1986.

Yava, Albert. *Big Falling Snow: A Tewa-Hopi Indian's Life and Times and the History and Traditions of His People.* New York: Crown, 1978.

Young, M. Jane. *Signs from the Ancestors: Zuni Cultural Symbolism and Perceptions of Rock Art.* Albuquerque: University of New Mexico Press, 1988.

Zolbrod, Paul. "When Artifacts Speak, What Can They Tell Us?" In *Recovering the Word*, ed. Swann and Krupat, 13–40.

Index

Abbey, Edward, 82, 105, 122, 201n2; *Desert Solitaire*, 4
Adams, Ansel, 85
Adams, Henry, 198n1
Alexie, Sherman (Spokane–Coeur D'Alene), 22, 31, 36
aliens: encounters between "aliens" and "natives," 1–2, 10, 187, 188, 191. *See also* American Indians; American Southwest; borders; Roswell, New Mexico
Allen, Paula Gunn (Laguna Pueblo), 35–36, 198n7; "Autobiography of a Confluence," 19–20, 31–33; on tribal identity, 31–33
Almanac of the Dead (Silko), 2, 8, 22, 46, 63–76, 77, 151–152; as migration narrative, 9, 14, 31, 34–40, 41, 75–76, 188–190, 195; as monstrous text, 188–190, 195; photography as resistance in, 64–65, 66–76
American Indian literature. *See* American Indians; autobiography; *and specific authors and titles*
American Indians: adaptability of, 28, 75, 92, 169, 191, 193–194; assimilation of, 5, 9, 57–58, 60–62, 74, 76, 77, 78, 139; dispossession of, 24, 26, 133–146 passim; Euro-American images of, 18, 22–23, 43, 78, 130, 197–198n3; intertribal relations, 15, 18–22, 25, 27–28, 31, 35, 40, 41, 63, 67, 68, 72, 171; as migratory, 2, 9, 17–22, 23–40, 68, 74, 77, 92, 187, 188–192, 194, 195; oral narratives and traditions of, 9, 20, 21, 23, 26, 29–30, 33, 52, 63, 189, 193; origin stories, 24–25, 26–28, 29, 31, 52; as outlaws, 44, 50; as "postcolonial," 5; prophecies of, 38–39, 41, 71; relationships to land, 6, 20, 26–27, 36, 38, 170–172; shape-shifting, 27; systems of trade, 23, 25; tribal sovereignty, 39–40, 62, 74–76. *See also* autobiography; women writers; *and specific authors, titles, and tribes*
American Rhythm, The (Austin), 113, 130, 131
American Southwest: "alien" topographies of, 2, 90, 92, 100, 105; and American nation, 5, 48, 80, 87, 93, 113, 114, 121, 152, 154–159, 161–162; and other American regions, 4; as site of cultural encounters, 3, 4, 13–16, 17, 85, 191; as site of migrations, 9, 15, 17, 31–40, 59, 183, 187, 190–191; as text, 3, 15, 84, 85–86, 90–91, 94, 116, 117–118, 119–120; defined, 4, 5–8; desert as "aesthetic spectacle" (Limerick), 46, 79, 81, 84, 86, 88–91, 93–94, 155, 198n2; desert as "economic resource" (Limerick), 86–88; desert as wasteland (Limerick), 84–85, 86–90, 100; outlaws in, 13, 41–50; paradox of preservation and improvement, 5, 78–83; problems of defining, 5–8, 35; recontextualizing, 9, 48, 49, 184–185; and urban spaces, 8, 153–162. *See also* aliens; American Indians; borders; *and specific authors, place names, and titles*
Ammons, Elizabeth: on Austin, 113, 114, 119, 120–121, 122, 123, 201–202n3; on Cather, 134; on Humishuma and Sui Sin Far, 125; on modernist appropriation, 131, 202–203n5
Anzaldúa, Gloria, 7

Apache people, 51–62, 86, 171. *See also* identity
appropriation, cultural, 10, 131, 138, 202–203 n5. *See also* Austin, Mary; Cather, Willa; *Professor's House, The*
Armory Show, 150
Asa Bazhonoodah (Navajo), 170–171
Austin, Mary, 5, 8, 14, 88, 147, 151, 157, 204–205 n8; *The American Rhythm*, 113, 130, 131; as critic of Turner thesis, 121–123, 154; as desert writer, 7, 113, 114–122, 123, 130–132; contrasted to Sarah Winnemucca, 113, 126, 127, 128; critiques of, as "Indian expert," 112, 113, 119, 123–124, 130–132; gender and authority in, 114–115, 116–117, 119, 120; *The Land of Little Rain*, 9–10, 92, 112–124, 125, 131–132, 154; *Lost Borders*, 121
autobiography: American Indian, 18–21, 27, 31–33, 51–62, 63, 85, 125–130, 175, 202 n4; role of Euro-American editors, 51–54, 58–59. *See also specific authors and titles*
"Autobiography of a Confluence, The" (Allen), 19–20, 31–33

Baker, Houston A., 184–185
Bandelier, Adolf, 88, 200 n4
Barnes, Jim (Choctaw), 22
Barrett, S. M., 2, 44, 51–54, 199 n2
Barthes, Roland, 199 n1
Beck, Peggy V., 172
Bering Strait land bridge theory, 24, 29
Berlitz and Moore, 12–13, 197 n1
Betzinez, Jason (Apache), 21, 42, 44, 57–62, 77, 86, 198 n1, 199 nns, 6; on Apaches as travelers, 59–61; as assimilated Indian, 57–58, 60–62; *I Fought with Geronimo*, 54, 57–62
Big Falling Snow (Yava), 27, 66–67
Billy the Kid, 14, 41–50, 53, 73, 90
Billy the Kid (Vidor), 49
Black Elk (Oglala Lakota), 21
Bloch, Robert: *Psycho*, 197 n3
Bone Dance (Rose), 17–19, 21
Bone Game (Owens), 190; influence of *Ceremony* on, 191–192, 206 n5
Boone, Elizabeth Hill, 26
borders, 3, 4, 10–11, 17, 85, 93; crossings of, 6–8, 26, 41, 42, 47, 151, 188, 189, 195; impermeable, 9, 35, 84, 90, 184;

international, 10, 189; permeable, 20, 26–27, 35, 91, 92, 184, 194; problems with term, 6–9; Silko on, 35–38, 188. *See also* American Indians; American Southwest; colonialism; postcolonialism
boundaries. *See* borders
Brill, Susan, 204 n1
Brown, E. K., 138
Brownlow, Kevin, 44, 173
Brumble, H. David, III, 52–53, 126, 127, 128
Burns, Walter Noble: *Saga of Billy the Kid*, 49
Burroughs, John, 114
Burroughs, William S., 189

Calderón, Hector, 88
Calloway, Colin, 19, 24–25, 26, 28
Canfield, Gae Whitney, 127
captivity narratives, 33, 55–56, 200 n6; photographs as, 74
Carlisle (Pennsylvania) Indian School, 52, 57, 61
Carr, A. A. (Navajo–Laguna Pueblo), 2, 22; *Eye Killers*, 14–15, 190, 191–195, 206 n4
Carr, Helen, 113, 119, 121, 125
Carson, Kit, 171
cartography. *See* maps
Castiglia, Christopher, 200 n6
Cather, Willa, 5, 8, 14, 92, 130, 131, 147, 151, 157; *One of Ours*, 134, 202 n1; *O Pioneers!*, 143; *The Professor's House*, 9–10, 133–146, 153
Cawelti, John, 49
Ceremony (Silko), 15–16, 31, 33–34, 190, 193; and *Almanac of the Dead*, 35, 39, 72, 188; influence on *Bone Game*, 191–192; influence on *Eye Killers*, 191–192, 194
Chaplin, Charlie, 148, 149, 185
Chase, Richard, 201 n3
Citizen Kane (Welles), 150
Clifford, James, 2–3, 195, 197 n1; on roots and routes, 10, 15, 17, 27, 92, 187; on Squanto, 22–23, 24
collage: and *Krazy Kat*, 150–151
colonialism, 3; American Indians, Euro-Americans, and, 6, 9, 24, 32, 53, 77, 92, 147, 171, 183, 195; in *The Professor's House* (Cather), 137, 138, 146. *See also*

aliens; American Indians; American
Southwest; borders; postcolonialism
conspiracy narratives. *See* aliens; Ros-
well, New Mexico
Cordell, Linda S., 6, 202n2
Coyote, 21, 22, 119
Coyote, Wile E., 157–158
Crane, Stephen, 88, 102, 154
Creole ethnicity, 147. *See also* Herriman,
George
Crook, General George, 43–44
Cubism, 149, 150
Cullick, Jonathan S., 201n4
Cummings, E. E., 148, 151, 153
Curtis, Edward, 74
Cushing, Frank Hamilton, 88, 200n4

Dada, 149
Daklugie, Asa (Apache), 51–52, 54
Dasenbrock, Reed Way, 6, 35
Dean, Thomas K., 201n4
Death of Bernadette Lefthand, The
(Querry), 190
Debo, Angie, 43, 54–55, 199n6
de Kooning, Willem, 149
Deloria, Ella (Yankton Sioux), 21–22
Deloria, Vine, Jr. (Standing Rock Sioux),
23–24, 28–29
Dene people, 26
Desert Solitaire (Abbey), 4
Dillinger, John, 37, 73
Dillingham, William B., 101–102, 110,
201n5
Dilworth, Leah, 55, 79, 119, 125
dime novels, 46, 47, 87, 93, 121
Dingbat Family, The (Herriman), 155–
156, 158–159
Dobie, J. Frank, 7
Donner party, 126–127
Doughty, Francis W., 46
Dracula (Stoker), 193
Drinnon, Richard, 43, 123
Duchamp, Marcel, 149
Durham, Jimmie (Cherokee), 45, 75

Earp, Wyatt, 44–45
Ellington, Duke, 148, 185
Erdrich, Louise (Turtle Mountain Chip-
pewa), 22, 206n3
Etulain, Richard W., 205n3
extraterrestrials. *See* aliens; Roswell,
New Mexico

Eye Killers (A. A. Carr), 190, 191–195,
206n4; as migration narrative, 14–15;
influence of *Ceremony* on, 191–192,
194, 195

Faris, James C., 74, 200n5
Fergusson, Erna, 7
Fonda, Henry, 45
Fools Crow (Welch), 26
Foote, Kenneth E., 12
Ford, John, 90, 170, 205n1; *My Darling
Clementine*, 44–45; *Stagecoach*, 172
Francisco, Nia, 172
Frankenstein (Shelley), 188
Frémont, John C., 86
frontier, 7–8, 42, 45–47, 49–50, 85, 121–
123; aesthetic of, 46, 50; as mythic
place, 46, 50; urban frontier, 155. *See*
American Southwest; borders; Limer-
ick, Patricia Nelson; Turner, Frederick
Jackson
frontier thesis. *See* Turner, Frederick
Jackson
Fuller, Henry B., 154

Garland, Hamlin: "Up the Coulé," 4
Garrett, Pat, 42, 46, 47, 48
gender, 3, 7, 8, 11, 13, 20–21, 37, 113–
114, 125–126, 128. *See also* Austin,
Mary; Cather, Willa; *Krazy Kat*; Winnemucca, Sarah; women writers
geography: alien, 2, 91; colonial, 37;
cultural, 12, 92, 155; sacred, 28, 34,
140
Georgi-Findlay, Brigitte, 202n4
Geronimo (Apache), 2, 5, 14, 37, 42, 43–
44, 45, 50, 51–62, 77, 124–125, 184,
198n1, 199nn2, 5, 6; in *Almanac of
the Dead*, 63–65, 66, 68–76; as critic
of U.S. officials, 51; *Geronimo's Story
of His Life*, 10, 44, 51–57, 63, 76, 131,
199n2; as prisoner of war, 51–52, 55–
56, 77; as resistance Indian, 9, 51, 53–
54, 63, 68, 70, 92; as world's fair exhibit and visitor, 55–56, 57; writing
process of, 52
"Geronimo Story, A" (Silko), 63–64
Ghost Dance, 71–72
Ghost Singer (Walters), 22
Gopnik, Adam, 148, 149, 156–157, 158
Grand Canyon, 77–81, 83–84, 88–89,
173

Graulich, Melody, 33
Guston, Philip, 149

Halberstam, Judith, 193, 206n1
Haraway, Donna, 152
Harjo, Joy (Muscogee Creek), 22, 25, 29, 35, 188; "Ordinary Spirit," 21
Harrell, David, 140
Harvey, Fred, 79
Hayes, Rutherford B., 129
Hearst, William Randolph, 156, 162, 172, 204n7
Hemingway, Ernest, 134, 135, 142–143
Herriman, George, 4, 5, 130, 204n4, 205n3; biography of, 155–157, 169, 170, 172–173, 178, 183–184; *The Dingbat Family*, 155–156, 158–159; ethnicity of, 147, 159, 184; *Krazy Kat*, 8, 147–168, 169–186; and Navajo people, 169–175, 178, 179–181, 183–184, 185
Hitchcock, Alfred: *Psycho*, 15, 197n3
Hofstadter, Richard, 80
Holland, Sharon, 189
Hollon, W. Eugene, 7
Holmes, Sherlock, 90, 200n5
home places, 3, 4, 5, 19–21, 24–25, 29, 60, 187
Hopi people, 18, 19, 25, 27–28
Hough, Emerson, 48
Howard, General O. O., 43, 128
Howard, June, 4–5, 96–97
Howells, William Dean, 101
Humishuma (Mourning Dove), 125
Hyde, Anne Farrar, 87, 89

identity: "alien," 2, 11–14; Anzaldúa on, 7; Apache, 52, 57, 58, 61, 69; Clifford on flexibility of, 3, 92; constructions and formations of, 10, 15, 19–20, 28, 68, 92, 169–170; mixed-blood, 18, 19, 31, 147, 190, 191, 193; tribal, 21, 27, 33, 36, 41, 68, 75–76, 169–170. *See also* Allen, Paula Gunn; Rose, Wendy; *and specific tribes*
I Fought with Geronimo (Betzinez), 54, 57–62; migration stories in, 59–61
imperialism. *See* aliens; borders; colonialism
Incidents in the Life of a Slave Girl (Jacobs), 126, 128, 199n1
Indian detours (Fred Harvey Company), 79, 89, 90, 91, 145

Jacobs, Harriet: *Incidents in the Life of a Slave Girl*, 126, 128, 199n1
Jennings, Francis, 29
Jewett, Sarah Orne, 154, 204–205n8; "A White Heron," 4–5
Joyce, James, 149
Jung, Carl, 157

Kane, Sean, 26
Kaplan, Amy, 10, 205n10
Kaywaykla, James (Apache), 42, 44
Keaton, Buster, 149
Kenny, Maurice (Mohawk), 18
Kiowa people, 29
Krazy Kat (Herriman), 147–168, 169–186, 204nn5, 7, 205n3; ethnicity in, 147–148; gender in, 147, 148, 152, 154; homoeroticism in, 148, 165; language in, 153, 159–162, 163, 168; as modernist text, 147, 150, 153, 168; and Navajo aesthetics, 169, 174–175, 178, 179–181, 183; and Navajo people, 150, 154, 169–175, 178, 179–181, 183–184, 185; and newspapers, 8, 147–152, 153–154, 155–156, 158–159, 162–168, 172, 174, 184, 185; railroads in, 163–165; as southwestern text, 147–148, 149, 149–150, 151, 152–154, 169, 170, 172–173, 174, 183–184, 185–186; and urban spaces, 149, 151, 152, 153–162, 163, 183
Krupat, Arnold, 53–54, 199n2; on Native American literature as post-colonial, 5

Laguna Pueblo people, 25, 31, 66
Land of Little Rain, The (Austin), 9–10, 92, 112–124, 125, 131–132, 154
Langlois, Karen S., 112, 113, 119, 123–124, 125
Laut, Agnes C., 157
Leavell, Linda, 203nn7, 9
Lee, Elsie (Navajo), 180
Lee, Hermione, 133, 136–137, 138
Leibsohn, Dana, 26, 36
Life among the Piutes (Winnemucca), 22, 125–130, 131, 132
Limerick, Patricia Nelson, 5, 7, 82, 83, 84–86, 89–90, 92, 115, 153
Lippard, Lucy, 65, 66
London, Jack, 154
Lost Borders (Austin), 121
Lummis, Charles, 88

Mann, Mary, 125, 127
maps, 6, 35–37, 40; cartographic history, 36, 37; and migrations, 35–40; and stories, 20; tribal cartography, 19, 26
Martin, Calvin Luther, 23–24, 205 n9
Martin, Paul, 23–24
Marx Brothers, 149
Massai (Apache), 60–61
McAllester, David, 175, 178
McDonnell, Patrick, 159, 169, 170, 172–173
McTeague (Norris), 2, 9–10, 92–111, 153; American Indian character in, 94–95; and American literary naturalism, 93, 95, 101, 102, 110–111; constructions of history in, 93–96, 97–99, 102–105, 106–108, 111; cultural contexts of, 93, 103–104, 107, 110; desert passages in, 93, 95–111; evolutionary language in, 107; narrative disruptions in, 93, 99, 100–105, 108; railroads in, 93–95; role of memory in, 95, 97, 98, 101, 102–103
memory, national, 5, 13, 36, 80–81
Mexico: in *Almanac of the Dead*, 35, 36, 37, 38, 39; in Billy the Kid legends, 49; boundary between U.S. and, 10, 13, 35, 36, 38, 39, 41, 42; defined as southwestern, 6; enmity between Apaches and Mexicans, 54, 59, 62; native maps of, 35, 36
Michaels, Walter Benn, 10, 97, 103–104, 133, 202 n3, 203 n9
migration, 10, 14–15, 17–22, 23–40, 47, 91, 194–195; as American Indian political strategy, 3, 5, 9, 14, 22; in American Southwest, 2–5, 9–10, 17, 59–61, 91; definition of, 2–3; and Euro-Americans in Southwest, 3–4, 9–11, 13–14, 15–16, 17, 18; problems with term, 6; and resistance, 3, 14, 68, 74, 75–76, 92; and textuality, 3, 8, 11, 14, 18, 20, 21–22, 25, 27, 29–40, 192; *See also* American Indians; home places; *and specific authors and titles*
Miles, General Nelson A., 125
Mitchell, Frank (Navajo), 175, 180–181
Mitchell, Lee Clark, 96, 199 n1
Mix, Tom, 173
mixed-blood identity. *See* identity
modernism, 17, 31, 130–132, 134, 135, 138, 146, 147, 150, 153, 168, 184–185. *See also* appropriation, cultural; *and specific authors and titles*

Momaday, N. Scott (Kiowa), 21, 29–31, 77, 200 n2, 205 n2; *The Way to Rainy Mountain*, 30
Muir, John, 114
My Darling Clementine (Ford), 44–45

nationalism, 10, 36
Native Americans. *See* American Indians *and specific authors, titles, and tribes*
naturalism, American literary, 93, 95, 96–97, 101, 102, 110–111
Navajo people, 28, 31, 169–175, 178, 179–181, 183–184, 185
Nelson, Robert M., 34
"Neon Scars" (Rose), 18, 19, 20–21
newspapers: and *Krazy Kat*, 8, 147–152, 153–154, 155–156, 158–159, 162–168, 172, 174, 184, 185; treatment of Euro-American outlaws, 47; treatment of Indians, 43
nomadology, 23, 29
Norris, Frank, 8, 85, 147, 151; *McTeague*, 2, 9–10, 14, 92–111, 153
Nye, Wilbur Sturtevant, 58–59, 199 n6

O'Connell, Karen, 159, 169, 170, 172–173
O'Keeffe, Georgia, 5, 80–82, 85, 89, 90, 115, 130, 131, 200 n2
One of Ours (Cather), 134, 202 n1
O Pioneers! (Cather), 143
"Ordinary Spirit" (Harjo), 21
Ortiz, Simon (Acoma Pueblo), 22
Orvell, Miles, 148, 149
outlaws. *See* American Southwest; Billy the Kid; Geronimo
Owens, Louis (Choctaw–Cherokee), 22; *Bone Game*, 190, 191–192, 206 n5

Paiute people, 86, 126–127
Pan-Indianism. *See* American Indians; identity
Paulson, Ronald, 149, 152
Pérez-Torres, Rafael, 6–7
Perrigo, Lynne I., 7
Perry, Donna, 31, 189
petroglyphs, 19–20, 174
photography: as evidence, 64, 66–67, 75; as magic, 65–67; as material product, 66; as representation, 64–67, 69–70, 71–72, 75–76; of urban spaces, 155. *See also Almanac of the Dead*; Lippard, Lucy; Riis, Jacob; Silko, Leslie Marmon; Tagg, John

Picasso, Pablo, 149

Pinchot, Gifford, 82–84, 87

Pizer, Donald, 100–101, 102, 201 n2

Pleistocene overkill theory, 23–24

Poe, Edgar Allan, 109

Pollock, Jackson, 181, 183

postcolonialism, 3, 5, 8, 12, 17, 74–75, 123, 163, 169, 183, 184, 186

postmodernism, 185

Pratt, Captain Richard, 57

Professor's House, The (Cather), 9–10, 92, 133–146, 153; commercial processes in, 133–134, 135–136, 137–138, 140, 143–144, 146; history and memory in, 133–146; Indians in, 133–134, 135, 136–142, 143, 144, 145–146; World War I and, 134, 135, 143–146

Pryse, Marjorie, 112, 122, 204 n8

Psycho (Bloch), 197 n3

Psycho (Hitchcock), 15, 197 n3

Querry, Ron (Choctaw): *Death of Bernadette Lefthand, The*, 190

railroads, 2, 78, 83, 87–89; in *Krazy Kat*, 163–165; in *McTeague*, 93–95

Rainey, Ma, 185

Randle and Schmitt, 11, 12, 14, 197 n1

Ration, Tom (Navajo), 181

Rauschenberg, Robert, 149

regionalism, 35, 152–153, 184, 195; connections between regions and nation, 4–5

Reid, E. Shelley, 200 n3, 206 n3

Remington, Frederic, 47, 121, 152–153

resistance. *See Almanac of the Dead*; American Indians; Geronimo; migration; Silko, Leslie Marmon

Revard, Carter (Osage), 22, 52, 57–58, 59

Reynolds, Guy, 202 n1

Riis, Jacob, 154, 155, 205 n10

Riley de Havenon, Georgia, 159, 169, 170, 172–173

Rinehart, W. V., 127

Road Runner, 157–158

Roberts, "Brushy Bill," 47

Roosevelt, Theodore, 5, 44, 46, 47, 77–83, 86, 88, 112, 114, 121, 134, 152; anti-Indian rhetoric of, 78; and Geronimo, 45, 51–52, 79

Rose, Wendy (Hopi–Miwok), 4, 17–21, 25, 29; *Bone Dance*, 17–19, 21; "Neon Scars," 18, 20–21; on tribal identity, 18, 19, 20–21

Rosemont, Franklin, 159

Rosowski, Susan J., 138

Roswell (New Mexico): alien spacecraft wreck, 1, 11–14, 187; conspiracy theories and theorists, 1–2, 3, 11–14, 187, 190, 197 n1; crash site, 12; space aliens, 1–2, 11–14, 187, 191; tourism, 11–12. *See also* aliens; Berlitz and Moore; Randle and Schmitt

"Roswell Report, Case Closed, The" (U.S. Air Force), 1, 197 n2

Rudnick, Lois, 113, 114

Ruoff, A. Lavonne, 31, 202 nn4, 5

Rushing, W. Jackson, 181, 183

Saldívar, José David, 88

Sands, Kathleen Mullen, 202 n6

Sarris, Greg (Miwok–Pomo), 53, 192, 195, 198 n7, 199 n2

Schurz, Carl, 129

Seldes, Gilbert, 148–149, 163, 183

Seltzer, Mark, 96–97

Sequoya-Magdaleno, Jana, 33–34, 192

Sergeant, Elizabeth Shepley, 157

Shelley, Mary: *Frankenstein*, 188

Silko, Leslie Marmon (Laguna Pueblo), 5, 21, 25, 26, 30, 32–40, 45, 92, 184, 198 n7, 206 n1; on "alien" identity, 2, 14; *Almanac of the Dead*, 2, 8, 9, 14, 22, 31, 34–40, 41, 46, 63–76, 77, 151–152, 188–190, 195; *Ceremony*, 15–16, 31, 33–34, 35, 39, 72, 188, 190, 191–192, 193; on Geronimo, 2, 9, 63–65, 66, 68–76; "A Geronimo Story," 63–64; influence on other American Indian writers, 191–192, 194, 195; on migration, 2, 9, 34–40, 41; on petroglyphs, 20; on photography, 31, 64–76; *Storyteller*, 33, 63–64, 188; on Tucson, 2, 35, 37

Sinclair, Upton, 154

Sister Carrie (Dreiser), 101

Smith, Patricia Clark, 25

Southwest. *See* American Southwest

Squanto (Patuxet), 22–23, 24

Stagecoach (Ford), 172

Steckmesser, Kent, 47, 48

Stein, Gertrude, 114

Steinberg, Saul, 156

Stoker, Bram: *Dracula*, 193

Storyteller (Silko), 33, 63–64, 188
Stout, Janis P., 202 n4
Sui Sin Far, 125
Sundquist, Eric J., 6–7
Surrealism: and *Krazy Kat*, 147, 149, 151

Taft, William Howard, 59
Tagg, John, 66, 67
Tatum, Stephen, 48, 49, 50, 198 nn2, 3
Teague, David W., 201 n1
Tewa people, 27
Thoreau, Henry David, 114
"Tom Outland's Story" (Cather). *See* Cather, Willa; *The Professor's House*
tourism: Euro-American, in Southwest, 77–80, 83–84, 88–89
Trachtenberg, Alan, 8, 77, 103, 150, 152, 204 n3
Trail of Tears, 171
travel. *See* American Southwest; home places; migration
Turner, Frederick Jackson, 13, 41–43, 45–50, 53, 141, 154–155; critiques of frontier thesis, 8, 77, 121–123
Tuska, Jon, 198 nn2, 3

Upson, Ash, 47
"Up the Coulé" (Garland), 4
Urgo, Joseph R., 144
Utley, Robert M., 42, 43, 47, 112, 124–125, 198 n2

Van Dyke, John, 154
Vidor, King: *Billy the Kid*, 49

Wallace, Lew, 43
Walters, Anna Lee (Pawnee/Otoe-Misouria): 172; *Ghost Singer*, 22, 190

Warner, Michael, 144
Warrior, Robert Allen, 6
Warshow, Robert, 149
Washington, Booker T., 185
Watterson, Bill, 204 n5
Way to Rainy Mountain, The (Momaday), 30
Weber, David J., 7–8
Welch, James (Blackfeet–Gros Ventre), 22, 26
Wheeler, Kathleen, 138, 139, 203 n8
White, Richard, 46–47, 49, 82
Wiget, Andrew, 28
Wilbur, Reverend James H., 127, 129
Winnemucca, Chief (Sarah's father), 127, 128
Winnemucca, Sarah (Northern Paiute), 86, 113, 125–132; *Life among the Piutes*, 22, 125–130, 131, 132
Winters, Laura, 146
Witherspoon, Gary, 174–175, 180–181, 183
women writers: American Indian, 20–21. *See also* gender *and specific authors and titles*
Wong, Hertha Dawn, 169–170, 171–172
Woodard, Charles L., 30
Writing without Words (Boone and Mignolo), 26
Wyatt, David, 104–105, 106, 120

Yava, Albert (Hopi–Tewa), 20, 25, 27–28, 35; *Big Falling Snow*, 27, 66–67
Young, M. Jane, 20

Zitkala-Sa (Yankton Sioux), 21
Zolbrod, Paul, 28
Zuni people, 20